WELCOME TO OUR WORLD

This book is designed to welcome people to this beautiful area. For those vacationing here, we've tried to point out the places of interest, restaurants, and shops that should be on the "can't miss" list. If you're a newcomer here or are thinking of moving to this special part of the world, we've provided information on communities, businesses and health care to ease your transition.

Read and enjoy the book. However, if the cover reads "Owner's Copy" it has been provided for you only while you're visiting. Please leave it behind so that others can enjoy it after you've gone.

Wilmington Today is for sale at Island Book Shop in Carolina Beach, Pomegranate Books on Park Avenue, Two Sisters Bookery at The Cotton Exchange, and Barnes and Noble at Mayfaire as well as online.

Thank you for leaving the book for others to enjoy.

www.wilmingtontoday.com

Photo by G. Frank Hart Photography

WILMINGTON TODAY

Wilmington Today LLC
1213 Culbreth Drive
Wilmington, NC 28405
910-509-7195

Publisher & Editor
Hazel White Jones

Director of Marketing
Tom Jones

Distribution Director
John Salsburg

Design Director
Jeremy Grissett
The Dude Design, Inc.

Writers
Elizabeth Biro, Emily Gorman-Fancy, Gwynne Moore, Terrance Moore

Photographers
G. Frank Hart, Brownie Harris
Cover photo:
Our area's beautiful beaches are a magnet for avid surfers.
Photo: G. Frank Hart Photography

Maps © 2015 Cape Fear Images, Inc.

All other material:
© 2015 Wilmington Today LLC.
No portion of this book may be copied, reproduced or used in any way except with the express, written consent of the publisher.
Printed in Hong Kong

ISBN 978-0-9729573-2-8

Scan to view website

Get the free mobile app at
http://gettag.mobi

www.wilmingtontoday.com

index

Historic Downtown	4
Communities	16
Entertainment & Nightlife	30
Festivals	36
Shopping	40
Healthcare	58
Topsail Island	66
Area Map	79
Attractions	80
Just For Kids	90
City Map	95
Business	96
Salons & Spas	104
Education	108
Weddings, Catering	116
Golf	126
Restaurants	134
Downtown Map	161
Hampstead	162
Carolina & Kure Beach	166
Wrightsville Beach	176
Films	184
Figure Eight Island	187

this is wilmington today

We are dedicating this edition of our book to Terrance Moore who with his wife Gwynne were the original exclusive writers we worked with in the early years of this project. For the last nine editions Terry has worked with us, always with great curiosity and enthusiasm. He died on February 27, 2015. We will miss his friendship and his humor.

Like Terry, we relocated here from a different part of the country. After 14 years here, we appreciate even more what this area has to offer.

Southern sensibilities and a casual lifestyle give our communities an inviting ambiance of cordiality, warmth and easiness. A positive spirit is evident; people like being here. This is a great place to visit, live, work, play, raise a family, make friends and generally enjoy life.

We have a delightful climate with just enough inclement weather to remind us to appreciate all the lovely days with bright sunshine and comfortable temperatures. We enjoy outdoor living at its best.

For its size, the Wilmington metropolitan area offers amazing diversity in cultural activities, restaurants, shopping, sports, theater and music.

The area's rich history is reflected in its well-preserved and restored homes in and around downtown as well as in surrounding towns. Several museums and events honor this deep heritage.

Of course our main attraction is the endlessly fascinating sea. Never the same from one day to the next, our ocean may be flat calm with waves gently lapping on the sand or it might be roaring indignantly, slamming itself against the shore.

Glorious sun, beautiful Carolina blue skies, salt-scented breezes and soft white sand provide unequaled relaxation opportunities. Surfers, sun worshippers, fishermen, and boaters alike can't get enough of our warm Gulf Stream waters.

Equally impressive is the Cape Fear River which provides both commercial and recreational possibilities. Downtown Wilmington's Riverwalk is the focal point of the 200 block historic district.

We're glad to have you here. Read on to find out more about this amazing place. And visit our continuously updated website, www.wilmingtontoday.com, to learn what's happening here.

Welcome!
Hazel and Tom Jones

The Cape Fear River is the backdrop for Wilmington's downtown, a shopping, dining and entertainment mecca.

explore historic downtown wilmington

Southern hospitality, historic charm, movie stars and modern thinkers. This is Wilmington, a 300-year-old port city that never goes out of style.

Horse-drawn carriages still click down cobblestone streets, and moss-draped oaks canopy stately old mansions along downtown's 200 historic blocks. Yet, Wilmington has a progressive vibe that captivates tourists, entrepreneurs and even residents who have lived here all their lives.

Variety supplies the city's steady beat

Tucked between the Atlantic Ocean and the Cape Fear River, Wilmington presents so many stunning vistas. To the east, the city overlooks sounds, barrier islands and the Intracoastal Waterway. The west borders the busy Cape Fear River. Downtown hosts a scenic, mile-long boardwalk, named The Riverwalk, which skirts the Cape Fear River.

Tour a World War II battleship or take a riverboat cruise. Bump into celebrities working with a movie studio 15 minutes from dowtown. Local actors as well as internationally known musicians and actors perform at ornate theaters, worth a visit for their architecture alone. Contemplate myriad works at 20 galleries or tuck into downtown's more than 100 distinctive shops. Refresh at some 50 delicious downtown restaurants, cocktail lounges and an award-winning craft brewery.

Downtown parking decks are centrally located and free for the first hour. Most city streets host meters, where parking is free after 6:30 p.m. Some venues have their own parking lots or neighbor public lots. A free city trolley traverses downtown, and wide sidewalks welcome pedestrians.

Battleship's on guard

Wilmington's top attraction makes the city unique. The mighty Battleship North Carolina stands at attention on the Cape Fear River's western shore, directly across from downtown's center. Commissioned in 1941, the 728-foot-long ship participated in every major, Pacific-area naval offensive during World War II, earning the vessel 15 battle stars.

Drive or take a water taxi to the ship for a full tour and special events like the Battleship Blast July 4 fireworks display.

The battleship is not the only floating marvel to see downtown. Tour the large U.S. Coast Guard cutter, Diligence, usually berthed just south of lovely Wilmington Hilton Riverside hotel. Be sure to look for "weed" decals on the bridge indicating the ship's number of successful drug busts. Now and then, tall ships dock here, too.

Pleasure cruising

The first documented explorers to visit what became Wilmington arrived in the 1500s on the Cape Fear River. Get a sense of the excitement this beautiful waterway must have stirred aboard the Henrietta III, a huge, old-fashioned riverboat docked downtown. Narrated tours outline the river's natural, historic and economic significance. Romantic dinner dance and murder mystery cruises are offered too.

The Capt. J.N Maffit, a former World War II liberty launch, runs shorter narrated cruises and water taxi service to Battleship North Carolina. It's a relaxing way to get across the river, and certainly more fun than driving. Kids love the taxi, yet it's also romantic for couples. Ask about the Maffit's four-hour, Black River nature excursion with a coastal ecologist. And keep private charters in mind for gatherings.

The newest way to explore the Cape

The Battleship North Carolina should be a must-see Wilmington attraction.

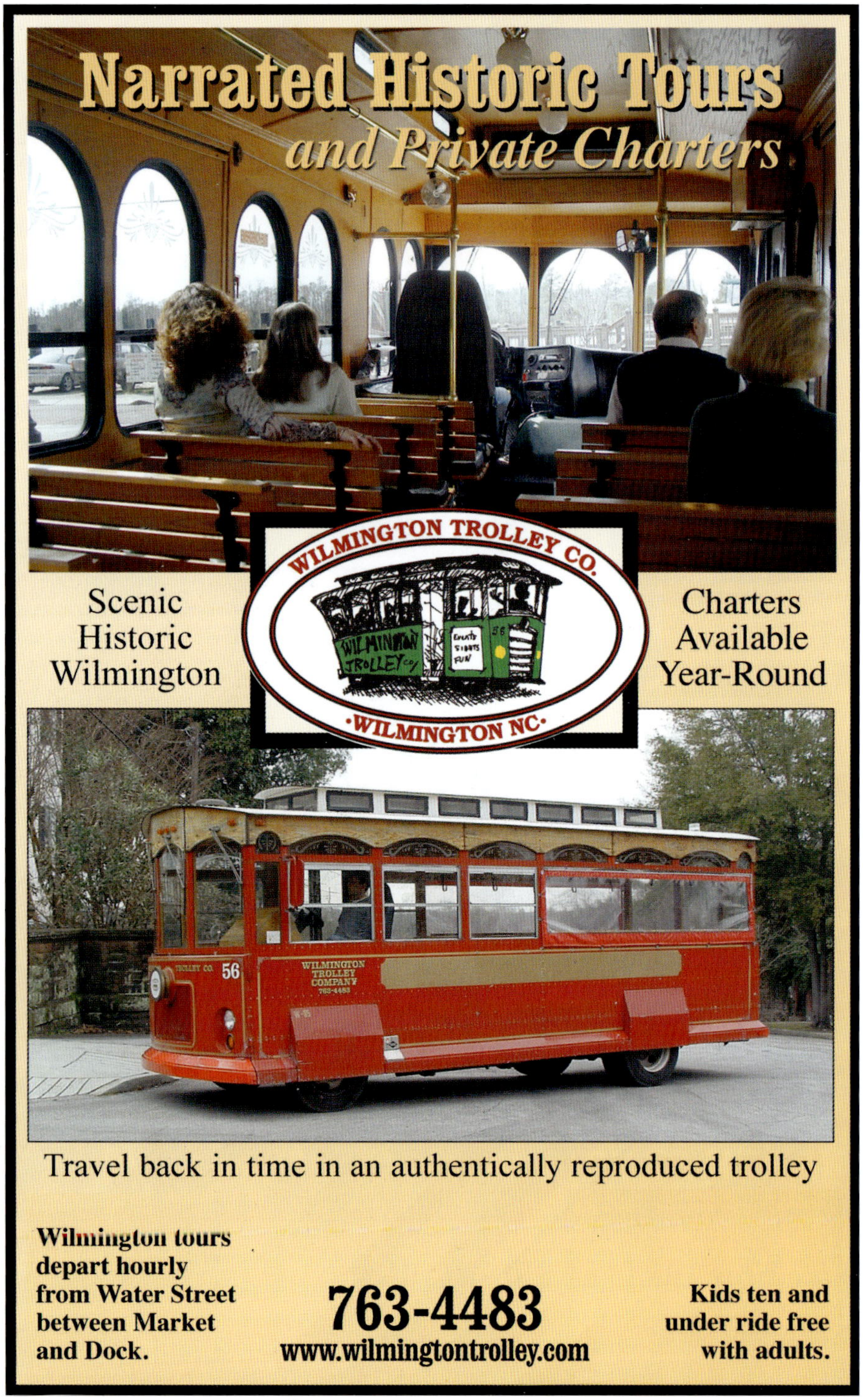

Fear River is aboard a luxury yacht. Wilmington Yacht Charter's Sanjema II is available by the day or week. Spending time aboard this vessel would be a wonderful way to celebrate such special events as engagements, birthdays, anniversaries or vow renewals.

The Sanjema II was built in 1986 to the highest standards by Hatteras Yachts and has been beautifully maintained since then. With either day or overnight charters available, trips to downtown Wilmington or further afield to the Southport area are possible.

A old-fashioned trolley ride through time

Wilmington Trolley Company's bright red and green trolleys are lined with arched windows, providing views of old and new downtown Wilmington as well as Christmastime lights. Narrators supply interesting anecdotes. Along the way, see numerous historic homes and buildings, many open for touring. Wilmington Trolley is also available for private charter. The Wilmington Trolley is a wonderful way to travel from the wedding ceremony to the reception.

There are several spectacular buildings downtown that shouldn't be missed. Thalian Hall theater, which once served as city hall. stands on Third Street, at Chestnut Street, next door to the showy, red brick New Hanover County Courthouse, built in 1892. Magnificent Bellamy Mansion and gardens are walking distance away on Market Street. Kids marvel at Cape Fear Serpentarium's reptiles and there are lots of them. Find the serpentarium on Orange Street.

Was that Ryan Phillippe?

Bump into actors live on location or end up sitting next to them in a restaurant. You never know where celebrities will pop up. Wilmington is nicknamed "Hollywood East" and "Wilmywood" thanks to EUE/ Screen Gems Studios on North 23rd Street, near downtown, and the annual Cucalorus Film Festival, an indie favorite.

Iron Man 3 and *The Longest Ride* are among dozens of movies that were filmed in and around Wilmington. The impressive palm-tree-fronted Federal

Building on downtown's waterfront was the location for many episodes of actor Andy Griffith's popular *Matlock* television series. The CW Network's *One Tree Hill* and *Dawson's Creek* were produced here. Look for Wilmington in many current programs, too, including *Under the Dome* and *Secrets and Lies*, the new ABC series starring Ryan Phillippe.

When Cotton Was King

At the turn of the 20th century, downtown Wilmington's Cotton Exchange was home to one of the world's largest and busiest cotton export companies. Trade at this century-old complex is alive and well. Eight brick buildings, one built before the Civil War, have been restored and converted into a multi-level maze of 29 shops and restaurants mingled with displays featuring the compound's history.

Stores stock clothing, stationery, jewelry, beads and gemstones, books, paintings, hand-made pottery and crafts, souvenirs, gifts, a vast selection of spicy sauces and gourmet delights.

Access the Cotton Exchange from

The U.S. Federal Building on Water Street downtown was a famous backdrop for the "Matlock" series that starred Andy Griffith.

explore historic **downtown wilmington**

It's Fork 'n Delicious!

Try our all house made high end bar food.
Full bar, craft beer and a thoughtful wine list.

CORK N CORK

122 Market Street • Wilmington NC 28401
910-228-5247
www.theforkncork.com

CAPE FEAR SPICE MERCHANTS
SPICES • TEAS • GIFTS

ALWAYS FRESH

OVER 150 LOOSE LEAF TEAS,
OVER 90 "HOUSE MADE" SPICE BLENDS,
& OVER 225 SINGLE SPICES

Located at 20 Market Street, Downtown Wilmington
(910) 772-2980

Front or Water streets' north ends. It's fun to enter on Front Street and depart on Water Street, which is a short stroll to The Riverwalk. From there, head less than a block north to encounter Best Western Coastline Inn, the Coastline Convention Center and the Wilmington Railroad Museum, a spot train aficionados adore.

Whether you take The Riverwalk or Front Street, you're bound to notice Market Street between the two pathways. Everyone recognizes it by the white, old-fashioned, horse-drawn carriages that park there. Take time to browse this little block's cafes, restaurants and stores. One of them is Cape Fear Spice Merchants. The massive global spice and tea collection harks back to a time when tall ships unloaded spices and other goods downtown. Wilmington's colonial port was at the intersection of Market and Water Streets. Shipping and trade is part of how the road got its name. Hand-mixed spice blends range from the exotic Persian 7-Spice blend with cloves and green cardamom to piquant rubs for ribs and roasts. Loose-leaf teas, more than 100, fill shelves as do oils, vinegars and sea salt blends. Consider the Lime Fresco Rimmer for your next margarita. Sip tea while perusing coffee, flavored sugars, gourmet foods, Mexican chocolates, cooking tools such as cutting boards and everything you need to make the perfect cup of tea.

Bites, sips and smiles

Wilmington adventures invariably intersect places to eat, drink and enjoy nightlife. Some people visit just to sample the city's fine restaurants. Chefs prepare a smorgasbord of Southern, contemporary American, Italian, Asian, Mediterranean and Middle Eastern fare, just to name a few. Fancy dress is not required even at the most high-end restaurants, many of which bill themselves as "upscale casual." Sit by the water, hide out on a romantic patio or see and be seen at a sidewalk café table or an indoor seat by the window.

Fork 'n' Cork on Market Street, between Front and Second streets, is one of downtown's newest and most popular restaurants. Chef James Smith traded in his hugely popular Patty Wagon burger truck for permanent gastropub digs. His comfort food twists served with impressive but affordable wines are like nothing else downtown. Scotch eggs and deep-fried, confit duck legs are famous here, as are creative mac 'n cheese combinations, one layered with brisket. The historic red brick building is so intimate and cozy you won't want to leave.

No matter where folks venture downtown, warm caramel, chocolate and sugar aromas eventually attract everyone to Kilwin's, a favorite after-dinner or dessert-first treat. Follow your nose to Market Street, between Front and Water streets. Choose from a huge assortment of ice cream flavors served in cups or fresh-pressed waffle cones continuously made fresh throughout the day.

Watch candy makers mix giant batches of creamy fudge. Flavors suit every taste, whether you're nuts for classic peanut butter and chocolate or a connoisseur seeking single-origin Peruvian chocolate fudge. Display cases are jammed with sweet delights such as truffles, chocolate-covered cookies and chocolate-dipped pretzels. Gift cards, seasonal treats and holiday and special-occasion baskets are available

One of downtown Wilmington's

most beautiful and most romantic restaurants, Aubriana's, features an American menu with European flair. Native North Carolinian chef Tyson Amick and his brigade, one of the city's best kitchen teams, present outstanding fare on a seasonally changing menu and a specials board that always impresses. Among entrees is a thick, tender, applewood bacon-wrapped Black Angus filet mignon served with Yukon Gold mashed potatoes, asparagus, wild mushrooms and green peppercorn reduction. Specials might showcase jumbo shrimp etouffee with housemade duck boudin. Dessert is always special. Silky gelato is made in-house. Layer cakes are spectacular, especially the creamy coconut cake. Aubriana's has a full bar serving classics and fresh twists. The wine list has earned an Award of Excellence from *Wine Spectator* magazine.

Old Wilmington City Market

Continuing along, turn south on The Riverwalk to find the Old Wilmington City Market. Another entrance is on Front Streets. Established in 1880 as a meat and produce market, it was considered one of the South's most beautiful shopping malls. Placards inside and out tell the place's history, as do some vendors who still remember selling and buying food there. Ever colorful, the restored market these days is lined with unusual shops.

A few blocks further south on Water Street, explore the Chandler's Wharf area, another historical treasure with restaurants and shops.

Remember to look up here and elsewhere downtown. The area's late 1980s resurgence and subsequent growth was thanks in part to the expanding availability of residential space. Downtown Wilmington sidewalks don't roll up when the area's businesspeople close in the evening. Condominium developments and town homes along with many residential accommodations above businesses help to keep the neighborhood vibrant day and night.

Lots More Shopping Options

Wilmington is a shopper's paradise that extends beyond downtown. Castle Street's antiques district is just a mile away, a pleasant drive or walk down Third Street, a shady lane lined with well-appointed historic homes and churches.

Antique, vintage clothing, music and art stores share Castle Street with cozy places to eat and drink.

The Forum, Lumina Station and Mayfaire shopping centers, all in north Wilmington near Wrightsville Beach, offer tony boutiques and/or national chains selling everything from fine wine to cookware, clothing, furniture and books. Many other shopping centers and malls are located around the city - some trendy and upscale, all worth exploring.

Laugh out loud

Don't expect downtown dining to put you in the mood for a nap. Exciting dining experiences are more likely to put you in the mood for more fun. Dead Crow Comedy Room fits the bill. A comedian founded this full-time comedy club on Front Street, between Grace and Chestnut Streets. Lots of national talent show up here, but the club also supports local up-and-comers. Take a shot yourself during open mic nights. The basement space is a cool hideaway with a full bar and a great pub menu of snacks.

Award-winning craft beer

Front Street Brewery's tall, vertical, neon sign is one of the most recognizable and sought-after landmarks in central downtown Wilmington. Brewmaster Kevin Kozak and team produce a changing array of micro-beers, some aged in bourbon or wine barrels, that have garnered national attention and gold medals. Flagship beers include light Coastal Kolsch, Port City IPA and the wildly popular Dram Tree Scottish Ale. Deep red and lightly hoppy, it's a natural with the kitchen's Scottish ale barbecue ribs or sweet cinnamon doughnut bites. The menu also includes Front Street's popular pulled chicken nachos as well as burgers, sandwiches, slow roasted brisket, Shepherd's pie, Buffalo shrimp and a bratwurst plate.

Front Street also boasts more than 275 spirits, including around 50 bourbons and whiskeys, and rare bourbon

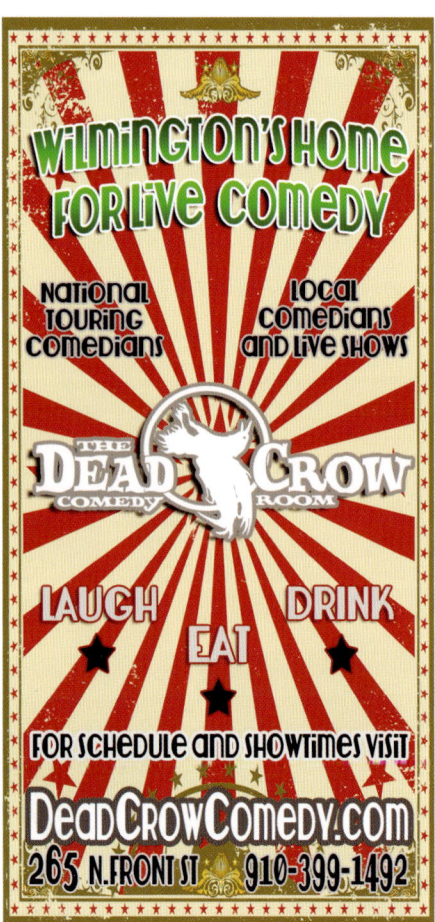

tastings. The spot stages special events, free brewery tours, free beer tastings and great lunch, dinner and appetizer specials daily. Front Street Brewery is open 11:30 a.m. to 2 a.m. on Friday and Saturday and 11:30 a.m. to midnight the rest of the week.

Watch the Cape Fear River's flow, and don't blame too many martinis when the water seems to be moving in two directions. The flow reverses when the ocean approaches high tide.

Grab your palette

The largest space for artists is in a revitalized part of the original Block Shirt Factory, located at 200 Willard Street just a mile from downtown. TheArtWorks is an art village showcasing Wilmington's vibrant visual, literary, and performing arts. TheArtWorks provides art studios, gallery space, educational opportunities, and an event venue with the mission to foster a creative environment for artists and enhance Wilmington's cultural community through art.

More than 45 artists actively create and sell their art through studios in TheArtWorks. The range of mediums for sale includes original fine art, sculpture, jewelry, pottery, photography, glass, and unique handmade gifts. The studios feature work spaces and mini galleries. With 9,000 square feet of beautiful gallery space, TheArtWorks is a perfect event place for a wedding reception, bar or bat mitzvah, trade show, or other special event.

TheArtWorks also includes classrooms where a wide variety of performing arts classes are taught, including voice, drums, and guitar, among other classes. Another educational offering is their Art Trash program, which provides arts education to economically disadvantaged members of the community from age 6 to adult.

TheArtWorks anticipates opening the gallery space six days a week in the summer of 2015. There is also space allocated for a coffee shop and a fine arts supply store, which they would like to offer in the future.

One of the artists at TheArtWorks is Sandy Nelson, winner of numerous national awards whose portraits and landscapes have been accepted for inclusion in national juried competitions from

explore historic **downtown wilmington**

More and more people are living, working, dining and shopping downtown.

HAND CRAFT USA

24 N. FRONT STREET, HISTORIC DOWNTOWN

WWW.CRESCENTMOONNC.COM

910.762.4207

CRESCENT MOON — CRAFT IN AMERICA

NOTHING IS MASS PRODUCED HERE EXCEPT ORIGINALITY!

Bring It! DOWNTOWN
Park FREE 1st Hour In City Decks

Maine to California. She was named one of the best 200 artists in 1993 by *Artists Magazine* and continues to produce amazing works with our area's marshes, ponds and open fields serving as inspiration. She also is a talented portrait painter who is happy to consult with those who might be interested in acquiring a portrait.

Arts and culture

Wilmington's many layers inspire artists who live and work here. As a result, the city is an art lover's dream spot. Works hang all over downtown in this supportive community where it's not unusual to see painters putting brushes to canvas along downtown sidewalks. Artists in residence work and teach classes in the loft space at Crescent Moon on Front Street, between Market and Princess Streets. The first-floor gallery features creations by more than 50 artists. As the store's slogan says, "The only thing mass-produced here is originality." Jewelry, sculpture, paintings, paperweights, holiday ornaments and stained glass represent a wee sample of the colorful display. Lifelike animal sculptures handmade from Sisal fibers must been seen to be believed. Custom and online orders are welcome, and gift cards are available at this so-friendly shop

Many artists launch their own galleries. Painter Dan Beck is one of them. His many awards from the Oil Painters of America include the 2011 Gold Medal from the organization's National Exhibition. Major galleries, collectors and museums around the world seek out his impressionist works – figurative, still-life and landscape. Using both oils and pastels, his paintings depict the artist's love of nature and deep respect for art. Beck's works evoke timelessness and dignity. Find Dan Beck Fine Art Gallery and Studio in downtown's Castle Street district.

Port of Wilmington

Just south of downtown on the Cape Fear River, the bustling Port of Wilmington loads and unloads ships from around the world. A deep river channel and four, 100 foot-gauge container cranes enable the port to handle heavy cargo, allowing the port to accommodate the largest ships arriving from the Panama Canal.

Port managers expect annual, double-digit growth.

Anticipating international trade to double by 2020, the North Carolina Port Authority acquired 600 acres on Cape Fear River's west side for a new International Port to handle more enormous container ships. The addition will catapult North Carolina into the ranks of the foremost East Coast ports.

Excellent healthcare, colleges

The port is one reason Wilmington is the financial center of southeastern North Carolina. Health care and higher education boost the economy, too.

New Hanover Regional Medical Center on 17th Street and its associated facilities throughout the area continue to improve, expand and earn recognition.

The University of North Carolina Wilmington on College Road is highly ranked both nationally and in the Southeast, and has won a number of awards for academic excellence.

The school, with an enrollment of more than 13,000 students, offers 52 bachelor's degree programs and 35 graduate programs. Among public institutions nationally, UNCW ranked among America's 50 Best Value Colleges.

Cape Fear Community College trains a workforce and inspires entrepreneurial spirit that helps Wilmington grow all sorts of small, medium and large businesses. The college was instrumental in bringing the large Verizon Wireless customer support center here in 2005. The school has a film studies program and a culinary school that operates a restaurant in spring and fall.

Beautiful beaches nearby

Wilmington has so much to offer that leaving town seems unnecessary, but adventurers will find even more to do beyond the city limits. Beautiful coastal communities fill Topsail Island, Figure Eight Island, Oak Island, Wrightsville Beach, Carolina Beach and Kure Beach.

Each town has its own flavor. Carolina Beach is known for deep-sea, surf and pier fishing. Ocean sports lovers rush to Wrightsville Beach for surfing, body boarding and sailing. See a Civil War fort and giant aquarium teeming with sea life at Kure Beach. Learn about endangered sea turtles at a Topsail Island turtle rescue center. Take a ferry from Pleasure Island to historic Southport, famous for its seafood and salubrious breezes.

Getting here is easy

Whether visitors are flying in for conferences, weddings, business, family vacations, to make a film or to spend time at their seaside homes, all of them are impressed with the ease of travel via Wilmington International Airport, also known as ILM. Polite, friendly and professional staff make arrivals and departures hassle-free pleasures. Even better is the airport's convenient location just minutes from the historic downtown district.

Wilmington's beautiful setting and uncomplicated access attracts growth. The city's population has doubled in the past 20 years, standing at around 110,000 people.

Dan Beck Fine Art Gallery & Studio
545 Castle Street
Wilmington NC 28401
910-299-8288
www.danbeckart.com

explore historic **downtown wilmington**

It is fun to explore the Cape Fear River on any type of water craft.

Retirees come for relaxed, affordable living on a warm, sunny coast. Singles and young families find an escape from big-city stress.

Entrepreneurs steadily uncover opportunities, while students begin their professional paths at respected institutions of higher learning.

How it all began

Much of Wilmington's present-day character, especially downtown, derives from a robust, eventful, sometimes-tumultuous and always-fascinating history.

The Cape Fear region's first explorer, other than Indians and pirates, was Giovanni de Verrazzano. The Italian, at sea for France, in 1524 set anchor near the Cape Fear River's mouth. He described the area as "open country rising in height above the sandy shore with many fair fields and plains full of mighty great woods…as pleasant and delectable to behold, as is possible to imagine." Some of his men encountered friendly Indians on shore, but strong "Northern winds," possibly from what coastal North Carolinians call "a nor'easter" storm, made the mooring unsafe, forcing the party to leave.

The following year, Spain sent a ship, and in 1526, ships carrying 600 settlers arrived from Hispaniola (now Dominican Republic). One of the ships was lost on the shoals, so the group stayed only long enough to build a new one. When it was done, they sailed for Winyaw Bay in what is now South Carolina.

In 1561, King Phillip II of Spain decreed Spain would make no more attempts to colonize Florida, as the area was known then.

Subsequently, Queen Elizabeth I decreed the right of the British to conquer and occupy land "not actually possessed on any Christian prince or people," opening the door for English colonization. In 1629, the Cape Fear area was incorporated as the Province of Carolina.

A group from the Massachusetts Bay Colony sent William Hilton in 1662 to explore the area for settling. He reported favorably, and in 1663, the group arrived here but were dissatisfied with the land and left a few months later.

In 1664 settlers from British Barbados arrived to establish Charles Town, 20 miles upstream from the ocean on the west bank of what is today named Cape Fear River.

By 1667, a multitude of problems including hostile Indians, mosquitoes, pirates and inadequate supplies forced the settlers to abandon Charles Town and migrate south, where they founded Charleston in South Carolina.

Notorious pirates

For the next 50 years, no settlements were attempted because of hostile Indians and notorious pirates, including Stede Bonnet. He ultimately was captured at the Cape Fear River mouth. Eventually, all the pirates were rounded up and the Indians driven off, making the area ripe for renewed settlement by the early 1700s.

Brunswick Town was founded on the west side of the river in 1726 (the ruins of which may be visited today). The community did not fare well compared with the more favorably positioned and protected area on high bluffs across the river and upstream, now known as Wilmington.

Setting roots, building ships

Initially settled in 1729 and subsequently known as New Carthage, New Liverpool and Newton, the town was incorporated as Wilmington in 1740 in honor of Spencer Compton, Earl of Wilmington and patron of Royal Governor Gabriel Johnston (possibly an early form of political patronage?).

During the formative years, Wilmington became an important port, shipbuilding center and processing location for lumber, pine products and cotton. At various times during the 1700s, Wilmington was North Carolina's capital. By 1760, the population reached 5,000.

In 1765, one of the American Colonies' first successful armed resistances to the British-imposed Stamp Act took place in Wilmington. Five hundred men, well-fortified from having planned their rebellion in local taverns, forced the stamp collector to resign. Thusly, Wilmington was drawn into the American Revolution, and by early 1781 British forces occupied the city. Late in the year, Lord Cornwallis arrived to lead the British to Yorktown, Va., where they were defeated.

During the years following the Revolutionary War, Wilmington prospered as an important port, and at one point was the largest city in North Carolina. However, after the turn of the century, the city began to decline because of infrastructure problems, river navigation difficulties, land transportation obstacles and various other problems.

With the advent of steam-powered vessels and the railroads, Wilmington bounced back, and by the 1840s was again an important port city for the export of cotton, lumber, naval stores, rice, flax and peanuts.

Civil war curtails trade

When the Civil War began, much of Wilmington's export trade was curtailed because of Union blockades. The port remained active thanks to the infamous and crafty blockade runners bringing supplies to the Confederacy at night from England and the Caribbean.

By 1864, Wilmington was the only Confederate port still open, but in 1865 Fort Fisher fell, the city was occupied, supply lines were closed, and the Confederacy was defeated.

Following the Civil War, Wilmington grew socially and economically as a major port and railroad center. By 1910, the city lost the distinction of being the state's largest, as tobacco and textiles fueled inland urban growth.

During the First World War, Wilmington shipbuilding and cotton export trade boomed, making for truly Roaring Twenties. Good times were not to last. The 1929 stock market crash and subsequent depression hit the city hard.

World War II rekindled prosperity. Thousands of people arrived to work on 243 ships built during the war. The North Carolina Port Authority was created, and Wilmington's port expanded significantly.

Railroad moves south

Development continued until 1955, when Wilmington was struck a nearly paralyzing blow by the movement of the Atlantic Coast Line Railroad's corporate headquarters to Florida.

Three hundred families and much of downtown's underlying economic strength departed. Downtown's decline was further exacerbated by economic growth in outlying areas, especially around modern shopping centers. Mom-and-pop shops closed and seedy bars opened. Downtown Wilmington seemed at its end.

Revitalization efforts

Although the situation appeared dire when the railroad left, despair didn't last long. During the 1960s, a dedicated group of businessmen and citizens unhappy with economic declines formed the Committee of 100, now known as Wilmington Industrial Development. The plan was to attract new and diversified industry and businesses to Wilmington.

Then, in 1977, the Downtown Area Revitalization Effort (DARE) was formed to help save existing businesses, attract new ones and preserve downtown's older buildings and historic character. That group is now known as Wilmington Downtown Inc.

All these efforts help residents and visitors acknowledge and appreciate the assets of Historic Downtown Wilmington.

Photo by G. Frank Hart Photography

Communities that are safe places to enjoy bicycle rides are becoming more and more popular.

a wealth of communities

More people each year are choosing to relocate to the Southeastern corner of North Carolina from many other areas of the country. This area is a desirable, premier location for retirees, corporate location, relocation and expansion, entrepreneurs and those seeking a better quality of life. New houses are being built, existing homes are selling, and the real estate and construction industries appear to be enjoying robust recovery and growth once again.

There are so many distinct areas that it's not easy to describe all the communities in the Greater Wilmington area. Of course, it's not possible to list all of them, but we'll mention a few that are continuing to develop in three basic areas: Brunswick County, which includes Southport and Leland; New Hanover County, which includes Wilmington, Carolina Beach, Kure Beach and Wrightsville Beach; and Pender County, just north of Wilmington.

We'll begin with Brunswick County, which experienced a 43.5 percent population growth during the '90s and was one of North Carolina's fastest growing counties. Although that rate slowed down during the economic downturn, it is expanding again. Growth of Brunswick County was not always so.

Fifteen years ago, the fishing village of Southport plus a few other sleepy communities were about all there was in Brunswick County. St. James Plantation south of Southport, probably the first of the major developments in the county, had just gotten underway. St. James today, actually an incorporated town now, is just one among many communities in the burgeoning Brunswick County real estate development scene.

Today, numerous, relatively new developments and neighborhoods exist in Brunswick County, many along North Carolina State Routes 133 and 211 from Southport, and along US Highway 17. A number are gated communities, sometimes called plantations, and quite a few have golf courses.

Brunswick Forest continues rapid growth

Once again Brunswick Forest, a 4,500-acre master-planned golf and residential community, is the fastest growing community in this area. More than 1,300 homes have been sold thus far. Located on Town Creek near Leland, Brunswick Forest is about 10 minutes from downtown Wilmington on US

16 ■ www.wilmingtontoday.com

Highway 17 South.

A number of distinctive neighborhoods include single-family homes and home sites, custom homes, town homes and cottages, all designed to offer a wide range of architectural and lifestyle choices. Home sites range from $80,000 and homes range from the high-$200s-$600s. Visitors can choose from among myriad model homes that are open for inspection and many of the models are easily customized. There is an extensive custom home building program as well.

There are a variety of different neighborhoods offering a host of options. The Woodlands at Meadow Park features low-maintenance, single-level home living. Cape Fear National offers premier home sites on the Championship golf course. Shelmore features luxury town homes, custom homes and exclusive home sites. You'll find Carolina and homes and home sites are available throughout the community.

Brunswick Forest's residents daily enjoy the Cape Fear National golf course, which opened in the fall of 2009 to outstanding reviews. Both *Golf Magazine* and *Golfweek* recognized Cape Fear National in 2010 as one of the best courses to play in North Carolina.

Other amenities include an 18,000 square foot Fitness & Wellness Center with tennis courts, indoor and outdoor pools and extensive fitness facilities, Hammock Lake Park & Pool, Town Creek River Launch serving as the center for boating and fishing, the Community Commons with a gourmet kitchen for cooking demonstrations, a picnic area and a lake with fishing gazebo and more than 100 miles of paths and trail ways, parks and natural areas.

The Villages at Brunswick Forest, a 160-acre major commercial center with shops, dining, entertainment and medical and professional offices, is located at the community's entrance. Among other tenants it is home to Lowes Foods, CVS Pharmacy, a 40,000 square foot building housing New Hanover Regional Medical Center professional offices and a variety of other professional and retail offerings.

Cape Fear National

Tim Cate, who is known for his attention to detail and imaginative routing, designed Cape Fear National. He has built a number of courses in the Carolinas that have won awards, but feels this is his best yet. The 18-hole Championship course offers premium public golf and winds through heavily undulating land and sweeps past large expanses of maple, oak and magnolia trees as well as cypress and pines. There are very picturesque vistas too, with wildflowers in bloom throughout the course, abundant water features including three waterfalls and several bridges cut through natural areas.

The driving range features grass hitting areas along with practice putting and chipping venues.

The large clubhouse at Cape Fear National has a fully stocked pro shop as well as both indoor and outdoor dining and/or bar areas. The club is happy to host golf outings and tournaments. It also is possible to rent the facility for such special events as rehearsal dinners, anniversary or birthday parties and family reunions.

For more information, call 888-371-2434.

With so many enjoyable activities available to fill the day, and with business

people working harder all the time, many homeowners prefer to let professionals maintain their lawns for them so that they have time to pursue other interests. Fortunately, a well-established, reliable service is just a phone call away.

Maintaining beautiful lawns

North State Gardens is a full-service residential and commercial landscaping business serving the greater Wilmington area since 1982. The company has serviced clients throughout the area, keeping lawns healthy and beautiful from Leland to Jacksonville.

This family-owned company prioritizes customer service, attention to detail, and sustainability. They provide a full range of lawn care services to hundreds of residential, commercial and industrial clients. With a highly experienced and knowledgeable staff, North State can handle properties of any size or complexity.

Their lawn maintenance services include mowing and lawn cleanup, edging, fertilization and pest control, all tailored to the individual client's lawn. North State's lawn service customers appreciate that the company does not require contracts. With a commitment to sustainability, North State composts and re-uses all grass clippings and lawn debris. They also offer the option of organic fertilizer upon request.

North State also is a full service landscaping contractor. Shrub and tree care, pruning, mulching, dune planting, seasonal color design, installation and maintenance are among the services offered.

North State is happy to provide free consultation and lawn analysis to new clients.

Older communities

Not far from Brunswick Forest on US Highway 17 are two older gated housing developments, one built around a golf course and one not.

Waterford of the Carolinas, in the Leland area on 575 acres, has a host of features and amenities almost too numerous to mention. Most of the 900 homes and home sites are located on the creeks, lakes and waterways within the community.

Scenic walking trails wind throughout the community, there are four lighted tennis courts and the lakes are large enough for small boat sailing, fishing, kayaking and rowing.

The Amenities Center has a sports events lawn for outdoor activities and parties, fitness facility, media room and library and gathering area with kitchen for parties. The large, resort-style swimming pool and walk-up beach are connected with the Clubhouse by a poolside screened porch.

Waterford of the Carolinas does not have its own golf course but dozens of courses are within easy driving distance.

At the entrance to Waterford, the Village Shops include a comprehensive medical center, restaurants, bank, animal hospital, pharmacy, dentist and much, much more, all only about five minutes from Wilmington.

Popular Italian spot

Waterford is home to Eddie Romanelli's, a popular Italian restaurant known for affordable prices and portions so large doggy bags make up a full meal.

Myriad appetizers include hot wings and hot crab dip for two. Among salads, consider the almond chicken salad with sliced chicken, spring onions, pineapple and fresh herbs with a bit of simple mayonnaise, all on a bed of lettuce in a tortilla bowl. Tomatoes, boiled egg and almonds are the garnish.

A large number of sandwiches, pizzas and calzones are featured, too.

Italian specialties include eggplant rollatini, chicken marsala, baked ziti and Mama Romanelli's cheesy lasagna. Shrimp Tuscany features sautéed shrimp with mushrooms, basil, tomatoes, scallions and prosciutto in a creamy alfredo sauce tossed with linguini.

Check the family-style, to-go menu for eight to 10 people, perfect for dinners, business lunches and parties. Don't forget curbside to-go service. Eddie Romanell's decadent strawberry cream cake is among family-style menu offerings.

The restaurant has a full bar and large wine list. Hours are 11 a.m. to 10 p.m. Sunday-Thursday. Hours are extended to 11 p.m. on Friday and Saturday. Look for drink and food specials on Monday and Tuesday nights. The

restaurant's event spaces can host up to 45 people.

Another golf community

Located adjacent to Waterford is Magnolia Greens Golf Plantation, a thriving community with acres of conservation areas studded with ponds and lakes. Magnolia Greens is built around a championship 27-hole golf course that received a 4 1/2 star rating from *Golf Digest*, the only golf course in the area with that rating.

The community contains a huge 8,000 square foot recreation center with all type of fitness equipment and aerobic and cardio rooms where a variety of classes are offered. There are two outdoor swimming pools, a covered grilling area and lighted tennis courts, among other features.

Home sites offer both water and golf course views. Everything from townhouses to patio homes to beautiful custom homes is available with Magnolia Greens.

At the entrance of Magnolia Greens is a retail and office complex where all types of shopping, dining and professional services are offered, including medical and dental offices, banking, insurance and salon and spa services.

Audubon community

One of the newer communities is Compass Pointe, set on 2,200 acres on the highest point in Brunswick County. The gated community will have a 27-hole golf course, an 18-hole putting course with two additional putting greens, two amenity centers, indoor and outdoor pools, tennis courts, a dog park, bike trails and a launch for canoes and kayaks.

Rick Robbins has designed the golf course in a style similar to what is found in Pinehurst, not to copy that area but because the topography and vegetation at Compass Pointe is like that of the sandhills region of North Carolina.

Compass Pointe is located ten miles from Historic Downtown Wilmington on Highway 74/76W. Compass Pointe is an Audubon International Gold Signature Community with a 70-acre sanctuary for native plants and wildlife.

New Hanover County

Although New Hanover County geographically is next to the smallest county in North Carolina, it's far from the smallest in residential development.

One of the fastest growing areas in the county is along River Road, which has been rerouted to facilitate some of this development. Not so many years ago, the only developments between Carolina Beach Road and River Road were The Cape, Beau Rivage Plantation and Echo Farms Golf and Country Club.

Today, thousands of homes have been built or are planned for this burgeoning corridor along the Cape Fear River from Downtown Wilmington to Pleasure Island with prices ranging from the low $200 to the millions.

Proximity to beaches and services makes this area particularly attractive. Wilmington's airport, the New Hanover Regional Medical Center and all the health facilities and medical offices around it, Carolina Beach, Kure Beach and Wrightsville Beach are a short drive away. The area's largest shopping centers are reachable in 15 minutes or less, making it easy to find whatever might be needed.

River Bluffs

A beautiful new community is taking shape in a wonderfully convenient location. Situated along the high bluffs of Castle Hayne, River Bluffs is a new, low-impact community offering 3,000 feet of navigable river frontage. Wilmington's airport, historic downtown, entertainment, major medical and destination shopping are just minutes from the gated entrance of River Bluffs.

River Bluffs presents a luxurious coastal waterfront lifestyle with a considerable number of community amenities. When complete, the River Club will offer a warm, inviting restaurant and lounge with riverfront views. The River Bluffs Marina Complex will feature 141 boat slips, 20- to 30-foot water depth, and floating docks to take full advantage of the community's riverfront location. Davis Square will offer a wide range of amenities, including a swimming pool, tennis courts, fitness center, children's playground, general store, post office and

WILMINGTON'S PREMIER RIVERFRONT COMMUNITY

RIVER LIFE IS GOOD!

MARINA & RIVER CLUB | VILLAGE CENTER | ORGANIC FARM
PARKS & TRAILS | BOAT LAUNCH & STORAGE

DISCOVER RIVER BLUFFS ~ Plan *your* property tour now!

Single Family Homes *from the mid $350's+* | Personal Tours by Appointment

1100 Chair Rd. Castle Hayne, NC 28429 | 910.617.4954 | RiverBluffsLiving.com

Equal Housing Opportunity. This is not intended to be an offer to sell or solicitation of offers to buy real estate in River Bluffs to residents of any state or jurisdiction where prior registration is required or where prohibited by law, unless registered or exempt from registration. The features, amenities and prices described and depicted herein are based upon current development plans, which are subject to change without notice. Renderings and artists' interpretations are for illustrative purposes only and no guarantee is made that the features, amenities and facilities described herein will be provided, or if provided, will be of the same, type, size or nature as depicted or described. Access to and rights to use recreational facilities within the development may be subject to payment of use fees, membership requirements, availability and other limitations, rules and regulations. © River Bluffs 2015

a wealth of **communities**

Photo by G. Frank Hart Photography
Many of our area's homes enjoy magnificent views of the water.

café. The organic farm, located just outside the community entrance, will grow certified organic produce available at the River Club and general store. More than one-third of the community's land (over 100 acres) has been preserved for walking trails, open green space, and a dog park.

River Bluffs will feature southern architecture reminiscent of riverfront homes in historic Wilmington, Charleston and Savannah. The Cape Fear River wraps around the property in a way that affords many opportunities for water access or simply enjoying the views. At completion, River Bluffs will include approximately 750 home sites within the 313-acre community. During Phase 1, 221 home sites will be built over 88 acres. Home sites range from one-fourth to one-third acre with prices for house and lot spanning from $300,000 to $500,000 and higher.

Developed on a philosophy of sustainability and environmental preservation, River Bluffs is certified as a Low Impact Development (LID) based on its water re-use, rainwater harvesting and storm water control techniques. The community is designed to preserve existing rolling terrain, native hardwood forests, coastal plants and high bluffs overlooking the river. LID communities enjoy improved water quality and the notable absence of storm water ponds.

Burrows Smith, managing partner in River Bluffs Development Group, is a native of Wrightsville Beach. His real estate construction and development experience in the area spans several decades, and notable projects include Masonboro Landing, Masonboro Forest, Landfall, Porters Neck, and Dockside Restaurant.

Downtown Wilmington

Downtown Wilmington continues to enjoy an upsurge in people living there as new condo developments spring up. This increase in downtown residency is a great part of what is fueling the strength of the downtown area.

A fair amount of residential construction has occurred on the north side of downtown where the new headquarters building for PPD Corporation opened in 2007. Add to all this the continued renovation of old homes and the growth of living quarters above shops and offices, and you have a recipe for a vibrant downtown Wilmington.

A major new apartment complex is about to open downtown and plans for a mixed used facility that will include condos is nearing approval.

Many more buildings are in the early planning stages. New hotels and new mixed-use buildings that will include residential spaces are being discussed since there is a need for additional housing downtown.

New neighborhoods galore

Getting away from downtown, growth of new neighborhoods is taking place all over the city and outlying areas, with much of it being concentrated along several corridors: the east side near Wrightsville Beach, especially along Eastwood Road; the southeast side along Carolina Beach Road down to Pleasure Island, and the northeast side along Market Street through Ogden.

On the east side of the city near Wrightsville Beach, quite a few new residential communities have developed. One of the communities that continues to develop is Landfall, with gated entrances on both Eastwood and Military Cutoff Roads.

Area's top community

Landfall is a community of nearly 2,200 acres that has developed over nearly three decades into North Carolina's premier coastal community. Located on the Intracoastal Waterway and Howe Creek in Wilmington, the community features over four miles of waterfront property as well as superb golf courses.

The 25 different communities that comprise Landfall include lakes, ponds and a wide variety of land and vegetative environments that are an ideal setting for the nearly 2,000 homes located there. Homes range from spectacular ones located on the Intracoastal Waterway to condos and patio homes that are preferred by some retirees. Landfall also has 29 miles of paved roadway and 320 acres of conservation areas.

With so many communities within Landfall, there is a wide range of home

Discover Landfall Today!

Nestled on 2200 acres along the Intracoastal Waterway, Landfall is the premier gated community in Wilmington. It's just minutes from Wrightsville Beach, with many shopping and dining options nearby. It's only a short drive from Historic Downtown.

Within the three gates of Landfall, there are a wide variety of amenities. Enjoy the walking trails throughout the community's 320 acres of conservation area. Landfall features several lakes, parks and gardens. Landfall Lake offers a mile long paved path with views of the Intracoastal Waterway. There is year round golfing on the Jack Nicklaus & Pete Dye Courses. The Country Club of Landfall offers various memberships that include golfing, fitness center, swimming and tennis. The community provides 24/7 security.

There are over 5000 residents in Landfall representing over 40 states & 20 countries. Community events include annual festivals, tournaments, concerts, fireworks and so much more. Landfall has over 1600 homes with 24 unique sub-communities with over 4 miles of waterfront properties. Home prices starting in the mid $300,000's and lots starting in the low $120,000's.

Forbes Magazine named the Landfall community as "Best Address" to live. Landfall was also just named "Best North Carolina Community Of The Year" by REAL ESTATE SCORECARD. Come see why our community is such a desirable place to raise a family or retire. Call for your own personal tour of our community. Discover the Landfall lifestyle today!

GARY NICHOLS
Broker/Resident
910-620-6925
gary.nichols@livinglandfall.com
www.livinglandfall.com

prices too. In 2014, the highest price paid was $2.9 million and the lowest $240,000.

Landfall offers plenty of things to do within its gates. Perhaps a walk or bike ride on the one mile paved path around Landfall Lake or a stroll through the nature trail beckons, while the kids play soccer, volleyball or basketball on the community recreational facilities.

Those who purchase membership in Country Club of Landfall will find 45 holes of the best golf in North Carolina minutes from their front door, with 27 holes designed by Jack Nicklaus and 18 by Pete Dye.

If racquet sports are preferred, there is tennis on the 14 varied court surfaces of the tennis complex set on 14 acres, arguably North Carolina's finest tennis facility. Perhaps a healthy workout in the Club's fitness center, a swim in its Olympic pool that features eight lanes, a toddler pool, snack bar and areas for relaxation, or dinner in its excellent dining facility is more what is desired.

Landfall is located only five minutes away from the ocean front town of Wrightsville Beach and just 15 minutes from historically interesting Downtown Wilmington, which is filled with restaurants, attractions, theaters and shops offering unique, superbly crafted merchandise.

A regional library offering a host of education programs, huge shopping complexes and many outstanding restaurants are just outside the gates.

Landfall is a controlled-access gated community, which is secured by three entrance gates that are either manned by security personnel or accessible via a barcoded entry system, 24 hours a day, seven days a week.

The professionally trained staff provides an array of services to the community that adds convenience to everyday life; they respond to resident inquiries, provide assistance to 911 calls, check homes while homeowners are traveling and basically assist residents in almost any capacity possible.

Superb custom homebuilder

Those who purchase building sites in Landfall or any number of other distinguished communities are always looking for a qualified, reputable homebuilder who can bring their vision to life. A builder with a sterling reputation is Mark Johnson Custom Homes, a licensed unlimited builder focused on new custom home building and remodeling. Locally owned in Wilmington, they provide the full range of residential construction services, including single-family custom homes, and energy-efficient, sustainable remodels and renovations.

As a small, family-owned business, the Mark Johnson team takes extraordinary pride in every new home and remodeling project they undertake. They carefully craft timeless homes built to last generations as well as remodel existing homes into beautiful, new living spaces for enhanced functionality and updates.

With a long list of outstanding client testimonials and referrals, Mark Johnson Custom Homes is consistently recognized for outstanding customer service, craftsmanship and safety. Because they are not a high-volume production manufacturer of homes, customers receive undivided attention and service. Prior to starting a new home construction or remodeling project, MJCH spends time getting to know their customers and

Wilmington's Premier Builder

MJ

MARK JOHNSON
custom homes

"We had a totally positive building experience with Mark Johnson Custom Homes during all phases of building our new home. Working with a builder when you are living out of state requires frequent and clear communication and a high level of trust, and MJCH more than met our expectations in those areas."
- Mark & Cindy Humphreville

Phone: 910.443.5422
Mark@MarkJohnsonCustomHomes.com
www.MarkJohnsonCustomHomes.com

identifying their needs and wants so that they can turn their dreams into reality.

Since every great home begins with a solid plan, Mark Johnson Custom Homes can work with an existing plan, find a pre-designed plan matching the customer's criteria, or build a custom design plan. The next step is to create a comprehensive budget outlining the final price based on allowances, layouts and specifications. Then the design team walks customers through the interior and exterior design selection process, including showroom visits. Once construction breaks ground, customers are kept in the know consistently with detailed production schedules and weekly progress photos. Throughout the construction process, the home is thoroughly inspected by independent home inspectors and quality control professionals. After completion of the home, the Mark Johnson team walks the clients through the house, providing a thorough orientation to all aspects of the house. Finally, MJCH provides a one-year builder warranty on each new house, and during the eleventh month, they follow up to address any touch-ups or warranty concerns.

MJCH is committed to smart, sustainable building and development. Indeed, they built Eastern North Carolina's first LEED Platinum Home. With the highest green-building certification, the LEED home had unparalleled efficiency, sustainability and safety.

More information about Mark Johnson Custom Homes can be found on their website. He also builds in areas away from Landfall.

Landscaping services

After your new home has been completed, many people turn their attention to creating outdoor living space that complements their home. Most people have neither the knowledge nor the expertise to make all the decisions about how to enhance their property. Fortunately, a long-established, talented design company is available.

North State Gardens is a full-service residential and commercial landscaping business serving the Wilmington area since 1982. This family-owned company prioritizes customer service, attention to detail, and sustainability. They specialize in design/build landscaping and maintenance, and the quality of their work speaks for itself.

The North State team relies on principles of design, art, horticulture and architecture to create a garden that will add beauty and value to the property. Each landscape design project begins with a meeting between the client and one of North State's designers. The designer will then develop a landscape plan to meet the client's goals and preferences, while taking into consideration the architecture of the house and the coastal North Carolina environment.

Upon approval of a landscape design, North State will manage installation of all the elements, from plantings and hardscapes, to irrigation, lighting, lawn care, and maintenance. Each project has a team, consisting of a designer and a field foreman, which manages the project from beginning to end.

North State is experienced with new landscape installations and renovations, and they personally select the plant material that is best suited to the project. Additionally, their team of craftsman can create the rights hardscape for any garden, including walkways, patios, driveways, walls, arbors and outdoor fire-

Outdoor Living Spaces

NORTH STATE Gardens

Expert landscape design, installation, maintenance, and lighting with a focus on form, function and sustainability. Call us today for a FREE consultation.

910-270-4702 • www.northstategardens.com

places.

The company values sustainability and employs sound environmental practices whenever possible in all of their services. Some of their sustainable practices include using drip systems in plant beds, rain sensors in their irrigation systems, and composting lawn trimmings.

North State also provides regular lawn maintenance service to hundreds of residential, commercial and industrial clients from Jacksonville to Leland. New clients are encouraged to contact them for a free consultation to discuss landscaping and maintenance needs.

Growth continues around Porters Neck area

An area that continues to see very rapid growth surrounds the intersection of Porters Neck Road and Market Street. Porters Neck Plantation and Country Club is on the Intracoastal Waterway about four miles north of Wilmington. Porters Neck is another of New Hanover County's upscale developments.

The 18-hole golf course at Porters Neck was designed by Tom Fazio and has been named "the #1 coastal course" in North Carolina by *Golf Digest*. Among the amenities at Porters Neck are a clubhouse, two large pools, seven lighted hydro-clay tennis courts, fitness complex and a boat ramp on the Intracoastal Waterway.

Lots in Porters Neck range from $75,000 to more than $200,000, and homes are priced from the high $300,000 to $1 million or more.

Forest Creek is a newer gated neighborhood in Porters Neck Plantation. Nestled among majestic southern oaks and beautiful magnolia trees, this quiet community features more than 20 classic home designs ranging from 2,200 to 3,500 square feet.

Members can enjoy all Porters Neck Country Club privileges, plus private walking paths, open green space and lighted streets.

Several huge apartment complexes are rising near Porters Neck and are adjacent to Marsh Oaks, a lovely community comprised primarily of single-family homes. The apartments, mostly rental, are in the building phase now with just a few ready for current occupancy.

Another new apartment complex is being built just north of Porters Neck Road, and a huge shopping complex that will include WalMart as its anchor is developing on Market Street just south of Porters Neck Road.

Buy, repair lamps

Once your home is designed, your landscaping is in place and you're settling into your new home, you may find that new furnishings are needed. An item that can make a huge difference in how a room looks is lighting.

Customers throughout the tri-county area have relied on D. Baxter's for the company's expertise for many years. D. Baxter's, located on Oleander Drive in the Anderson Shopping Center, does a beautiful job repairing lamps and light fixtures of all types. They have been in business since 1993 and have helped thousands of customers in that time.

In addition to top quality repairs for lamps and chandeliers, they have an enormous selection of frames. They also have the people with the talent to do a superb job of matting and framing all types of artwork, diplomas and other objects that people want to display.

D. Baxter's has by far the largest selection of lamps, replacement shades, and finials and pulls in the area. They can produce a lamp out of most anything; people with a favorite vase or sculpture that they would like to turn into a lamp can have it done here. They also refinish brass and silver and expertly repair porcelain and glass.

Building kitchens to suit

Homeowners know that in order to maximize their own enjoyment and resale value, investing in their home to keep it up to date is a good idea. For many, the kitchen is considered the most important room in the house. Kitchens are no longer hidden behind closed doors; today many people choose to make them an integral part of their living and entertaining space. As a result, the quality and design of the components in the kitchen takes on added importance.

A company that has been designing, installing and delivering kitchens since 1990 is Kitchen Blueprints, located on

We can do this...

Wood·Mode®
FINE CUSTOM CABINETRY

Kitchen BLUEPRINTS
3115-J Wrightsville Avenue, Wilmington NC 28403
910-763-2536 • 910-763-2536
www.kitchenblueprints.net

Building a new home to an individual's specific taste is very satisfying.

Wrightsville Avenue. The staff at Kitchen Blueprints is happy to work with a client's architect or builder, or is content to work directly with clients to deliver the kitchen of their dreams.

Kitchen Blueprints is the exclusive Wood-Mode Fine Custom Cabinetry dealer in the Wilmington area. Wood-Mode cabinets are proudly made in America, with a nearly infinite choice of cabinets, inserts, styles, drawers and combinations.

Wood-Mode products also are used for baths, libraries, closets and any place else where beautiful cabinets would fit.

Many homes in older communities that are about to go on the market have kitchens that need to be updated, and homeowners who have lived with inadequate kitchen space are remodeling. Kitchen Blueprints also does a wonderful job in redesigning and redoing dated kitchens. Their installers are first rate, and clients can rely on having the job done professionally. The job will be completed on time and on budget, and to the customer's complete satisfaction.

Rapid expansion to north

New housing developments have spread into Pender County too, just north of Wilmington. People who work at GE and Corning, two of the area's larger employers, can reach their offices quickly thanks to the new bypass. As a result, several communities in Hampstead are now nearly built out.

Castle Bay Country Club in Hampstead is a private community developed around a golf course that features acres of protected wetlands sheltering a variety of very rare, prized native plants, numerous ponds and a lake.

A Scottish links golf course, huge clubhouse, sidewalks, pool, tennis, and fitness center are some of the amenities. Access to Pender County's highly ranked schools, proximity to the beaches of Topsail Island, and availability of the cultural activities in Wilmington attract families with children as well as empty nesters to Castle Bay. There are only a few empty lots remaining in Castle Bay and the community will be completely built out in a year or so. Patio homes, townhouses and custom homes are available.

Just a few lots that can be built on remain at Olde Point, a community developed in the late 1970's that stretches from US Highway 17 to the Intracoastal Waterway in Hampstead. Olde Point members also have tennis courts and a swimming pool available for their use.

Homes of all types - from relatively modest wooden villas to more than million dollar waterfront homes - are present in the development that features beautiful mature trees and plantings.

Belvedere Country Club also stretches from US Highway 17 to the Intracoastal Waterway. Belvedere is built around an 18-hole golf course that welcomes players of all abilities.

Custom homes, townhouses, patio homes and homes facing a beautiful marina are found at Belvedere. There are relatively few home sites left in this community and all lots facing the golf course have been sold.

Golf & private beach

North Shore County Club is a golf community located in Sneads Ferry, about 40 minutes north of Wilmington. Homes in the development are built around a beautiful 18-hole golf course that features everything from woodland to marsh views since it is built along the Intracoastal Waterway.

North Shore homeowners enjoy all the amenities one could expect, including tennis, golf and swimming.

There is a clubhouse too where residents and their guests can enjoy food and beverages while mingling with their neighbors.

Homeowners also enjoy private oceanfront beach access on Topsail Island, located just over the bridge from the community.

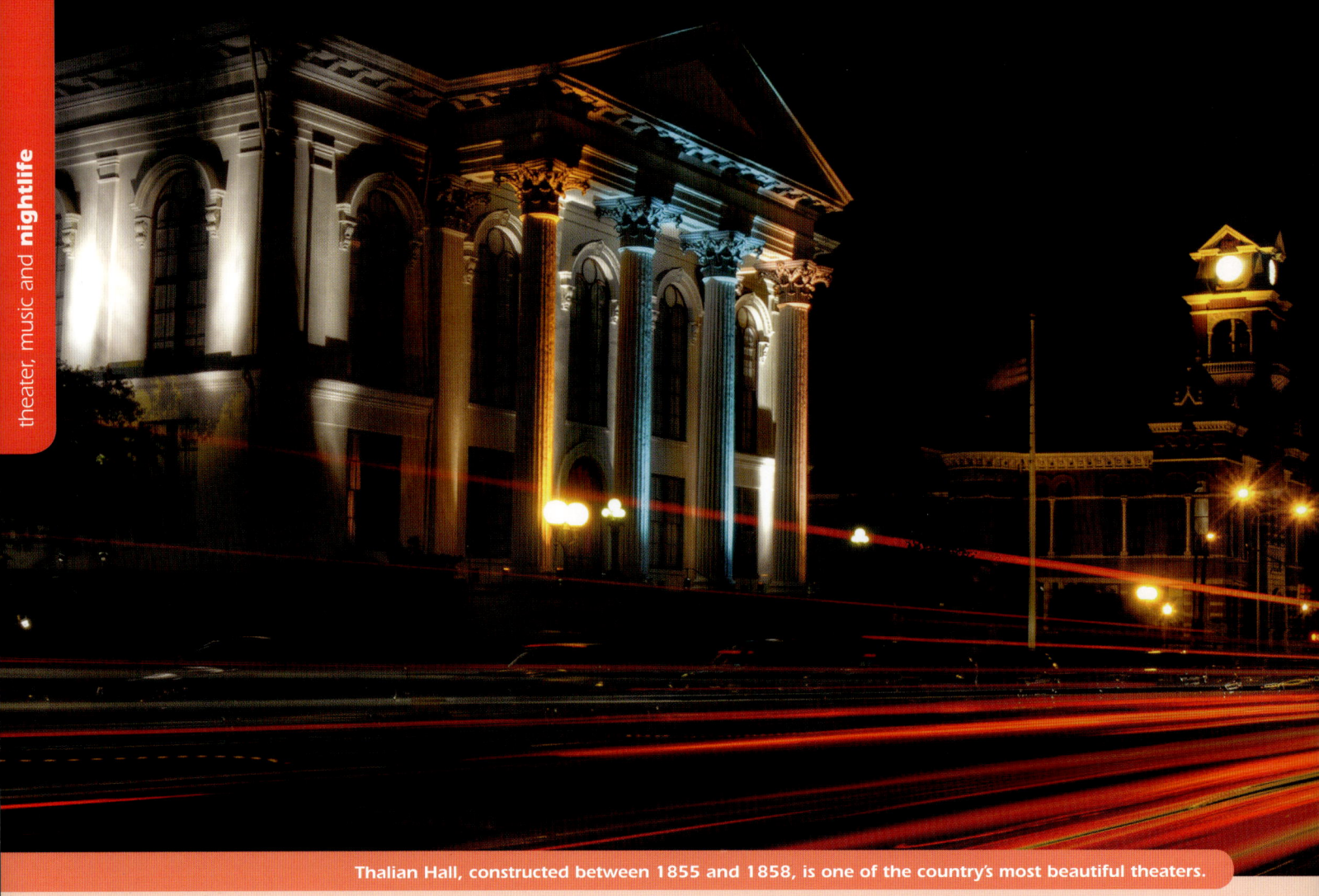

Thalian Hall, constructed between 1855 and 1858, is one of the country's most beautiful theaters.

entertainment and **nightlife**

Residents have enthusiastically encouraged and supported artistic endeavors all throughout Wilmington's history.

The focal point, and certainly the earliest venue in our cultural scene, is that venerable jewel, Thalian Hall. One of the oldest and most beautiful theaters in the nation, Thalian Hall was built between 1855 and 1858 to satisfy both the cultural and governmental needs of the city.

It originally served as a combination opera house and a seat for local government, with a library thrown in for good measure. When the theater opened on October 12, 1858, it seated 950 people.

Who performed at Thalian?

As a major stop on the national touring circuit, Thalian Hall hosted well-known entertainers including Lillian Russell, Buffalo Bill Cody, John Phillip Sousa, Maurice Barrymore and Sir Henry Lauder. After the turn of the century, the facility was renovated and updated for electricity, but by the thirties, with the decline in traveling road shows, activity at Thalian Hall dwindled.

Thalian Hall had a few close calls with demolition during the thirties and forties, but the citizens always rallied to its support. The theater was restored to its turn-of-the-century splendor in 1973, and activity increased. During the eighties, with funds from the city and state plus contributions from the citizens, $5 million was raised for an 18-month renovation and expansion project.

250 annual events

Thalian Hall hosts more that 250 performance events per year, including concerts, stage plays, popular musical attractions, a children's theater and Cinematique, which presents artistic films. With beautiful renovations completed in 2011, new seating, new lighting equipment and a new HVAC system make an evening in the theater much more comfortable and enjoyable now.

One addition worthy of special note is the fabulous chandelier that was donated to the theater. Affectionately named Alice, the audience cheers every time the chandelier is raised before a performance.

A newer addition is the exterior lighting, which was turned on for the first time on February 28, 2013. Designed by the same company that lit the Washington Monument, Statue of Liberty and the White House, the system uses 32 energy efficient fixtures that consume approximately the same amount of energy as two household microwaves. The beautiful historic building is now

Visit historic Thalian Hall where shows are playing most every night!

Thalian Hall Center for the Performing Arts, Inc.

310 Chestnut Street, Wilmington, NC 28401

Box Office: 910-632-2285; toll-free: 1-800-523-2820

www.thalianhall.org

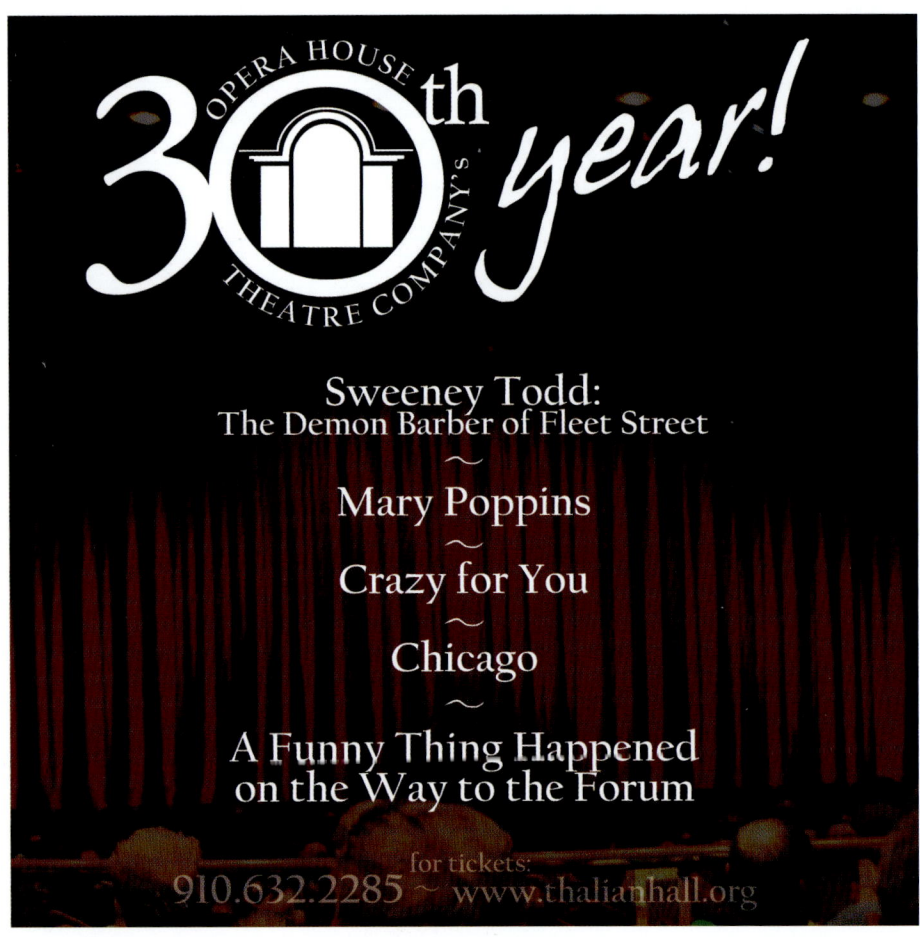

much more visible at night.

The most recent major renovation was just completed in February 2015, when the Ruth and Bucky Stein Theatre was completed. The space, previously known as the Studio Theatre, has now been redone with stadium seating, digital film equipment and state of the art light and sound equipment. The new theatre will be used for film half the time, and for live performances the rest of the time.

NC's community theater

When Thalian Hall was constructed, Wilmington was a bustling and growing city with an active theatrical group, the Thalian Association, dating back to 1788.

The goal of the founders was to bring arts education and performing arts to the growing city. Continuing to this day, Thalian Association, celebrating its 227th anniversary in 2015, has contributed substantially to Wilmington's cultural scene. Its importance was recognized in 2007 when it earned the honor of being named the Official Community Theater of North Carolina. Signs announcing that designation are proudly displayed on major roads leading to Wilmington.

Each year, Thalian Association produces five major productions – musicals, drama and comedies – on the Main Stage of Thalian Hall. Through the years, thousands of local actors, directors, choreographers, conductors, musicians, designers and technicians have developed their craft while enjoying the opportunity to work with Thalian Association.

Children share limelight

Young thespians are given the opportunity to perform also; children ages 7-10 can participate in workshops throughout the year. The Thalian Association Children's Theatre (TACT), founded more than 30 years ago, stages five productions annually on the Second Street Stage at the Hannah Block Historic USO/Community Arts Center, each showcasing the talents of youngsters ages 6-17.

Thalian Association added a summer season at the Red Barn Studio in 2014 and is continuing to stage shows there. Red Barn is an intimate theater founded by former Wilmingtonians Linda Lavin and Steve Bakunas.

Thalian Association's activities are not limited to theater productions. They present the Orange Street Arts Fest in May each year. They also manage the Hannah Block Historic USO/Community Arts Center for the city of Wilmington, making space available for classes in a wide array of artistic disciplines. Performing and visual community arts groups can rehearse, perform, display and teach their various art forms at little or no charge thanks to Thalian Association's management of the community arts center.

Opera House continues

Lou Criscuolo, a former Broadway performer who never shied away from a theatrical challenge, founded Opera House Theatre Company. He died on December 13, 2014, at age 80, one month before he was due to be honored with a well-deserved lifetime achievement award for his contribution to local theater.

Criscuolo came to Wilmington in 1983 to appear in the 125th anniversary show at Thalian Hall. He moved to Wilmington and started Opera House the following year. Since that time, Criscuolo mentored many of the talented local performers. He was much beloved and revered by those who benefitted from his wise counsel and support.

Opera House will continue, and their new season began with a wonderful presentation of Sweeney Todd: the Demon Barber of Fleet Street. This Tony-award winning musical featured a wonderful local cast, set, lighting and staging. Based upon that production, it seems safe to assume that Opera House will continue to collect a sizable number of Wilmington Theater Awards for the performers and productions they stage.

Big Dawg Productions

Big Dawg Productions moved into a new space, the Cape Fear Playhouse on Castle Street, in 2010.

The non-profit company presents both new and well-known plays and is coming into its own as a force in the Wilmington theater scene.

Several Big Dawg productions, including *The Hermit of Fort Fisher*, have received accolades and awards in recent years. The play was so popular that it sold out completely not only in Wilmington, but in Southport as well.

UNCW Stages Events

There are additional theatrical venues away from downtown too.

At the University of North Carolina Wilmington, outstanding University Theatre productions are presented in conjunction with the UNCW Theater Department.

In September 2006, the university opened its new $32 million, 104,830 square foot academic and performance facility, the Cultural Arts Building, which includes two theatres.

Other locations used by various theatre groups include the Scottish Rite Temple on South 17th Street, the Minnie Evans Art Center on the campus of Ashley High School, and Murray Middle School on Carolina Beach Road.

Live theater is not the only artistic discipline that is celebrated in this area. Many other endeavors are recognized and nourished by public and private groups, especially by Wilmington's own Arts Council.

Devoted fans in the area continue to support classical music programs. UNCW's Kenan Auditorium and Cultural Arts building host the Wilmington Symphony Orchestra, operatic productions, the Wilmington Symphony Youth Orchestra and the North Carolina Symphony plus a variety of national touring groups brought in by the Wilmington Concert Association.

The UNCW Department of Music's 280-seat Recital Hall is a state-of-the-art facility where Chamber Music Wilmington makes its home, bringing to campus a wide variety of world-class chamber musicians.

Brown Coat Pub & Theatre

Brown Coat Pub and Theatre on Grace Street downtown is dedicated to presenting new or less frequently seen works by playwrights. Richard Davis formed the non-profit group in 2004.

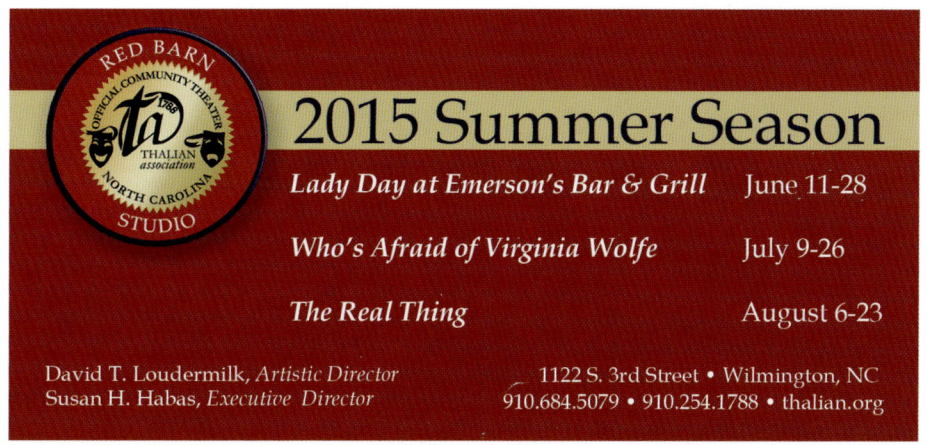

Gallery won the best play at the Wilmington Theater Awards in 2015 along with three other awards. Every Monday at 8 p.m. free movies are shown, followed by karaoke at 10 p.m. In fact, karaoke is so popular that it's featured each night at the same time.

Wilmington's Guerilla Theatre Company's live productions at Brown Coat are staged without glitzy sets, special effects or amazing costumes. As a result, an actor's ability to convey the spoken words is the sole emphasis.

Comedy tonight

Dead Crow Comedy Room, the successor to Nutt Street Comedy Room, is bringing talented comedians back to Wilmington now that it has found a great location on North Front Street downtown. It is a favorite gathering spot for locals and visitors to experience live comedy. The intimate basement venue provides a special environment to see comedians from Comedy Central, HBO, BET, Conan O'Brien, Jimmy Fallon and Last Comic Standing.

Local comedians get a chance to perform too: Thursday night is open mic night when all are welcome. Dead Crow serves very reasonably priced pub food and has specials on beer and drinks too. Dead Crow opens at 7 p.m. and closes at 2 a.m., seven days a week.

City Stage Co.

Nick Gray and Rachael Moser, the co-artistic directors of new City Stage Co., are off to a rousing start. They have staged three productions thus far, all of which have been very successful.

Their latest effort, Triassic Parq, was a raucous, bawdy adult musical that had the audience laughing out loud throughout the show.

The mission of the company is to produce shows that have never been seen in Wilmington. They are doing a wonderful job of restoring the City Stage space too so that it is a much more comfortable and welcoming venue. The future looks very bright for this group.

Music lovers choices

No self-respecting city situated between a river and sandy beaches would be complete without music and nightlife, and Wilmington has more than its share of both to offer. For the most part, music and nightlife in the downtown area are intertwined. Restaurants, bars, lounges, cafés, clubs and theaters offer a wide variety of musical genres including cool and smooth jazz, rompin' stompin' blues, rock, Hawaiian, country and western, indie rock, Caribbean and pretty much everything else.

A newer nightspot downtown is Bourgie Nights, a wine bar located next door to Manna, one of Wilmington's best restaurants. Bourgie Nights particularly supports talented bluegrass music and musicians thanks to the efforts of Billy Mellon, owner of both the restaurant and the music venue.

Downtown draws crowds

Downtown, thousands of college students from UNCW and Cape Fear

Community College descend on the central city music scene with regularity and frequency, fueling the tremendous popularity of live music. Coupled with the tourists, Marines from Cape Lejeune and regular residents, it makes for a lively situation. On-street parking places can be harder to find in the evening than in the daytime, but several conveniently located downtown parking decks and lots are available 24 hours a day.

Because of North Carolina's unique and somewhat outdated liquor laws, the popular music scene is a bit more complex than in many other cities. If a music venue - for example, a restaurant and lounge - derives most of its revenue from food, there are no restrictions on accessibility. However, if a music venue gets most of its revenue from liquor sales or offers no food, it must function as a private club. Not to worry though, you can buy a membership, effective in three days, for a very nominal sum, and you can be admitted immediately as a "guest" of a member. Some of the jumping downtown venues, including those known as dance clubs, usually offer rock or some variation thereof. Throughout the greater Wilmington area, the nature of the music scene is similar to downtown except for the large clubs. Many of the entertainers and groups appearing downtown also appear at other locations around the city or in suburban and beach venues on other nights.

Late night food, drinks

Hell's Kitchen is a popular sports bar downtown that features live bands most weekends. The venue was seen on *Dawson's Creek*, the popular television series that was filmed in Wilmington. There are food and drink specials each weeknight; Wednesday features $6.66 burgers and $3 pints, which is always a good combination.

Front Street Brewery, Wilmington's original and award-winning craft brewer, serves a full menu until midnight each night. Their filling sandwiches, salads or delicious appetizers are a terrific choice to satisfy your hunger after the theater or a concert downtown.

Slice of Life also serves late in their new, much larger space downtown. Slice

Continued on page 65

Downtown Wilmington has lots of places where people can celebrate.

The Azalea Belles serve as ambassadors during the largest annual Wilmington festival.

celebrate our festivals

The Wilmington area draws a large number of visitors who come to attend the festivals that are held here each year. Several of the celebrations have been recognized as outstanding regional or national events. With such an abundance, we have room to highlight only the current major festivals and make mention of some of the rest. The Wilmington Today website, www.wilmingtontoday.com, carries additional information that is updated throughout the year.

Azalea Festival

From its beginning in 1948, the North Carolina Azalea Festival has blossomed into a five-day event showcasing exquisite gardens, great artwork and our rich cultural history and heritage. It is held in April each year at the height of azalea blooming.

The Azalea Festival includes a parade complete with Azalea Queen, street fair, circus, concerts, horse show, major entertainment, home and garden tours, children's tea, pageantry from a bygone era and much of the charm and culture that makes Wilmington a proud Southern city.

The festival officially kicks off with the arrival of Queen Azalea, followed by the parade and two-day street fair. In all, more than 125 events are included.

Naturally, the Queen has a court, comprised of gorgeous young ladies escorted by Summerall Guards, handsome military cadets in full dress uniform from the Citadel's senior elite drill team. In addition, the Azalea Princesses, a group of outstanding local high school students who have participated in the Princess Scholarship Pageant, are present.

In 1969, the tradition of the Azalea Belles was introduced, and since then has grown to more than 100 young ladies, all dressed in gowns that reflect the style of the antebellum period. Azalea Belles primarily serve as hostesses at the garden tours and they definitely add a note of gracious beauty and heritage from bygone days.

The Azalea Festival has a $50 million impact on the area, according to the most recent study done by the University of North Carolina Wilmington. The study found that 165,000 people attended the event, with the vast majority of them (93 percent) local.

30th Carolina Beach Music Festival

The 30th annual Carolina Beach Music Festival takes place on Saturday, June 6, 2015 where else - on the beach! The gates open at 10:00 a.m. with people coming from everywhere to enjoy the sun, music and beer. Of course, a little shaggin, a favorite dance in these parts, is thrown in too.

This festival is one of the longest running beach music festivals in the United States. Coolers, beverages and food are allowed, though for safety's sake glass containers are prohibited.

Independence Day Fireworks Shows

Wilmington's Fourth of July Riverfront Celebration features a street fair along the riverfront and culminates with spectacular fireworks over the river from Battleship Park. The hallmarks of the Port of Wilmington Maritime Day Festival are entertainment and tours of the port. The fireworks are visible from far enough away so that it is not necessary to be right on the riverfront to enjoy them. Park several blocks away and you can still see the sky light up while avoiding the parking and traffic difficulties.

Many of our coastal towns and beaches have fireworks at this time too. Carolina Beach will have its largest fireworks display on July 2, 2015 by the sea on the beach near the Carolina Beach Boardwalk. There also is entertainment at the gazebo. In fact, Carolina Beach has fireworks and entertainment each Thursday from Memorial Day through Labor Day weekend at this location. Gazebo entertainment begins at 6:30 p.m. with fireworks scheduled at 9:00 p.m.

Surf City on Topsail Island will have its Independence Day Fireworks display on July 3, while Holly Ridge and Sneads Ferry will celebrate on July 4.

Cape Fear Blues Festival

Wilmington hosts the 20th annual Cape Fear Blues Festival, an extravaganza of authentic blues music featuring three days of local, regional and national blues group performances, all-day blues jam, kickoff party, and blues workshops. Performances take place both indoors and outdoors as well as in local clubs.

A highlight of the event is the famous Blues Cruise on the Henrietta III riverboat offering three blues bands on three decks with three bars plus local cuisine, all in an exciting evening sunset cruise on the beautiful Cape Fear River. The event will take place July 24-26, 2015, with the Blues Cruise on July 24. Watch for a full schedule of events and musicians.

45th Shrimp Festival

North Carolina's Official State Shrimp Festival will take place in Sneads Ferry from August 8-9, 2015. The Festival features entertainment all day long, a wine and beer garden, rides for the kids, numerous arts and crafts vendors, and shrimp prepared in all sorts of ways. There will be plenty of other types of food available as well, with such festival favorites as funnel cakes, candy apples, cotton candy and gyros among the popular choices.

Sneads Ferry is located approximately 30 miles north of Wilmington. Marines from Camp Lejeune, the headquarters for the Marine Corps 2nd Division, are on hand with military equipment that children can explore and adults can learn about and view.

52nd Annual Spot Festival

The 52nd annual North Carolina Spot Festival takes place in Hampstead, 10 minutes north of Wilmington, September 25-27, 2015. Spot dinners are the highlight: a spot is a tasty little pan fish (about 8 oz.) that is fun to catch and good to eat, especially when served with cole slaw and hush puppies. Beer and wine is sold at the event too.

The event includes performances by several bands who play all day, vendors of many types, arts and crafts, rides for the kids and such festival requisites as funnel cakes, hot dogs, sausages, blooming onions and cotton candy.

Riverfest in October

Wilmington's Riverfest, October 2-4, 2015, runs from the foot of Market Street to Cape Fear Community College. Currently drawing more than 100,000 people, Riverfest began in 1979 as a modest two-day event and has expanded to three fun and food-packed days.

Riverfest has over 200 craft and food vendors plus fireworks, continuous entertainment on two stages, the Great Waiters Wine Race, Run the River 8K Race, various exhibits and a children's area.

Additional Riverfest activities include skateboard competitions, street dance, wakeboard competition and a musical Battle on the River by a number of bands, a film festival, and Art in the Garden tours of gorgeous private

Many of the festivals held throughout the year feature musicians who draw ardent crowds of fans.

and public gardens enhanced by art and music.

During Riverfest, the Invasion of the Pirates is a kind of festival within a festival, beginning with the arrival of the "pirate ship" on Friday evening, followed by the Pirates Ball.

On Saturday, kids can participate in a treasure hunt and pirate costume contest.

Pleasure Island Seafood, Blues and Jazz Festival

Seafood, blues and jazz have proven to be a winning combination for the Pleasure Island Chamber of Commerce. The Pleasure Island Seafood Blues & Jazz Festival, slated for October 10-11, 2015, is sure to be a big hit once again. The event will sell out, so it is always best to buy tickets early. The Festival continues to attract record-setting crowds and there is every reason to believe that the upcoming event will do so again.

The Festival celebrates its 22nd anniversary in 2015. With nationally recognized performers, wonderful coastal cuisine, natural beauty and crisp salt air, the Festival committee produces a great event each year. The Fort Fisher Military Recreational Area in Kure Beach is the site for the Festival.

Autumn with Topsail

Fall is a wonderful time to visit Topsail Beach and there is a good reason to do so in October. The 25th Annual Autumn with Topsail festival takes place on October 17-18, 2015. The highlight of the Festival is a juried Artists Show that attracts many regional artists who display and sell their wares.

Other features include live beach music, a variety of food vendors and games and rides for kids of all ages. The festival is staged in and around the Assembly Building in Topsail Beach.

Poplar Grove's popular Haunted Halloween

One of the fun annual events is the Haunted Halloween extravaganza that takes place over two weekends at Poplar Grove Plantation. From October 16-18 and October 23-25, 2015, brave souls can visit a Haunted Barn or take a Haunted Hayride if they are courageous enough to face ghouls and goblins and things that go bump in the night. A 5K Zombie Fun Run/Walk through the Abbey Preserve was added in 2014 on the first Saturday of the event.

There are inflatable carnival rides for kids, a little kids' fun house, non-scary hayrides during the daytime for those who prefer rides without chills, and pony rides for children.

This is the largest fundraiser of the year for Poplar Grove Plantation, which was one of the oldest peanut plantations in North Carolina and was owned by the same family for more than six generations.

Poplar Grove opened as a museum in 1980 and its mansion is on the National Register of Historic Homes.

Festival Latino

Festival Latino celebrates the music, dance, arts, crafts, and food of the

Bringing the best of Classic Jazz by World-Class Musicians To Wilmington since 1980!

Join us for our 36th Annual Traditional Jazz Festival ▪ February 4-6, 2016
Wilmington Hilton Riverside, Wilmington, NC 28401

All evening concerts start at 7:30 pm
General admission tickets Thursday $40, Friday & Saturday $60
Military $25 ▪ Students $15 all nights
Two or three night plus musical brunch Patron Tickets also available

Thursday ▪ Special Event Night ▪ Something For Everyone!
Professor Cunningham's Old School Tribute to the Big Band Era
Ladies of Jazz featuring singer Stephanie Nakasian with Hod O'Brien on piano
All-Star Jam led by Ed Polcher
Friday & Saturday nights ▪ 15 Jazz All-stars entertain in 6-7 sets each night

For more information go to www.ncjazzfestival.com
e-mail ncjazzfest@yahoo.com or phone 910-793-1111

NORTH CAROLINA JAZZ FESTIVAL

diverse Latin-American community in the Cape Fear region. The 17th annual event, which has grown in popularity each year from a very modest beginning, takes place at Ogden Park on Saturday, November 7, 2015, with lots of special events geared towards kids. The festivities will continue on Sunday, November 8 at Market Street and Gordon Road where residents are invited to share in the celebration. There will be lots of food and music on Sunday, but no special events for children that day. This cross-cultural event draws more visitors each year and spots for vendors and music are always snapped up.

This is an outreach event that embraces the fundamental goal of Amigos Internacional, which is to celebrate, advocate and provide resources for the Latino Community.

Cucalorus Film Festival

The Cucalorus Film Festival presents its 20th annual festival of independent films November 11-15, 2015.

This non-competitive event showcases more than 200 independently produced films from all over the world and has been cited by the Southeastern Tourism Society as a Top 20 Event.

In addition to feature films, documentaries and experimental short films, workshops and panel discussions are available for aspiring filmmakers and others interested in the film industry.

Cucalorus has added annual another event, An Evening on the Red Carpet, which serves as a fundraiser for the Festival. The party takes place on the evening of the Academy Awards and features cocktails and a catered dinner.

Wrightsville Beach Holiday Flotilla

The Holiday Flotilla draws a crowd each year to Wrightsville Beach. The two day event, now in its 32nd year, takes place on November 27-28, 2015. The event begins with a Christmas tree lighting ceremony and appearance by Santa Claus at Wrightsville Beach Town Hall. The Holiday Flotilla follows, showcasing elaborately decorated and lighted boats that parade through the Intracoastal Waterway for all to see and enjoy.

On Saturday, the Festival in the Park is held. It features a large children's play area that includes several inflatable slides and bounce houses and a coloring contest. Of course, festival food is featured and local artists and merchants set up arts and crafts booths. Another popular feature is an antique car show with lovingly maintained cars on display for all to enjoy.

North Carolina Jazz Festival

The oldest of the music festivals held in the area is the North Carolina Jazz Festival, which celebrates its 36th anniversary from February 4-6, 2016. This three-day event, held in the ballroom at the Wilmington Hilton Riverside, features nationally known as well as local jazz musicians.

Fifteen jazz all-stars play seven sets each night on Friday and Saturday nights while Thursday is a Special Event Night featuring different styles of jazz.

Thursday night's kickoff in 2016 will feature Professor Cunningham's Old School Tribute to the Big Band Era, then Stephanie Nakasian with Hod O'Brien on piano presenting Ladies of Jazz. The evening will end with an All-Star jam led by Ed Polcer.

Mardi Gras at The Cotton Exchange

The fourth annual Mardi Gras Celebration will take place in early February at The Cotton Exchange in downtown Wilmington. The festival includes fun for the whole family, with live music, magicians, face painting, balloon twisting and a traditional King cake cutting at noon for the Saturday event.

Many of the 30 shops and restaurants will be offering discounts and specials during the event. Some of the shops also will have giveaways for those who register.

20th Pleasure Island Chowder Cook Off

The 20th Annual Pleasure Island Chowder Cook Off is scheduled for

Continued on page 65

You'll find whatever you need in the shops of all types located throughout the Wilmington area.

you can shop 'til you drop

This area is blessed with an embarrassment of riches. In addition to fabulous beaches, a huge historic district, wonderful weather, friendly people, low taxes, modest housing prices, and superb medical facilities, we also have terrific places to shop. A huge number of stores in our area offer unique, handcrafted, fabulous merchandise. If you can't relocate to our area today, at least do yourself a favor and sample as many of our retail establishments as you can. You'll be glad you did.

Lumina Station Shops

Lumina Station, located on Eastwood Road just before you cross the Causeway Bridge leading to Wrightsville Beach, is the place to visit for a truly local kind of shopping experience. Inspired by the Wrightsville Beach dance pavilion that was once central to the East Coast social scene, Lumina Station is so true to its historical roots that it won Coastal Living magazine's first-ever award for contextual design. Beautiful landscaping, whimsical sculptures and storybook bridges complement the wooded campus, making strolling a very pleasant way to pass the time.

The shops at Lumina Station are as unique as the setting, with all shops owned and operated by local merchants. Here you'll find a high-fashion women's clothing store, a men's emporium with superb clothing, several stores with out of the ordinary shoes and accessories, a superb home furnishings store and a wonderful gift shop among several others. You'll even find a fitness center at Lumina Station, perhaps a good thing since Lumina Station is home to one of Wilmington's best restaurants.

Port Land Grille is a class act from cocktail to dessert. It is known nationally, too, recently receiving a Distinguished Restaurants of North America Award of Excellence.

Locals, visitors and the famous (Wilmington is home to a busy movie studio) relish well-spaced tables and a warm, stylish ambiance. The restaurant's long-standing reputation is thanks to outstanding service and the extraordinary dishes by chef/owner Shawn Wellersdick. He began offering farm-to-table fare years before it was cool.

Some selections are from the "port," for instance pan-seared, wild-caught grouper over blue crab meat, English pea, pancetta risotto, butter-wilted baby organic spinach and a roma tomato, saffron, basil, melted sweet onion "fondue" sauce. Other selections are from the "land," such as the chef's personal favorite: a pork porterhouse chop served alongside roasted butternut squash, balsamic glazed cabbage and "red neck" potato gnocchi with heirloom pork barbecue. Savory bacon jam and sweet and tangy balsamic plum barbecue sauce finish the presentation.

Changing seasons and the chef's

SHOP DINE RELAX

Lumina Station
THE SHOPPING VILLAGE BY THE BEACH

FIND SOMETHING *Special*

APPAREL

AQUA FEDORA
Trendy apparel, accessories and more

BEANIE + CECIL
The best of NYC fashion

GENTLEMEN'S CORNER
Fine men's clothing and accessories

ISLAND PASSAGE
Clothing, shoes, and elixers

J. MCLAUGHLIN
Classic American clothing and accessories

JENNIFER'S
Embellished sportswear and accessories

LILIES AND LACE
Fine lingerie and swimwear

MONKEE'S
Fine shoes, ladies' clothing and accessories

ZIABIRD
Artisan jewelry, handbags and more

FOOD & SPIRITS

19 HUNDRED
Tapas restaurant and lounge

BRASSERIE DU SOLEIL
French Mediterranean bistro

THE DIRTY MARTINI
Sophisticated fun martini bar

PORT CITY JAVA
Coffee house and café

PORT LAND GRILLE
Fine dining

HALLIGAN'S PUBLIC HOUSE
Family style Irish restaurant and pub

ARTS/GIFTS/DÉCOR

AIRLIE MOON
Bed, bath and home

PAYSAGE
Home furnishings and accessories

TICKLED PINK
Sophisticated boutique collective

HEALTH & BEAUTY

BLUSH HAUS OF BEAUTÉ
Fine cosmetics, skin care and salon

HARBOUR CLUB DAY SPA & SALON
Day spa and salon

SITO CHIROPRACTIC
Family chiropractic care

SERVICES

INTRACOASTAL REALTY
Sales, vacation rentals and financing

Located just a 1/2 mile before the Wrightsville Beach bridge.

LuminaStation.com | 910.256.0900

imagination regularly bring new selections and tweak more regular offerings. Don't miss soft-shell crab season at Port Land Grille. The chef is a master with these fresh delicacies.

Port Land Grille also presents snacks, tapas-style plates to share, homemade soups and "not your ordinary salads." The roasted beets, baby organic kale, fennel and gold beet "carpaccio" salad comes with candied walnuts, boursin cheese, fennel pollen and vanilla bean-clover honey-citrus vinaigrette.

Find room for dessert, especially the famous and oh-so-tall, caramel-drizzled coconut layer cake filled with mango coulis.

It's fun to watch the chefs in the kitchen while you sample classic and signature cocktails from the tables in the bar. A remarkable wine list, with labels you'll find no place else in the area, enhances meals, and servers really know their stuff when describing, pairing and pouring wine.

Spectrum Art & Jewelry

Spectrum Art & Jewelry, a long-time fixture at The Forum shops, has grown so much that they now occupy two stores. One is devoted primarily to fine custom jewelry, where you'll find the work of superbly talented designers Star Sosa and Susan Drake. If you have an old piece of jewelry that no longer works for you, they can turn it into a piece you'll treasure. And if you have an idea for a design, they can interpret it for you. Fine jewelry can be repaired here too.

The quality of the workmanship has been recognized nationally; both Ms. Sosa and Ms. Drake continue to be honored for their work. Ms. Drake was the 2015 J.A. Case first place winner for her zephyr diamond necklace.

The second shop owned by Spectrum carries the products of more than 100 American artists working in all media. You'll find paintings by outstanding artists Nancy Noel May, Sam Allerton Green, and Jane Faudree, among several others; hand-painted, exquisite scarves, beautiful glass vases, bowls and other accessories from sources including Vitrix Hot Glass Studio, regarded as one of America's prominent contemporary glass studios, and Glass Eye Studio, whose works are sought after by collectors around the world. You'll also find fantastic pieces done in metal by talented artist Anne Cunningham, who has been working exclusively with materials such as copper, brass, and aluminum since 1990. There is a reason this shop won two Top Retailer Awards in 2009, as you'll find by visiting this friendly store.

Special dining spots

Two restaurants serving totally different types of fare are located at The Forum shopping center on Military Cutoff Road. The two restaurants share a thing in common however; an outstanding chef who is passionate about the quality of the food he serves leads each.

Although Bento Box is frequently recognized as Wilmington's best sushi restaurant, it's also tops for delectable Asian appetizers, small plates and full-size entrees. The bar's sake selection is outstanding. Everything is prepared with great skill and care from the highest-quality ingredients. Sit at the sushi bar to watch the masters at work. Consider the signature Delicious Roll, made with either spicy tuna or salmon twirled

with avocado, seaweed salad, wasabi tobikko, sesame seeds and crisp tempura crumbles. Any roll is delicious, but better yet, ask owner/chef Lee Grossman to customize sushi for you. Don't miss Thai, Vietnamese, Korean and Japanese specialties. Pork belly lettuce wraps are crispy mother lodes. Vietnamese ginger beef is a beef tenderloin and vegetable stir-fry in ginger sauce. Pickled sweet red onions and crispy potato straws crown the mix. Oftentimes, diners choose several dishes and share them to enjoy all. The restaurant is open 11:30 a.m. to 9 p.m. Monday through Wednesday, 11:30 a.m. to 10 p.m. Thursday and Friday and 5 to 10 p.m. Saturday. Chef closes on Sunday so he and the staff can have quality family time.

At dinner only, enjoy honest farm-to-table fare at Pembroke's. A native North Carolinian who grew up in the state's coastal plain, Pembroke's chef James Doss describes his cooking style as "seasonally inspired, ingredient-driven, Southern cuisine." He sources local produce, meat and seafood for the menu, which changes daily. Everything here is made from scratch, and seeing cooks at work and smelling the delicious aromas that rise from the kitchen make this restaurant feel like home. Choose a seat with a kitchen view or tuck into a cozy corner. A private dining area is perfect for groups. A friendly, partially enclosed bar – with truly comfy stools – is perfect for a toasty bourbon apple tart or one of the craft bar's various takes on the Old Fashioned. Outdoor seating is available on the front patio. Be sure to make a date for Sunday brunch and bring a strong appetite. Pembroke's is open for dinner Tuesday through Sunday. Friday and Saturday nights may bring live music, never too loud for conversation. Sunday brunch happens 10 a.m. to 3 p.m., usually with a serving of live, soft jazz.

Mayfaire Town Center

Mayfaire Town Center is located on Military Cutoff Road just north of Eastwood Road on the far east side of Wilmington, almost to Wrightsville Beach. Situated on 400 acres, the mixed-use development is unlike any other in the area. It offers a huge and diverse number of stores, with more than 80 chain stores, specialty shops, salons and businesses that provide a complete range of goods and services.

Mayfaire also has the largest movie complex in Southeastern North Carolina, Cinema 16, with - you guessed it - 16 movie screens.

As you stroll through Mayfaire's village-like streets, you'll find major chain stores Ann Taylor, Talbots, and J. Jill. Men's retailers include J. Crew, Jos. A. Bank and Men's Wearhouse. Home furnishings are available at Williams-Sonoma, Pier 1 Imports and World Market, among many others. Children's wear, bridal shops, book and stationary stores, crafts shops and many others are located at Mayfaire. A must-see for sure is The Gallery of Fine Art.

Dr. Seuss Lives Here

If you love the enchanting stories of Dr. Seuss, you can't miss The Gallery of Fine Art at Mayfaire.

The Gallery is one of just 99 in the world that was chosen to present the Secret Art of Dr. Seuss and was honored again in 2013 among a very select group

you can shop 'til you drop

All types of jewelry from fun to fine is available in our local stores.

chosen to present "Hats Off To Dr. Seuss," a show with Dr. Seuss's never before seen hat collection exhibited alongside his little-known group of "Midnight Paintings."

Young George Pocheptsov, who began painting at the tender age of 17 months and went on to receive great acclaim while still a teenager, also is represented by this gallery. Fabio Napoleoni and Shaw Lackey are among the other artists represented.

In addition to paintings, the Gallery also has jewelry, pottery, sculpture and hand-blown glass. They offer custom framing too.

When you've had your fill of shopping or are hungry after seeing a moving, try the restaurants at Mayfaire that are sure to please.

Are you hungry?

If you've shopped 'til you're ready to drop, you can regain your strength with meals at two of Mayfaire's favorite dining spots.

Tokyo 101 is a popular Japanese restaurant just steps away from Cinema 16. An extensive sushi menu and traditional Japanese food are served in a beautiful, serene setting.

Be sure to check weekday lunch specials. The prices are fantastic. Tokyo 101's bar showcases different cocktail specials every day. Special sushi prices come Monday through Thursday. Hibachi choices are vegetables, chicken, steak, and five types of seafood, offered either singly or as combinations. Like noodles? The kitchen sends out udon soup and yakisoba creations stir-fried with chicken or seafood. Deep-fried shrimp-and-crab-stuffed jalapenos are among dishes with a fusion feel. There also is a moderately priced children's menu for kids under age 12.

The Melting Pot is a fondue restaurant located directly across the street from Tokyo 101. It is a fun place to share a meal with friends and family. Often diners choose the four-course experience, which includes cheese fondue, salad, entree and dessert. Others prefer just cheese fondue paired with a glass of wine. Still others find that moderate cravings can be satisfied with chocolate fondue, which is even better accompanied by a wonderful full-bodied red wine. Four-course experiences include a cheese fondue, salad, premium entrees and chocolate fondue. The question is which chocolate fondue. Eight are offered, including a create-your-own option. Perhaps the wisest approach is to start at the top, then work down the list on return visits.

Rejuvenate

Mayfaire is home to the area's only Aveda salon. Van Davis Aveda Salon and Spa offers whatever rejuvenation services men, women and children might want. In addition to haircuts and styling, many other hair services are available ala carte. Either before or after a major shopping trip, a trip to this salon would be refreshing.

Full spa treatments are available at Van Davis Aveda as are all types of hair care services, from cut to color to extensions. The staff at Van Davis Aveda salon and spa will happily consult with you to determine what services best meet your needs.

Dragonflies

Dragonflies is a rarity among gift shops: a specialty boutique housed in a spacious, 9,700 square foot store. This large store serves as a one-stop resource for the entire family, as they carry unique baby and children's items as well as women's and men's clothing and accessories. Many of the gift items and home decor have a distinctly coastal theme and a Southern flare, which carries throughout the store.

Dragonflies is the perfect place to buy gifts for any occasion, including weddings, baby showers, Christmas, birthdays or "just because." They offer a wide array of home décor, including handmade signs, decorative and functional glassware, lamps, and candles. Cooking aficionados will appreciate the selection of cookbooks, tableware, and cooking utensils.

The boutique sells a large selection of Pandora charms, bracelets, earrings and necklaces, with a corner of the store dedicated to the line of jewelry. Other popular items include their large assortment of bright, colorful Scout bags, Wil-

LET YOUR STYLE *blossom.*

Sterling silver charms from $25
Introducing the 2015 Spring Collection from PANDORA

Experience at:

4106 Oleander Drive
Wilmington, NC 28403
910.796.9997

PANDORA®

Some jewelry displayed patented (US Pat. No. 7,007,507) • © Pandora • PANDORA.NET

low Tree ceramics, Spartina jewelry and handbags, and Hobo wallets and purses. Additionally, they sell Cotton Colors handcrafted pottery and Nora Fleming kitchen platters.

Dragonflies welcomes wedding and baby shower gift registries. For added customer convenience, gift-wrapping is complimentary.

Dragonflies Baby, a specialty boutique within Dragonflies, caters to children from infant to school age. Dragonflies Baby features a selection of handpicked items to beautifully outfit and equip babies and children, from infant christening gowns and raincoats to bathing suits and hair bows, and virtually everything in between.

They carry top boutique brands for clothing and shoes, including Kissy Kissy, Livie and Luca, Johnnie-O, and Aden and Anais. Their clothing section features a selection of casual and dressy items in sizes infant to seven.

The boutique offers many items for young babies, such as baby carriers, diaper bags, swaddling blankets, and bibs. They even sell a gentle line of baby and children's shampoos, lotions, and soaps.

They also carry a smattering of unique toys, books, puzzles and dolls. Dragonflies Baby welcomes baby shower gift registries. For added customer convenience, gift-wrapping is complimentary.

Blue Moon Gift Shops

With more than 100 artisans and retailers filling 8,500 square feet with their wares, Blue Moon Gift Shops is a premiere shopping destination for locals and tourists. Located off Racine Drive convenient to midtown Wilmington and Wrightsville Beach, Blue Moon features a treasure trove of locally made items.

Blue Moon offers a unique selection of furniture, home accessories, art, clothing, décor, jewelry and much more. The focus of Blue Moon remains on showcasing the handcrafted work of talented local artisans and entrepreneurs.

If you can't find exactly what you are looking for in stock, they offer custom ordering, and as an added convenience, gift-wrapping is complimentary. These small touches make Blue Moon stand out. Indeed, for several years running, Blue Moon has been voted the area's

"Best Gift Shop" due in large part to their excellent customer service and unmatched selection.

Prepare to spend some time browsing Blue Moon for a one-of-a-kind shopping experience. As they like to say, "Why be ordinary … when you can Moon somebody!"

Eclipse at Blue Moon

Eclipse at Blue Moon spotlights the handmade, one-of-a-kind work of local and regional artisans. A new addition to Blue Moon Gift Shops in November 2013, Eclipse showcases original paintings, jewelry, photography, custom-built furniture, sculpture, pottery and alpaca bedding, setting it apart from a traditional gallery.

Each piece is displayed beautifully with a well-planned flow throughout the artisan boutique, inviting customers to browse and enjoy. To further enhance the customer experience, Eclipse offers commissioned custom orders and complimentary giftwrapping. In celebration of the local art community, Eclipse regularly hosts featured artists meet and greets and artist demonstrations.

Eclipse has already caught on as a favorite art gallery with the community, earning the distinction of Best Art Gallery 2014. Visit Eclipse and you will see why it is called "a gallery with a personality all its own."

Lou's Flower World & Vintage Market

For nearly 20 years, Lou's Flower World has been the premiere one-stop resource for all things floral in the greater Wilmington area. Lou's 20,000-square-foot facility carries an unmatched selection of flowers, plants, unique furniture and gifts.

With more than 30 years of experience, the designers at Lou's Flower World can create beautiful arrangements for every occasion, including weddings, birthdays, and funerals. Additionally, they have a large selection of trees and shrubs that can be rented for special events.

Need a gift for a garden enthusiast? Lou's garden center offers an extensive selection of gifts for the home and garden, including bird feeders, lawn pagodas and home décor.

As if their flower selection was not enough, Lou's features a large Vintage Market full of unique furniture and accessories that you won't find anywhere else. From beach cottage to shabby chic to antiques and estate pieces, they carry every style of furniture imaginable. The inventory changes regularly and prices are quite reasonable.

For enhanced customer service, they deliver to the Wilmington, Wrightsville Beach and Carolina Beach areas. Stop by Lou's today to see why they say, "There's something for everyone at Lou's!"

The Ivy Cottage

Without doubt, the best selection of quality consignments is found at The Ivy Cottage, a Wilmington institution that opened in 1998. The name now is a misnomer because The Ivy Cottage has expanded to four buildings totaling more than 25,000 square feet of space as well as two outdoor garden areas. The buildings are adjacent to each other and to the

Your one-stop shop for
Full-service florist services
Indoor, outdoor and bedding
plants • Trees • Shrubs • Gifts
Vintage, shabby and antique
furniture and accessories
Garden supplies • Clothing
Jewelry • Birding items and bird
houses • Koi fish • Venus flytraps
Organic seeds and fertilizers

If you've never been to this store, you owe it to yourself to come see what all the talk is about!

Lou's Flower World
5128 Oleander Drive
Wilmington NC 28403
910-395-1004
www.lousflowerworld.com

you can shop 'til you drop

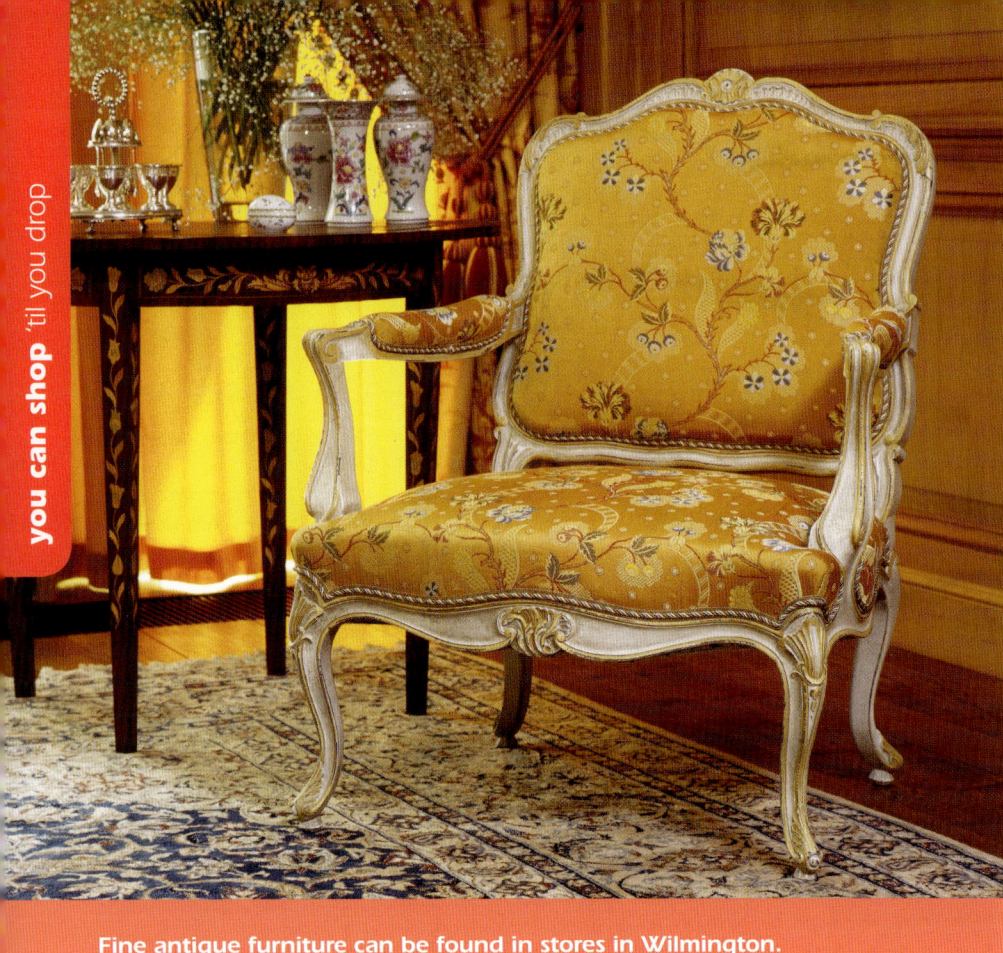

Fine antique furniture can be found in stores in Wilmington.

original site in the 3000 block of Market Street.

The Ivy Cottage is famed for its ever-changing inventory that includes classic furniture and antiques, lamps, Oriental rugs, crystal, china, sterling and other silver, fine porcelains, accessories, superb linens, paintings, garden ornaments, wrought iron tables and chairs, and most anything else you could want or need.

The Ivy Cottage also has a vast collection of fine jewelry, including beautiful vintage diamond, platinum and gold pieces as well as lovely gemstone necklaces, bracelets, rings and more.

Knowledgeable shoppers visit The Ivy Cottage often since 300-400 new items come in every day. Those who shop at Ivy Cottage definitely understand the benefits of recycling since the quality of the merchandise offered here is vastly greater than one would find for a comparable price.

Crabby Chic

Crabby Chic is a shopper's haven for handcrafted and unique items, custom furniture, home décor, lamps, and decorative accessories. The store embraces Wilmington's coastal environment, with a milieu that is decidedly beachy, including sea stars, starfish, octopus, anchors, and mermaids.

Crabby Chic offers a large selection of jewelry, including sought-after brands like Echo of the Dreamer and Mars & Valentine. They carry sea glass, nautical charms, and jewelry accented with initials.

With a variety of candles, diffusers, French luxury soaps and picture frames in a range of price points, Crabby Chic has an unmatched selection of gifts. The store also features local and regional artwork with beach-inspired themes. If you like the store's coastal motif, consider exploring their redecorating services to bring Crabby Chic's style to your home.

Albert F. Rhodes

The finest full service, traditional jeweler in Southeastern North Carolina is Albert F. Rhodes Jewelry, located on Floral Parkway just up from Independence Mall.

There is a reason this store has been a Wilmington institution since 1948 – the integrity of the company is demonstrated by its designation as a Rolex authorized dealer. Albert F. Rhodes has some of the finest diamond jewelry in the area and definitely has the most knowledgeable and helpful staff. Don't even consider buying a fine piece of new diamond jewelry without visiting them.

Headed today by Wayne Rhodes, shoppers can get an education if needed for true comparison-shopping. Ask any staff person and they will explain the four "Cs" of diamond grading to you. It is critical that you understand how stones are graded before you invest in a diamond.

Jewelry is not limited to Rolex watches and diamonds. They also have a tremendous selection of gold or sterling silver earrings, rings, bracelets and necklaces both plain and set with rubies, sapphires, emeralds and other precious stones. Pearls in many forms and colors are on display and jewelry set with many types of gemstones is available too.

Albert F. Rhodes also carries china, silver and crystal giftware, making it easy to find the perfect gift whether you're

910-799-4216 • 4107 OLEANDER DRIVE • WILMINGTON, NC

The Ivy Cottage
DISTINGUISHED CONSIGNMENTS

Wilmington's Finest Consignment Shop

THE LARGEST FURNITURE CONSIGNMENT STORE IN THE SOUTHEAST!

FEATURING...

ANTIQUES, FINE FURNISHINGS (CLASSIC, ANTIQUE, MID CENTURY, MODERN, & RECLAIMED), FINE JEWELRY, CHINA, CRYSTAL, STERLING SILVER, ORIENTAL CARPETS, LAMPS, MIRRORS, CHANDELIERS, COLLECTIBLES, STAINED GLASS, FINE ART, DECOR FROM AROUND THE GLOBE,

and more...

OPEN 7 DAYS A WEEK

HUNDREDS OF NEW ITEMS EVERY DAY

FOUR BUILDINGS... OVER 25,000 SQUARE FEET!

3020-3030-3100 MARKET STREET   WILMINGTON, NC 28403   910.815.0907

WWW.THREECOTTAGES.COM

We *can* do that!

Custom Picture Framing
Lamps & Lampshades
Custom Made Lamps
Lamp & Chandelier Repairs
Brass & Silver Refinishing
Porcelain & Glass Repair

D. BAXTER'S

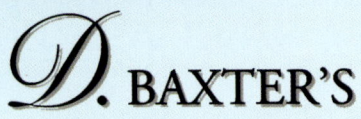

910.791.8431
4113-D Oleander Drive
Wilmington NC
www.dbaxters.com

Many people use accessories to personalize their home or office.

shopping for yourself, your fiancé, your wedding attendants or your mother.

Visitors and locals alike feel right at home at Independence Mall on Oleander Drive and Independence Boulevard. Anchored by Belk, Dillard's, JC Penney and Sears, this is the areas only totally enclosed shopping mall with an ever-changing group of stores.

D. Baxter's Lamps

A wonderful lamp shop on Oleander Drive has been in business since 1993. They specialize in two things, lamps and framing. Customers throughout Southeastern North Carolina have come to rely on D. Baxter's for their expertise in repairing lamps and helping people choose the right shade for lamps that need a replacement. Thousands of happy customers have purchased their products and services.

In addition to top quality repairs for lamps and chandeliers, they have an enormous selection of frames. They also have the people with the talent to do a superb job of matting and framing all types of artwork, diplomas and other objects that people want to display.

D. Baxter's has by far the largest selection of new lamps, replacement shades, finials and pulls in the area. They can produce a lamp out of most anything; people with a favorite vase or sculpture that they would like to turn into a lamp can have it done here. They also refinish brass and silver and expertly repair porcelain and glass.

New River Pottery

As you head north on Market Street you'll find New River Pottery, a huge store with an inventory of most everything under the sun. Glassware, china, gift wrap, vast numbers and types of candles, garden ornaments, pots, yards and yards of ribbon, artificial flowers in silk and other materials, live plants during the growing season, lamps, furnishings and linens are just a few of the items in stock.

Few stores carry more seasonal merchandise than you will find here. Indoor or outdoor wicker furniture is available and the store carries a huge assortment of cushions for tables, chairs and chaise

you can shop 'til you drop

Downtown Wilmington has many shops that carry unique merchandise.

lounges. As different holidays draw near, we're sure you'll find exactly what you want to decorate for Easter, Thanksgiving and other holidays.

No one in the area carries more Christmas decorations than New River Pottery. Trees, a vast selection of ornaments, lights and other trimmings, nutcrackers, ribbons, wreaths, candles and most everything else you can imagine is available. New River Pottery offers a customer loyalty program and there is no question that you will want to return again and again.

Downtown's unique shops

You can meander downtown along the streets in Wilmington's Historic District to browse the art galleries and small shops that are in abundance there. Most of the stores are independently owned and feature out-of-the-ordinary merchandise. Antiques, vintage clothing, crafts including woodcarvings, pottery, wall hangings, original art, new and vintage furniture, aromatherapy, beachwear, books and jewelry are on display. You'll be fascinated by the variety, and you won't get bored, that's for sure.

Front Street, Water Street, Market Street and several side streets are still the best shopping places downtown. From Ann Street and Chandler's Wharf on the south end of the Riverwalk to the Cotton Exchange at the northern end, you'll have more than enough places to explore in a day.

Moving north from Chandler's Wharf, be sure to go into The Old Wilmington City Market since the building itself is worth the visit. Built in 1879, the block-long brick and stucco arcade houses kiosks, specialty shops and boutiques offering wonderful treasures, exotic woods, plants, jewelry, clothing and works by local artists.

See the Cotton Exchange

When you've made your way up to The Cotton Exchange, between Front and Nutt streets, stop in the lower level vestibule and take time to read about its history and how these eight buildings, once part of the world's largest cotton-exporting company, were converted to a shopping and dining complex in the early 1970s. This tri-level mall is a really fun place to shop.

Today there are 30 unique shops and restaurants at The Cotton Exchange. Several of the shops specialize in art works of various types and all are worth a visit.

Port City Pottery & Fine Crafts is dedicated exclusively to handmade, one-of-a-kind, three-dimensional works of art. Pottery, fiber art, basketry, woodworking, jewelry and mixed media sculpture are found in the shop presented by jury-selected coastal North Carolina artisans.

The Golden Gallery opened in the Cotton Exchange in 1977 and now is in its fifth location there. The artists are what make the Golden Gallery unique; with one small exception, they are all Golden! On display are the works of Mary Ellen Golden, a watercolorist; John W. Golden, son of the owners, a photographer with a large catalog of images of the Cape Fear region, and Melissa Manley, a metal smith and honorary Golden. John D. Golden, a folksinger and storyteller, has CDs available.

If you enjoy working with beads, head to Carolina Beads and Gemstones, which has 1,100 square feet of fine quality beads, gemstones, findings and stringing materials. Those who are interested in learning to work with beads are invited to attend a variety of classes that take place in the shop, which has been located in Wilmington since 1995. Carolina Beads and Gemstones can also repair your jewelry or create an earring for those who have lost just one.

Two Sisters Bookery is an independent bookstore that welcomes browsers. The store features both classic and contemporary books and has a selection of first editions, collectibles, and signed books as well. The Bookery has a wide variety of bookmarks, unique greeting cards, reading glasses, umbrellas, Groovy Girls and Ugly Dolls too. Whether you're looking for a Coastal Carolina cookbook, regional ghost tales, any of Pat Conroy's titles or most anything else, you'll find it in this friendly store. And if you need a recommendation, don't hesitate to ask. They're happy to help.

If you love spicy food, you need to visit Fire & Spice Gourmet. The store is loaded with every kind of hot sauce you can imagine, and probably some you'd never thought of too. Hot sauces, blend-

Over 30 Local Shops & Restaurants

IN WILMINGTON'S HISTORIC RIVER DISTRICT
AT THE CORNER OF GRACE & FRONT STREETS

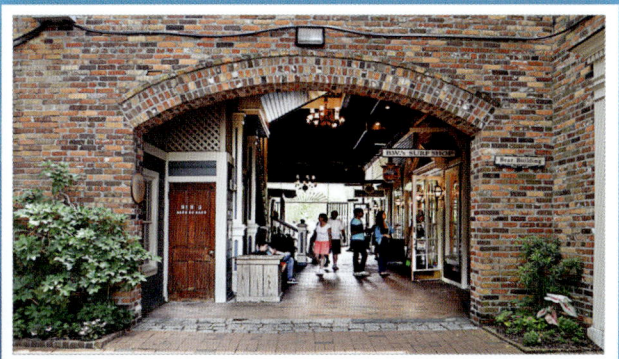

FREE PARKING WHILE SHOPPING & DINING

Monday-Saturday 10am-5:30pm • Sunday 12-4pm
Some Shops Open Later, Restaurants Always Open Late!

ShopCottonExchange.com • 910.343.9896 • 321 N. Front Street Wilmington, NC 28401

ed spices, jams, jellies, dips, salsas and a whole lot more are in ample supply. The "en Fuego" (on fire) salsa, made right here in North Carolina, is aptly named. Fire & Spice also has numerous kitchen gadgets, pickled vegetables, imported wines and various other kitchen or outdoor grilling items. There is even a room dedicated exclusively to North Carolina products.

The Olive Shoppe is a great place to find superb balsamic vinegars and delicious olive oils. Foodies regard their 5-star traditional aged balsamic vinegar as the best available in this area. Jars of hand-stuffed olives and several types of spreads are in stock, as are cocktail mixers. Any of these items make a wonderful souvenir or hostess gift. Tasters are always welcome at The Olive Shoppe and if you would prefer to have your purchases shipped, the shop does that too.

Occasions…Just Write is a delightful store that should be a must-see for all your stationery needs. The shop does a wonderful job in helping a bride choose the perfect wedding invitation that fits her style and budget. They also can design the right invitation for corporate announcements and events, birthday or anniversary parties and whatever else clients might need. Occasions…Just Write also stocks a broad selection of greeting cards, note cards and fine gifts.

Fidler's Gallery and Wrigley's Clocks has been in the Cotton Exchange since 1978. The owners of Wrigley's Clocks are skilled enough to take care of your heirloom grandfather clock, since they've been repairing and servicing clocks for more than 30 years. They also are expert framers and provide professional picture hanging services too. You'll find 4,000 square feet of gifts here, including three-dimensional art, vases, hand-made beaded fish, statuary, candles and, of course, clocks. Prices range from $5 to $100.

Artists' havens

Artists in residence work and teach classes in the loft space at Crescent Moon on Front Street, between Market and Princess Streets. The first-floor gallery features creations by more than 50 artists. As the store's slogan says, "The only thing mass-produced here is originality." Jewelry, sculpture, paintings, paperweights, holiday ornaments and stained glass represent a wee sample of the colorful display. Lifelike animal sculptures handmade from Sisal fibers must be seen to be believed. Custom and online orders are welcome, and gift cards are available at this very friendly shop.

Many artists launch their own galleries. Painter Dan Beck is one of them. His many awards from the Oil Painters of America include the 2011 Gold Medal from the organization's National Exhibition. Major galleries, collectors and museums around the world seek out his impressionist works – figurative, still life and landscape.

Using both oils and pastels, his paintings depict the artist's love of nature and deep respect for art. Beck's works evoke timelessness and dignity. Find Dan Beck Fine Art Gallery and Studio in downtown's Castle Street district.

Sandy Nelson, winner of numerous national awards whose portraits and landscapes have been accepted for inclusion in national juried competitions from Maine to California, has a studio and gallery at TheArtWorks. She was named one of the best 200 artists in 1993 by *Artists Magazine* and continues to produce amazing works with our area's marshes, ponds and open fields serving as inspiration. She also is a talented portrait painter who is happy to consult with those who might be interested in acquiring a portrait.

TheArtWorks is an art village showcasing Wilmington's vibrant visual, literary, and performing arts. TheArtWorks provides art studios, gallery space, educational opportunities, and an event venue with the mission to foster a creative environment for artists and enhance Wilmington's cultural community through art.

More than 45 artists actively create art and sell their wares through studios in TheArtWorks. The range of mediums for sale includes original fine art, sculpture, jewelry, pottery, photography, glass, and unique handmade gifts. The studios feature workspaces and mini galleries. TheArtWorks is located just one mile from the heart of downtown at 200 Willard Street.

Refuel

When you're reading for a treat, you can get a quick jolt of energy by

See great shops at The Cotton Exchange

Kitchen, Hot Sauce & Spice Headquarters
Fire & Spice Gourmet
910-762-3050

Wedding Invitations, Greeting & Note Cards, Fine Gifts
Occasions...Just Write
www.occasionsjustwrite.com • 910-343-9033

A huge selection of quality beads & supplies
Carolina Beads & Gemstones
www.carolinabeads.com • 910-343-0500

Independent Book Store & Gift Shop
Two Sisters Bookery
www.twosistersbookery.com • 910-762-4444

Local Hand-made Pottery and Crafts
Port City Pottery & Fine Crafts
www.portcitypottery.com • 910-763-7111

Framing, Gifts, Clocks and More
Fidler's Gallery/Wrigley's Clocks
www.fidlersgallery.com • 910-762-2001

Find the best of all things olive!
The Olive Shoppe
www.BeachOliveOils.com • 910-859-OILS (6457)

Original Paintings, Photos and Music
The Golden Gallery
www.thegoldengallery.com • 910-762-4651

Free parking. Friendly service. Fabulous choices. Shop today.
Visit The Cotton Exchange in Historic Downtown Wilmington at Front and Grace Streets.

Ad sponsored by the above eight merchants.

visiting either of two shops on Market Street. Kilwin's is a wonderful emporium where fudge, kettle corn, nut brittles and waffle cones made on the premises emit sugary aromas.

Just beyond the fudge factory, visible through the front window, fudge bricks in various flavors greet you near the door. Next is a line of chocolate candies and chocolate-dipped madness. There's chocolate-dipped pretzels, chocolate-dipped sandwich cookies, chocolate-dipped candied orange and chocolate-dipped strawberries, to name a very few. Next up, ice cream freezers full of wonderful flavors are available in cups or in one of those crispy waffle cones you smelled on the way here.

Kilwin's has plenty of take-away selections that are pre-bagged and boxed. Perhaps you'll need just an ice cream filled waffle cone to give you the strength to continue your shopping trip, but it's always a good idea to have extra sweets along too.

One of downtown's newest shops is Cape Fear Spice Merchants. The massive global spice and tea collection harks back to a time when tall ships unloaded spices and other goods downtown.

Wilmington's colonial port was at the intersection of Market and Water Streets. Shipping and trade is part of how the road got its name. Hand-mixed spice blends range from the exotic Persian 7-Spice blend with cloves and green cardamom to piquant rubs for ribs and roasts.

Loose-leaf teas, more than 100, fill shelves as do oils, vinegars and sea salt blends. Consider the Lime Fresco Rimmer for your next margarita. Sip tea while perusing coffee, flavored sugars, gourmet foods, Mexican chocolates, cooking tools such as cutting boards and everything you need to make the perfect cup of tea.

New at Porters Neck

Honeybee is a new shop that opened in the Porters Neck Center early in 2015. The store is owned by Julie Voorhees, who moved her downtown shop called Dang! to Porters Neck to be closer to her customers. The residents in this area are delighted that she located Honeybee here, since this area didn't have a store offering good, stylish women's clothing, accessories, handbags and a terrific selection of gifts until she arrived.

The merchandise at Honeybee, a sister store to Bumblebee located in Surf City, changes often. As a result, it is smart to visit the store frequently to see what's new.

When visiting Porters Neck, you can have your car cleaned by TLC Autowash, which offers superb service at very reasonable prices. Everything from an express wash to fine auto detailing is available. The friendly, efficient staff is impressive; they want their customers to be happy with the service every time.

Topsail Island shops

Shops within shops are located at The Fishing Village in Surf City. Island Outfitters has island wear for men, women and children, with accessories for all ages too. Columbia sportswear, Sperry deck shoes, terrific T-shirts, sunglasses and books plus lots of other merchandise are in stock. On Shore Surf Shop has surfboards, clothing, swimsuits, surf lessons and board rentals. The shop is operated by surfers and for surfers. Topsail Island has a dedicated group of surfers who come out any time the surf's up.

South End Outfitters is stocked with clothing from such well known, high quality brands as Tommy Bahama, Vineyard Vines, Southern Tide and Peter Millar, labels that are offered for the first time on Topsail Island. This also is the place to find Sperry Top-Siders, the perfect shoe for boating, fishing and ambling on the island. South End Outfitters also offers bicycle rentals, the perfect way to get around the island. Stand up paddleboards, including the top-of-the-line Bōte boards, are in stock too.

"Something for everyone" could be the slogan at Bumblebee. Several lines of designer jewelry including Freshie & Zero, John Wind, Lucky Feather and Dune please women. The store has numerous monogrammed jewelry pieces, too. Apparel, handbags, organizers, gloves and scarves are in stock.

Adorable baby and kids things include puzzles, plush toys and activity books. Slippers for little ones are so cute. Think home décor with high-quality napkin, coasters, aprons and towels. The kitchen/gourmet department is filled with items you won't find elsewhere including pasta shaped like N.C. State and

UNC-Chapel Hill logos.

Keep your Topsail Island time close to your heart even when you're away from the beach with the stunning creations at Mystic Treasures Jewelry. Owner Tommy James is a jewelry designer especially known for his bracelets, namely the Topsail Island Bracelet. Designed and crafted on the island, the sterling silver band with 14-karat gold rope trim cleverly incorporates Topsail Island's initials – T and I – in a delicate, linked script. James' other numerous designs feature sea creatures, mermaids, pirates, seashells and nautical themes. Other designers who fashion lovely items using enameling, glasswork, unusual gemstones and contemporary influences join him.

The only bad thing about the beach is having to leave, which may convince you to buy a Topsail Island home or redecorate your mainland home with some seaside style. Either way, visit Beach Furniture Outfitters on North New River Drive in Surf City for just the right look. The pastel array at this huge store embraces ocean blues, sea foam whites, sandy neutrals, sunset brights and sunny yellows. The one-stop shopping program means you can meet all your furniture, mattress and home accessory needs at affordable prices, plus find carpet, vinyl and installation service. Local delivery, setup and installation are free.

Edgar "Johnny" Herring opened Herring's Outdoor Sports on North New River Drive in 1962. Back then, it was a bait and tackle shop known for topnotch fishing supplies, good bait and friendly service. The space and inventory have grown, but folks here are as friendly as ever. You'll still find fishing supplies, everything from cast nets to waterproof cases for your cell phone. Buy the beach gear you need, whether its sunglasses, T-shirts, hats, sandals or suntan lotion.

A large Life is Good selection offers apparel, beach towels, water bottles and mugs. Kites, pocketknives, lanterns, hammocks, even ukuleles fill shelves at this one-stop store.

Southern Emporium is stocked with beautiful housewares, jewelry and clothing that reflect true southern tradition and New South flair. Jewelry cases feature gold, silver and rainbow tones in bold and restrained pieces for every occasion. Love the nautical look? Check out anchor-shaped wall hangings and navy blue-and-white-striped shirts and children's clothing. Lamps, frames, linens, pottery, silver, glassware and throw pillows, many with a cozy, beach house feel, are among home décor objects. There are baby gifts, Mom and Dad gifts and lots of just-because gifts, perhaps a new, floppy beach hat, a great new piece of jewelry, or a colorful beach bag. Visiting this store should be a must.

Shops on Pleasure Island

Island Tackle and Hardware is a two-story emporium dedicated to supplying an exceptionally complete offering of fishing equipment and supplies coupled with most everything the homeowner or contractor might need in hardware and materials from a True Value dealer.

In addition to apparel ranging from sunglasses and hats to shirts, shorts and shoes, they offer a full selection of rods and reels including electric, boating accessories and trailer supplies, bait for both fishing and crabbing, licenses, official weighing, local nautical art and, of course, free advice.

Squigley's, a wonderful ice cream shop, has a gift shop too. Squigley's Gift Gallery boasts four rooms filled with great finds. A treasure trove of handmade craft items, local art, jewelry, one-of-a-kind specialty items and stained glass is available at prices "ranging from affordable to very high end." One thing is certain; you'll always get value for your money here.

Island Chic is a first class consignment boutique featuring designer and boutique clothing and accessories. Owner Regina Scruggs strives to carry "the best designer brand names, the latest styles, at the best prices!" A truly fun place to shop, here you'll find affordable shoes, clothing, handbags, jewelry and seasonal items all either new or in just slightly used condition. Island Chic also offers new gift items, including hats, wallets, frames, monogrammed totes and scarves, among many other things.

There is a wonderful local bookstore in Carolina Beach. Whether light hearted beach fare or the latest political tome meets your criteria for a fun read, you'll want to visit Island Book Shop. They have a wide range of both new and used books for adults and for children. Ask for recommendations.

Visit Topsail Island's must-see shop!

No trip to Topsail Island is complete without a visit to this charming store, filled with beautiful housewares, jewelry, clothing and so much more.

Southern Emporium

208J North New River Drive • Surf City, NC 28445
910.541.0138

The quality of healthcare available in this area is important to both visitors and residents.

outstanding healthcare

The Cape Fear Region continues to attract a large number of high-caliber medical practitioners who want to live and practice in the Greater Wilmington area, Pender and Brunswick counties. We're fortunate that outstanding healthcare services, providers and facilities not only exist in abundance in this area, but also are among our greatest assets. Rapid population growth, real estate development, new businesses and the influx of retirees have spurred major hospital expansions too.

Without question, New Hanover Regional Medical Center (NHRMC) in Wilmington is the cornerstone and leader when it comes to providing a comprehensive and sophisticated array of services. For close to 50 years, NHRMC has served the residents of southeastern North Carolina and beyond. A tertiary referral center, NHRMC provides a broad range of medical specialties with some of the state's finest physicians, nurses and staff.

NHRMC includes the main 17th Street campus, NHRMC Orthopedic Hospital on Wrightsville Avenue and the management of Pender Memorial Hospital in Burgaw. NHRMC also provides Emergency Medical Services (EMS), critical care ground and air transport through VitaLink and AirLink, services through Health & Diagnostic Centers and outpatient rehabilitation. Through the NHRMC Physician Group, NHRMC provides primary care, specialty services and urgent care throughout the region. NHRMC is also affiliated with NHRMC Home Care, adding another dimension to the closely coordinated services that help provide more seamless, high-quality care from physician office to hospital to home.

N.C.'s ninth-largest healthcare system

New Hanover Regional Medical Center is the ninth-largest healthcare system in the state and the largest employer in the region, with a dedicated team of about 6,000 employees, 560 physicians and 760 active volunteers. NHRMC is licensed for 769 beds, including those at NHRMC Orthopedic Hospital.

As a public, not-for-profit hospital, NHRMC offers care to everyone who

When in need of urgent care, *know where to go.*

Why choose NHRMC Urgent Care? When you are a patient of New Hanover Regional Medical Center, NHRMC Urgent Care or any NHRMC Physician Group practice, you become part of a network with access to the same electronic health record across the continuum of your care. Add those things together and your healthcare team now has a more complete picture of your medical history – and so do you.

Learn how coordinated access to your electronic medical record benefits you.

Visit **nhrmc.org/nhrmcmychart** for more information.

WILMINGTON
1135 Military Cutoff Road, Suite 103
910.256.6222

WALLACE
112 Medical Village Drive, Suite G
910.285.0333

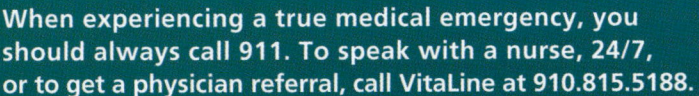

When experiencing a true medical emergency, you should always call 911. To speak with a nurse, 24/7, or to get a physician referral, call VitaLine at 910.815.5188.

outstanding **healthcare**

Our local medical staff provides excellent care to people of all ages.

needs it, regardless of ability to pay. On an annual basis, NHRMC provides more than $145 million in charitable and uncompensated care to the community. Its volunteer board of trustees is appointed by New Hanover County Commissioners with representation from Pender County. NHRMC receives no local tax support for its day-to-day operations.

Recognized for patient care

New Hanover Regional Medical Center has been recognized for the quality and safety of its patient care by The Joint Commission, which named New Hanover Regional Medical Center a 2013 Top Performer on Key Quality Measures® for attaining and sustaining excellence in accountability measure performance for heart attack, heart failure, pneumonia and surgical care. NHRMC was ranked as one of the 2013 and 2014 HealthStrong™ Hospitals in the United States, a top hospital delivering better care, higher quality and lower costs than 99% of rated U.S. hospitals.

New Hanover Regional Medical Center
2131 S. 17th Street
Wilmington, NC 28401
910-667-7000

NHRMC is a teaching hospital and regional referral center. As the tertiary care center for a seven-county area, the medical center offers specialty medical and surgical care. It is one of nine trauma centers in the state certified at Level II or above. Other specialty services include: four adult intensive care units, neonatal and pediatric intensive care, neurosurgery, pediatric surgery, open heart surgery, vascular surgery and oncology services.

In addition to advanced medicine and exceptional staff, NHRMC offers a beautiful environment for patients to receive care and heal. The hospital expanded in recent years with the addition of a 186,500-square-foot Surgical Pavilion and the 150-bed Betty H. Cameron Women's & Children's Hospital.

The hospital's patient tower has also been renovated, including private rooms, all-new interiors, a soothing and quiet design, room for family, and access to caregivers who are never far from the patient's room.

NHRMC Orthopedic Hospital
5301 Wrightsville Avenue
Wilmington, NC 28405
910-667-8100

NHRMC Orthopedic Hospital serves as NHRMC's home for orthopedic services. The NHRMC Orthopedic Hospital, designated as a Blue Distinction Center+ in Knee and Hip Replacements by BCBSNC, features designated orthopedic nurses, therapists, technicians and surgeons who are board-certified or eligible in orthopedic surgery. The dedicated orthopedic hospital includes specialists in hand and shoulder, foot and ankle, and spine as well as arthroscopic surgeries, sports medicine and joint replacement. More than 7,000 orthopedic procedures are performed each year at NHRMC Orthopedic Hospital – more than at any other hospital in the region. NHRMC also operates a 24-hour Emergency Department at this location.

NHRMC Orthopedic Hospital has received a number of quality recognitions, including being named a Blue Distinction Center+ in Knee and Hip Replacements by Blue Cross and Blue Shield of North Carolina and recognition as a Total Joint Replacement Specialty Center by UnitedHealth Premium®. The orthopedic hospital was also recognized as a top four hospital in the state overall, as well as in patient picks, and a standout hospital for orthopedics by *Business North Carolina*.

Pender Memorial Hospital
507 Fremont Street
Burgaw, NC 28425
910-259-5451

Pender Memorial Hospital gives residents of Pender and surrounding counties a convenient and friendly place to receive a wide range of services. Pender Memorial Hospital and NHRMC Home Care have received national recognition for a telehealth program designed to help reduce hospital readmissions for congestive heart failure patients, one of only five critical access hospitals in the country recognized by The National Rural Health Resource Center for innovation in delivering health care in rural communities. The Emergency Department is staffed 24 hours a day by the same group of physicians who provide emergency care at NHRMC and NHRMC Orthopedic Hospital. The 86-bed hospital also has rehabilitation and diagnostic facilities, and a surgical and endoscopy center. Pender Memorial Hospital's Skilled Nursing Unit provides a comfortable and caring environment for residents who need long-term care and help with daily activities. The post-acute care unit offers patients who no longer require hospital care a place to receive short-term rehabilitation before leaving the hospital.

Betty H. Cameron Women's & Children's Hospital
910-667-7360

NHRMC Betty H. Cameron Women's & Children's Hospital offers expert women's and children's care including obstetrical care for routine and high-risk deliveries. The unit handles about 3,700 births each year. Other services include the state's only all-private-room Neonatal Intensive Care Unit that cares for babies born prematurely or critically ill. The NHRMC Betty H. Cameron Women's & Children's Hospital also has the only pediatric intensive care unit and pediatric surgery program in the region. These specialized services address the medical and surgical needs of children who need hospitalization. Comprehensive pediatric subspecialty care is provided through the Nunnelee Pediatric Specialty Clinics. The clinic is able to offer children with ongoing medical needs the opportunity to receive advanced pediatric care close to home.

The NHRMC Betty H. Cameron Women's & Children's Hospital is a two-time winner of the Studer Excellence in Patient Care Award, presented by a nationally recognized healthcare consulting firm, to recognize facilities for outstanding achievement in areas of patient safety and quality care. NHRMC Betty H. Cameron Women's & Children's Hospital is also designated as a Baby-Friendly facility, recognized for offering an optimal level of family-centered care and education on infant feeding and mother/baby bonding.

NHRMC Rehabilitation Hospital
910-667-7845

A 60-bed CARF-accredited inpatient and outpatient rehabilitation facility on NHRMC's main campus, the NHRMC Rehabilitation Hospital helps patients with debilitating injury or disease recover mobility and independence, both through inpatient treatment and the Day Hospital Program.

The hospital has a 3,000-square-foot therapy gym and treats patients suffering from stroke, chronic conditions such as arthritis or multiple sclerosis, as well as patients who have suffered a traumatic brain or spinal cord injury. The focus is on improving a patient's mobility, self-care, communication and social skills.

Outpatient therapy is provided at two Wilmington locations– Independence Rehabilitation and Oleander Rehabilitation – as well as Pender Health & Diagnostics-Rocky Point. Services include neurological, pediatric, vestibular, orthopedic and back rehabilitation as well as hand, communication and swallowing therapy.

NHRMC Behavioral Health Hospital
910-667-7787

Located on the hospital's main 17th Street campus, the NHRMC Behavioral Health Hospital is a 62-bed psychiatric crisis stabilization hospital providing inpatient psychiatric programs for adults, older adults, and those with co-occurring mental health and substance abuse disorders.

Accredited by the Joint Commission, the NHRMC Behavioral Health Hospital is staffed by a comprehensive team of mental healthcare professionals, including board-certified psychiatrists, psychiatric nurse practitioners, nurses, psychotherapists, clinical social workers, certified addictions counselors, recreation and movement therapists.

A Network of Primary and Specialty Care

NHRMC Physician Group
www.nhrmcphysiciangroup.org

NHRMC Physician Group's affiliation with NHRMC means patients benefit from a collaboration that allows access to high-quality resources, clinical skills and a shared electronic medical record. Care is better coordinated between hospital and practice, and patients have access to MyChart - a secure portal to ask their physician a question, get tests results, request an appointment and get prescription refills.

With locations in New Hanover, Brunswick, Onslow, Columbus, Duplin and Pender counties, the NHRMC Physician Group offers services for the entire family from primary and urgent care to specialty care.

New Hanover Medical Group and Wrightsville Beach Family Medicine have been recognized by the National Committee on Quality Assurance and the American Diabetes Association for delivery of quality diabetes care. Cape Fear Cancer Specialists has been recognized for excellent care through the QOPI Certification Program, an affiliate of the American Society of Clinical Oncology.

NHRMC Heart Center nationally recognized

The NHRMC Heart Center is one of North Carolina's leading heart programs and is nationally recognized for delivering high-quality care including emergency treatment for heart attack patients twice as fast as the national standard. It has the area's only open-heart surgery program, houses a 16-bed Coronary Care Unit and a 14-bed Cardiovascular Intensive Care Unit, as well as cardiac catheterization, electrophysiology and cardiovascular labs. With more than 30 board-certified cardiologists, 12,000 procedures a year are performed at the NHRMC Heart Center. NHRMC Heart Center also includes the Chest Pain Center, where patients experiencing chest pain get specialized monitoring and care in the six-bed unit, and a heart valve program for the diagnosis and treatment of valve conditions.

NHRMC Heart Center received the American Heart Association's highest award for heart attack care as a recipient of the Mission: Lifeline Gold Plus Quality Achievement Award for its STEMI program - which is its protocol for rapidly delivering patients in cardiac arrest to the care they need. NHRMC Heart Center has also been nationally recognized for delivering high-quality cardiac care and as a standout hospital for cardiology and heart surgery by Business North Carolina.

NHRMC Heart Center Outpatient Services
1415 Physicians Drive
Wilmington, NC 28401

The newly opened three-floor, 62,300-square-foot NHRMC Heart Center - Outpatient Services facility offers a centralized location for patients to meet with cardiologists and advanced clinical practitioners as well as have easy access to cardiac imaging and rehabilitation services in one convenient location. The NHRMC Heart Center-Outpatient Services facility also includes NHRMC Heart Center's Cardiac Rehabilitation Program, which offers heart patients access to classes on diet and stress management, as well as exercise classes monitored by registered nurses and exercise physiologists.

NHRMC Zimmer Cancer Center
910-667-7787

NHRMC Zimmer Cancer Center has been nationally designated as a teaching cancer program by the American College of Surgeon's Commission on Cancer – a designation awarded to just 25 percent of hospitals in the country. The Zimmer Cancer Center combines outpatient treatment so patients can access the care they need in one convenient and comforting place. Treatments include radiation therapy, chemotherapy and infusion. The center also houses the hospital's cancer clinical trials program, giving local residents a chance to participate in national treatment studies. In addition, NHRMC offers ongoing support and resources for patients and loved ones. NHRMC Zimmer Cancer Center is a recipient of the Outstanding Achievement Award from the American College of Surgeon's Commission on Cancer.

Surgical Pavilion

NHRMC's Surgical Pavilion on the main campus combines access to highly advanced equipment and experienced specialists in a convenient and comfortable setting. Opened in 2008, the Surgical Pavilion houses 26 operating rooms at 600 square feet each, with each room designed to accommodate the entire surgical staff along with some of medicine's most advanced surgical equipment. This includes the da Vinci and Mazor robotic surgical systems, which allow surgeons greater visibility and precision when performing complex minimally invasive procedures. NHRMC was the region's first to use the robotic surgical system and has the largest team of experienced robotic surgeons in the region. These surgeons perform robotic gynecology, urology, prostate, gynecologic oncology and orthopedic procedures.

Bariatric program

NHRMC is designated as a Blue Distinction® Center+ for Bariatric Surgery by Blue Cross Blue Shield Association. In 2014, the American Society of Metabolic and Bariatric Surgery re-designated NHRMC as a Bariatric Center of Excellence. In 2013, Blue Cross and Blue Shield of North Carolina recognized NHRMC as a cutting edge hospital for its bariatric program.

NHRMC health & diagnostics

NHRMC offers advanced diagnostic services at several locations throughout the region. Services include a PET/CT scan for diagnosis of cancer and Alzheimer's disease. The medical center has an open bore MRI, capable of accommodating patients up to 450 lbs., and decreasing the incidence of claustrophobia for most patients, while providing physicians with high-quality readings. The addition of a 64-slice CT also helps improve diagnostic imaging services. Interventional Radiology, Nuclear Medicine, CT, Ultrasound and Digital Mammography are also offered to provide residents with advanced diagnosis and treatments close to home. A centralized scheduling number, 910-667-8777, connects patients to convenient locations throughout Wilmington and Brunswick County.

NHRMC Home Care
910-259-1224

An affiliate of New Hanover Regional Medical Center and Pender Memorial Hospital, NHRMC Home Care offers continuing care inside the comfort of the patient's home. NHRMC Home Care serves the seven-county area and offers skilled nursing, medication management, wound care, physical, occupational and speech therapy. The NHRMC Home Care team ensures continuity of care from hospital to home.

Trauma and Emergency Medical Services
2131 S. 17th Street
Wilmington, NC 28401
910-667-7000

NHRMC's Emergency Services Department is highly integrated to help ensure patients get the best care possible. It includes the region's only Level II Trauma Center and Emergency Departments at New Hanover Regional Medical Center, NHRMC Orthopedic Hospital and Pender Memorial Hospi-

tal. The hospital will expand its emergency services with the 2015 opening of NHRMC Emergency Department North for more convenient access to those living in the northern part of New Hanover County.

Trauma and Emergency Medical Services also incorporates New Hanover Regional EMS - one of only three hospital-operated EMS systems in North Carolina - which provides advanced pre-hospital care and emergency transport, allowing patients throughout the region access to the level of care they need. Services are provided by AirLink helicopter, VitaLink's adult and pediatric intensive care vehicles, ambulance, or patient care transport.

NHRMC Emergency Medical Services and AirLink VitaLink Critical Care Transport teams are among the first in the nation to receive the Mission: Lifeline EMS Silver Recognition Award - the highest award for transport agencies. NHRMC's AirLink VitaLink Critical Care Transport program is one of only two flight programs in the nation to receive this award.

VitaLine
910-667-5188, 1-888-815-5188

For patients with medical questions who are unsure if they need a doctor's office visit or trip to the Emergency Department, NHRMC offers VitaLine, a 24-hour nurse call system. VitaLine offers health information, answers to routine questions and physician referrals any time of day.

Brunswick County hospitals

In March 2006, Novant Health, a private, not-for-profit health care chain, took over management of the 60-bed Brunswick Community Hospital located in Supply. Just fourteen months later, in May 2007, North Carolina state officials approved Novant's certificate of need proposal to build a new, replacement hospital in Brunswick County.

The new facility has 74 acute care rooms, four observation rooms, four surgical operating rooms, one c-section room, 24-hour emergency department, maternity center, intensive care unit and extensive support services, including physical therapy and cardiac rehabilitation. All patient rooms are private and the hospital, Brunswick Novant Medical Center, opened in 2011.

Dosher Memorial Hospital in Southport is Brunswick County's hidden jewel. Owned by the citizens of Smithville Township for 80 years, the hospital has 36 acute care and 64 skilled nursing beds and offers a comprehensive scope of acute care health services using state-of-the-art technology. Having partnered with New Hanover Regional Medical Center, Dosher has been able to expand its services, share resources and provide joint outreach programs such as screenings, educational activities and support groups. Also, the alliance has facilitated a broader spectrum of physician specialties, services and technology.

Dental facilities abound

The Wilmington area has many dental facilities serving all disciplines. In addition to those who practice general dentistry, the Cape Fear area has specialists in public health dentistry, endodontia, periodontics, pedodontics, oral surgery and orthodontics, maxillofacial surgery, cosmetic and restorative dentistry.

Atlantic Dental Group
1301 Physicians Drive
Wilmington, NC 28401
910-270-1222
www.atlantic-dental.com

For more than 50 years, Atlantic Dental Group has been providing dental care to the Wilmington area. At their state-of-the-art facility located in midtown Wilmington, Atlantic Dental provides comprehensive dental treatment, including diagnostic and preventative, restorative, and cosmetic dentistry.

Atlantic Dental's four dentists pride themselves on offering excellent customer service and dental treatments with a personal, gentle touch. Dr. G. Barry Frazelle II, a graduate of UNC School of Dentistry, has practiced with Atlantic Dental for more than 25 years. Dr. Carter W. Lee joined Atlantic Dental in 1996, upon graduation from UNC School of Dentistry. Dr. Sarah E. Pless, who received her dental degree from the University of Illinois at Chicago, has practiced with Atlantic Dental since

G. Barry Frazelle, DDS • Carter W. Lee, DDS
Sarah E. Pless, DDS • Yulia Paterson, DDS

"I can't say enough about the wonderful people and the treatment you get here. They make you feel like part of the family."

—Sheri, patient of 10+ years

1301 Physicians Drive • Wilmington, NC 28401
P: 910-762-0958 • atlantic-dental.com

Serving the Wilmington Community for over 50 years.

2006. In 2014, Dr. Yulia Paterson joined Atlantic Dental after several years of dental practice in New York. She graduated from the New York University College of Dentistry in 2006.

Their longevity in the area translates to their ability to develop multi-generational relationships with patient families. From regular cleanings to a full smile makeover, Atlantic Dental is known for offering friendly and professional service. For added customer convenience, appointments can be requested and payments can be made through their website. They welcome new patients and accept nearly all types of dental insurance.

Pierpan Family Dentistry
14544 US Highway 17, Suite 10
Hampstead, NC 28443
910-270-1222

An outstanding family practice is Pierpan Family Dentistry located in Hampstead, just north of Wilmington. A husband and wife team, Drs. Henry and Monica Pierpan, who received their D.D.S. degrees from UNC School of Dentistry in Chapel Hill, head the facility.

Dr. Henry is passionate about providing his patients with high quality, state-of-the-art dental care. He completed his surgical residency for implant placement in Washington, D.C. in 2007 and is a fellow in the International Congress of Oral Implantologists. He also is a Captain in the U.S. Navy Reserves and serves as a Dental Corps officer at Camp LeJeune.

Dr. Monica's goal in her practice is to treat every patient as family. She strives to be gentle and caring while providing the highest quality of dental care. She is a member of the Port City Study Club, which is committed to dental excellence in all areas.

Pierpan Family Dentistry provides preventative care for young and old with the goal of keeping a patient's teeth and mouth free of disease that can lead to tooth and gum loss. Their talented dental hygienists have proven their ability to prevent further erosion in those suffering from gingivitis and other periodontal disease.

Since 2006, Pierpan Family Dentistry has provided implant services for their patients, including surgical placement and restoration to help replace missing teeth. They were the first office in this area to use a Cone Beam Dental CatScan to help in diagnosis & placement of implants. This state-of-the-art technology enables patients to replace missing teeth with a more natural feel; preserving bone and helping patients chew with confidence.

Pierpan Family Dentistry accepts most dental insurance plans and provides a means for patients to apply for credit through a dedicated private dental financing provider.

Physical Therapy

Hampstead Physical Therapy
25 N. Hampstead Village Drive
Hampstead, NC 28443
910-270-6026
2017 NC Highway 172, Suite B
Sneads Ferry, NC 28460
910-327-0418

There has always been a need for rehabilitative physical therapy to help those with broken bones, torn ligaments, and ruptured tendons regain full mobility. And even more therapists are required as the aging population has hips, knees and other joints repaired or replaced.

Just north of Wilmington is an outstanding service, Hampstead Physical Therapy, which is doing wonders with its patients in this location as well as in the office in Sneads Ferry. The talented staff has gained a reputation for getting their patients back to normal quickly.

Medical Infrastructure

Legions of freestanding clinics and medical offices of all descriptions and sizes are an integral part of our health and medical care infrastructure. Rehabilitation, surgery, urgent care, orthopedic and specialty centers, teen health, diagnostic clinics, infusion therapy, public health, dialysis, and imaging are among the many support services. And, supporting the support services is another industry – retail businesses including pharmacies, opticians, prosthetic devices, surgical garments, home medical supplies, and so forth. Alternative and complementary health care is widely available in coastal communities. You'll easily find chiropractors, massage therapists, herbalists, acupuncturists, and others who practice Naturopathic Medicine, Chinese Medicine and biofeedback. Many businesses in our area focus on natural remedies, nutrition, holistic health, wellness, organically produced foods and healthy lifestyles. Wilmington even offers holistic chiropractic care and acupuncture.

The Wilmington area has some excellent retirement and progressive care communities, which appeal to many of our seniors. Also available are assisted living, skilled nursing and memory care residences. In-home services, both medical and non-medical, are available in all counties, as is hospice care. Adult day care centers are located only in Wilmington, but they accept out-of-area participants. Southeastern North Carolina has a full complement of support groups and civic health organizations, too. Each county has a governmental department that acts as a resource for seniors and can help locate needed services such as Meals on Wheels and transportation for medical appointments. They are: the New Hanover County Department of Aging, in Wilmington, Brunswick Senior Resources, Inc., in Bolivia, and Pender Adult Services in Burgaw.

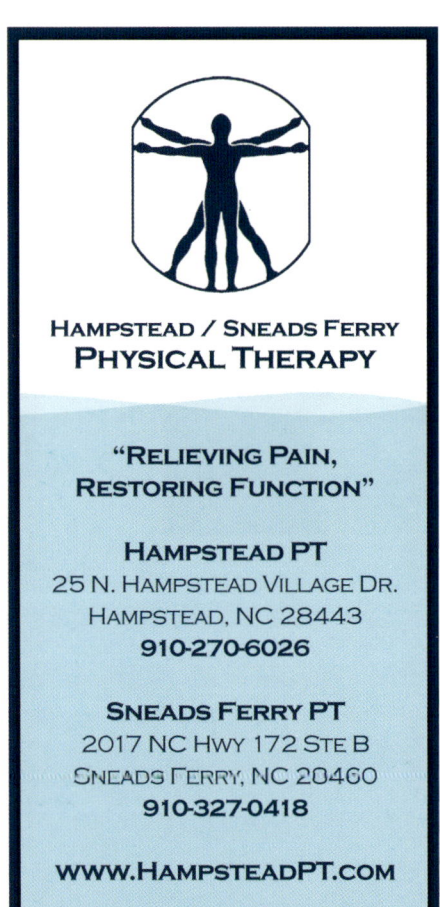

theater, music and nightlife
Continued from page 35

of Life is often recognized in readers' choice awards for producing Wilmington's best pizza.

Fork 'n Cork was voted best new restaurant in the 2015 readers' choice awards. They serve until midnight on weekends, offering really delicious sandwiches, salads, craft cocktails and specialty mac 'n cheese dishes.

A relatively new establishment in Leland, Willoughbys, is becoming the place to be for entertainment in Leland. Willoughbys, named after an episode of the *Twilight Zone*, opened in February 2013. Billed as "not your ordinary tavern," it is located on Ocean Highway just south of Magnolia Greens. The owner is dedicated to keeping prices very affordable and has created a comfortable, cozy atmosphere. Live entertainment is offered frequently and there are popular weekly trivia and karaoke nights. The restaurant has an outdoor area and a place for a fireside chat. Look for a beautiful fire engine red Willoughbys food truck that is in front of the tavern.

celebrate our festivals

April 9, 2016. The fun event features chowder from several restaurants in the area, all competing for the chance to brag about being judged the best. Bands play throughout the event, which lasts from 11:30 a.m. to 5:30 p.m. Ticket prices are moderate; children 12 and under are free.

Orange Street Arts Fest

With so many talented artists in Southeastern North Carolina, it's very fitting that there should be a festival showcasing their wares and talents. The 21st Annual Orange Street Arts Fest, the largest art festival in the area, takes place over the Memorial Day weekend, May 28 and 29, 2016. Artists also will be in the Hannah Block Historic USO building. Visitors are also invited to tour the World War II exhibits displayed at the Hannah Block USO.

Among the art works displayed are ceramics, jewelry, painting, photography, sculpture, cloth goods and much more. Food, a wine tent and a variety of live

Continued from page 39

entertainment are offered also. Thalian Association, the Official Community Theater of North Carolina, produces this first-class event.

Greek Festival

The Greek Festival is held at St. Nicholas Greek Orthodox Church and features the food, traditional dances, music, and wines of the Greek Isles. The 21st annual event is May 13-15, 2016; nearly 20,000 people attend each year. One of the highlights of the festival is the homemade Greek pastries that are prepared by church members and sold by the thousands at the Festival. Traditional Greek food, wines and beer are consumed in great quantities over the three days.

Especially popular are the dances performed to authentic Greek music on authentic instruments, with the dancers in traditional costumes. Particularly charming are the dances performed by young Greek children in native dress.

Willoughbys

Full Service Bar
Karaoke • Live Music
Fireside Chat Area • Special Wine & Cheese Nights
Chef Prepared Menu • Very Affordable Pricing
Outdoor Area • Cozy Atmosphere
Breakfast, Lunch & Dinner • Special Sunday Brunch

Our mission is to deliver fresh quality food and drinks at affordable pricing.
Step back in time for a more peaceful, stress free time and enjoy yourself and your company.

Check us out. Be sure you make "A Stop at Willoughbys"

8951 Ocean Hwy., Leland, NC 28451
910-383-1270

Find Us On Facebook
WilloughbysLeland

Photo by G. Frank Hart Photography

Topsail Island's relatively uncrowded beaches are enjoyed by visitors from both near and far.

traipsing along topsail island

Days glide along at Topsail Island. Vintage beach houses pepper maritime forests, wide beaches and friendly canal neighborhoods. A string of communities dotting the 26-mile-long shore host family businesses that bolster the small-town feel. Think of Topsail as paradise with a simple charm.

You can still drive an old-fashioned swing bridge to reach this narrow band, just 500 to 1,500 feet wide. Vistas stretch from sound to sea. One of the region's least populated beaches, Topsail Island is void of super high-rise hotels and condominiums. Locals still come to weekend homes that have been in their families for generations. Public parking, wooden fishing piers and watermen selling fresh shrimp from coolers on their tailgates keep this beach a favorite day-trip destination.

Make sure you say the name correctly. It's not pronounced like the "top-SAIL" on a schooner, although that may be what the island is named after. Rather, local dialect demands "top-SUL."

Topsail Island is the next barrier island of any significant size north of Wrightsville Beach. The strip is split between the two counties.

Onslow County's northern half includes the town of North Topsail Beach. You may hear someone call it by the original name, West Onslow Beach. If that happens, you'll know you've encountered a true local. Politicians changed the name when the town incorporated in 1990. Just over the high-rise bridge to the mainland sits Sneads Ferry. The fishing village has sprouted many new homes, but the community maintains its quaint character.

Surf City and Topsail Beach lay in Pender County. That swing bridge takes you to Surf City, where you can still shop a little grocery and meet locals at seafood steam bars. Serene Topsail Beach is the island's southernmost town.

Year-round populations in these towns are small. Numbers swell into the thousands in summer. Yet, the area never feels crowded.

Topsail's storied history

Island history dates back to prehistoric times. The first written records were made in the 1500s when early explorers described abundant seafood beds. According to legend, two prominent pirates, Blackbeard and Stede Bonnet, buried treasure hereabouts, and visitors toting metal detectors keep looking for it.

Those pirates may have given Topsail Island its name. Legend claims that they hung out in the sound between the island and the mainland spying merchant ships to plunder.

Eventually, merchantmen figured this out and kept their eyes open for the topsails of pirate ships hiding in sound-side marshes and woods.

World War II influx

Topsail Island was mostly uninhabited for years. There were no bridges to the island. Boats brought picnickers and anglers. A few fish camps were here and there. Occasionally, a mainland farmer drove his cattle over sand bars at low tide to feed on seaside grasses.

World War II changed everything. After the war, the U.S. Navy took the island. In conjunction with Johns Hopkins University Physics Laboratory, the Navy began "Operation Bumblebee." The top-secret project was designed to develop and test ramjet missiles advanced America's jet aircraft and missile programs and helped launch the country's space program. Roads, a fresh water supply, a bridge and other improvements were made as the military directed research operations from nearby Camp Davis in Holly Ridge on the mainland.

As you drive along Topsail Island, look for concrete observation towers from which scientists monitored rocket launches. Rockets were assembled and stored at an arsenal that still stands on the sound side of the island. Launching pads stood oceanfront.

More than 200 rockets were shot between 1946 and 1948, proving the feasibility of ramjet engines that could propel aircraft beyond the speed of sound.

Missiles and More Museum

Missiles and More Museum at Topsail Beach houses World War II artifacts from Camp Davis and exhibits related to Operation Bumblebee. The museum is located in the original arsenal building, known as the Assembly Building. Rocket models are displayed. Videos show how rockets were launched.

One exhibit features WASP, Women Air Force Service Pilots who served at Camp Davis during World War II. Also see displays of local pirate lore. Flora and fauna are highlighted, too. Don't miss the large seashell collection.

Each October, the Autumn at Topsail festival takes place around the Assembly Building. It showcases a juried Artists Court. Live entertainment, food vendors and games and rides for the kids are part of the event. Proceeds fund Assembly Building maintenance.

Annual festivals

No big surprise that two big Topsail Island festivals celebrate seafood. Fishing for a living has been going on here for years. Look for wooden shrimp trawlers offshore in summer. Some fishermen sell their catch at roadside stands.

Locals and visitors alike cherish Sneads Ferry's annual Shrimp Festival, August 8-9, 2015. Delicious shrimp platters are the big draw. Live music is a close second. Beach music masters The Embers play this year. Days also feature arts and crafts vendors, a beer and wine garden, cooking demonstrations, a car show and carnival rides. Nearby Camp Lejeune Marine Corps base brings interesting exhibits.

A month later, hit Hampstead's N.C. Spot Festival, usually the last weekend in September. Spots are local fish, usually weighing about a pound. Locals like the tender, mild meat dusted in cornmeal and fried. That's how cooks fix spots at the festival. Live m[...] vendors, cotton candy, funnel[...] carnival rides are included. Hampstea[...] on U.S. Highway 17, just south of Surf City.

Surf City here we come

It's not just a name. Surf City has long been a favorite spot for surfers. There's more than tasty waves at Topsail Island's largest town. Chartered in 1949, the municipality of around 2,000 people possesses the island's only traffic lights.

An old-fashioned, two-lane swing bridge remains Surf City's link to the mainland, although state leaders propose replacing it soon with a modern structure. Many people want the old bridge to stay.

With more than 30 beach accesses, many boat ramps, an ocean pier and a lovely waterfront town park with a playground and picnic areas, Surf City equals seaside fun. This Topsail Island business center has experienced rapid growth. Recent commercial development on mainland Surf City includes a large Lowe's home improvement center and Harris

Spectacular water views exist on the sound as well as the ocean side of Topsail Island.

Photo by G. Frank Hart Photography

Visit the Greater Topsail Area

**Home to
26 miles of Beach
Intracoastal Waterway Sports
Dining and Shopping**

Karen Beasley Sea Turtle Rescue and Rehabilitation

Missiles and More Museum

Poplar Grove Plantation
and more

THE GREATER TOPSAIL AREA
Chamber of Commerce and Tourism

Plan your next day trip with us!

www.topsailchamber.org

Teeter grocery store.

In 2006, a new 17,000-square-foot community center was built and the town park was completed. The swing bridge's approach hosts many new shops and condos.

Get your bearings

GREATER TOPSAIL CHAMBER

As you arrive near the swing bridge headed toward the beach, look for The Greater Topsail Island Chamber of Commerce on N.C. Highway 50. Staff is happy to provide visitors with whatever information they need to make their Topsail Island time pleasurable.

Get your questions answered and pick up a free information packet, especially useful if you're visiting the area for the first time. You'll find details about shops, restaurants, events and activities.

SURF CITY WELCOME CENTER

Once on the beach, check in at The Surf City Welcome and Visitors Center, 102 North Shore Drive.

It's in the heart of Surf City, just a few yards north of the wooden Surf City Pier and next door to popular Daddy Mac's restaurant. There is ample parking and a beautiful view of the ocean is just outside the door.

The center's information stash about holidays and events proves Surf City is a worthy year-round destination.

December's Christmas Flotilla, when boats are decorated and prizes are awarded for the best design, is as exciting as Fourth of July's fireworks display near Surf City's park.

Shop Surf City

SOUTHERN EMPORIUM

Southern charm. How do you put your finger on it? Hospitality, of course, but a certain look, too. Colorful but refined. Elegant yet at ease.

Find it at Southern Emporium in the heart of Surf City. Beautiful housewares, jewelry and clothing reflect true southern tradition and New South flair.

The shop's aqua walls, wood floors and lovely displays are sure to give you decorating ideas as soon you step inside. Start shopping to uncover an array of goods.

Jewelry cases feature gold, silver and rainbow tones in bold and restrained pieces for every occasion. Love the nautical look? Check out anchor-shaped wall hangings and navy blue-and-white-striped shirts and children's clothing.

Lamps, frames, linens, pottery, silver, glassware and throw pillows, many with a cozy, beach house feel, are among home décor objects. There are baby gifts, Mom and Dad gifts and lots of just-because gifts for that special someone or yourself, perhaps a new, floppy beach hat. a great new piece of jewelry, or a colorful beach bag.

Holiday décor might mean shell wreaths or amusing signs saying things like "Merry Christmas to y'all." Southern Emporium recognizes other holidays, too. Kitchen items take center stage at Thanksgiving.

You'll love it so much here that you may want, as Southerners say, "to sit a spell." And that's quite alright with the friendly staff.

68 ■ www.wilmingtontoday.com

Southern sensibility at its best!

No trip to Topsail Island is complete without a visit to this charming store, filled with beautiful housewares, jewelry, clothing and so much more. The selection is worth the trip from anywhere in the Cape Fear area.

Southern Emporium

208J North New River Drive • Surf City, NC 28445
910.541.0138

traipsing along topsail island

BUMBLEBEE MARKET

"Something for everyone" could be the slogan at this shop just over the bridge. Several lines of designer jewelry including Freshie & Zero, John Wind, Lucky Feather and Dune please women.

The store has numerous monogrammed jewelry pieces, too. Apparel, handbags, organizers, gloves and scarves are in stock.

Adorable baby and kids things include puzzles, plush toys and activity books. Slippers for little ones are so cute. Think home décor with high-quality napkin, coasters, aprons and towels.

The kitchen/gourmet department sells pasta shaped like N.C. State and UNC-Chapel Hill logos. Cat and dog lovers find pet and paw shapes. The cookie cutter section pairs unique recipes with fun shapes like palm trees and dinosaurs to provide the ultimate in cookie creativity.

MYSTIC TREASURES JEWELRY

Keep your Topsail Island time close to your heart even when you're away from the beach with the stunning creations at Mystic Treasures Jewelry in Surf City.

Owner Tommy James is a jewelry designer especially known for his bracelets, namely the Topsail Island Bracelet. Designed and crafted on the island, the sterling silver band with 14-karat gold rope trim cleverly incorporates Topsail Island's initials – T and I – in a delicate, linked script. As James says, "The TI bracelet represents all that is special about Topsail Island – from the flowing wave like caps on the T and I to the simple yet elegant design of the band. There is no doubt you are sporting a memory of Topsail Island." James' other numerous designs feature sea creatures, mermaids, pirates, seashells and nautical themes.

He's joined by other designers who fashion lovely items using enameling, glasswork, unusual gemstones and contemporary influences. Many items, such as a gold and silver crab holding a gem in his claws, may be worn as pendants or fitted into the Armada Double Hook interchangeable-look bracelet. Even when you're not in the store, you can shop online, which is handy to know for birthdays and holidays.

Mystic Treasures Jewelry

121 S. Topsail Dr Surf City, NC 910-328-6300 www.MysticTreasuresNC.com

BEACH FURNITURE OUTFITTERS

The only bad thing about the beach is having to leave, which may convince you to buy a Topsail Island home or redecorate your mainland home with some seaside style. Either way, visit Beach Furniture Outfitters on North New River Drive in Surf City for just the right look.

Tickle Imports and BeachCraft Rattan wicker and rattan pieces for indoor and outdoor spaces are on the sales floor. Papila Design lamps and artwork add just the right finishing touches. Choose all-weather BeachFront Furniture that can withstand the elements no matter where you live.

The pastel array at this huge store embraces ocean blues, sea foam whites, sandy neutrals, sunset brights and sunny yellows. The one-stop shopping program means you can meet all your furniture, mattress and home accessory needs at affordable prices, plus find carpet, vinyl and installation service. Local delivery, setup and installation are free.

Fishing and watersports

FISHING VILLAGE

Everything anglers need to enjoy a day of fishing may be found in a Roland Avenue building aptly named the Fishing Village. The complex hosts East Coast Sports, the area's most complete tackle shop. Rods and reels, rod racks, fishing carts, and all other supplies required for landing fins are here.

Island Marine Supply sells hardware and safety equipment, electronics, and water sports gear for boats and trailers. Interested in fishing charters? Topsail Charter Fishing books both inshore and offshore charters. Boats and kayaks may also be rented.

The Fishing Village is home to two other businesses, as well. Island Outfitters stocks island wear and accessories for men, women and children. Columbia sportswear, Sperry deck shoes, terrific T-shirts, sunglasses plus books and lots of other merchandise are stocked.

Preparing to hang ten? Check out On Shore Surf Shop's surf boards, clothing, swim suits, surf lessons and board rentals. The shop is operated by and for surfers.

The fish are always biting

Visitors from near and far relish Topsail Island's many opportunities to hook the big one. Surf cast, drop a line off a pier or reserve a charter boat. The fish are always biting on Topsail Island it seems.

TOPSAIL CHARTER FISHING

Headquartered in the Fishing Village, Topsail Charter Fishing docks 10 different boats and captains.

Each skipper is Coast Guard Certified and trained in first aid and CPR. Book half, three-quarter and full days of fishing.

Fish the Gulf Stream for tuna and mahi, or stay inland for trout. That's just a few of the some 150 edible species off North Carolina.

Topsail Island hosts three major fishing piers: SeaView Pier in North Topsail Beach, Jolly Roger Pier in Topsail Beach and Surf City Pier in Surf City. Numerous fishing tournaments happen throughout the year.

traipsing along topsail island

Photo by G. Frank Hart Photography

Locals love the old-fashioned swing bridge that leads to Topsail Island.

HERRING'S OUTDOOR SPORTS

Edgar "Johnny" Herring opened this Surf City store on North New River Drive in 1962. Back then, it was a bait and tackle shop known for topnotch fishing supplies, good bait and friendly service.

The space and inventory have grown, but folks here are as friendly as ever. You'll still find fishing supplies, everything from cast nets to waterproof cases for your cell phone. Buy the beach gear you need, whether it's sunglasses, T-shirts, hats, sandals or suntan lotion.

A large Life is Good selection offers apparel, beach towels, water bottles and mugs. Kites, pocket knives, lanterns, hammocks, even ukuleles fill shelves at this one-stop store.

Don't feel like packing all the stuff you need at the beach? Herrings rents bikes, umbrellas, fishing gear, beach chairs, kayaks, surfboards, body boards, paddleboards and games like corn hole and bocce. Book a kayak tour that takes you into tidal creeks and backwaters you might otherwise miss. Kayaking experience is unnecessary. The patient staff happily shows you how easy it is to get out on the water.

Surf City restaurants

MAINSAIL RESTAURANT

Seafood fans find lots to love at Mainsail Restaurant on N.C. Highway 50 in Surf City. Popular Calabash-style fried seafood platters mean a choice of flounder, shrimp, sea scallops or oysters individually or as combinations. Maryland crab cakes and grilled fish served with a choice of delicious sauces are popular. A raw bar features oysters steamed or raw on the half-shell. Steamed snow crab legs are on the menu, too. Landlubbers enjoy the Friday and Saturday night prime rib special. Filet mignon, New York strip and chicken marsala mark the regular menu, along with other meat and pasta dishes. Sandwiches and salads please those who prefer lighter meals. The restaurant serves beer, cocktails and moderately priced and high-end wines. Check the cocktail list for chocolate martinis and fresh fruit daiquiris. Mainsail accommodates large parties, and reservations for large groups are accepted. A separate room downstairs may be reserved for private parties. The upstairs Commodore Room works for wedding receptions, rehearsal dinners or anniversary parties. Mainsail is open for dinner from 5 to 9 p.m. daily during the summer season. Call for off-season hours.

DADDY MAC'S BEACH GRILLE

From fresh seafood accompanied by tasty sauces, to crab cakes done three ways, to the best baby back ribs on Topsail Island, Daddy Macs aims to please every taste. Ribs are slow-roasted, as they should be, so tender the meat falls from the bone. Select sweet Vidalia onion or Cajun beer barbecue sauce. The ribs, fried seafood platters and shrimp and grits are among entrees. Sandwiches are available in the evening. They make great lighter fare after a long day on the beach, just steps away. Daddy Mac's sits oceanfront. A wide deck set with dining tables affords a beautiful view. Few things are more pleasurable than enjoying a good

meal while watching and hearing waves break in the background. Steaks are cut in-house. Glorious, freshly ground half-pound burgers might get stuffed with feta cheese. Wasabi aioli spikes ahi tuna sliders with avocado and fresh cucumber. Cajun oysters and Lowcountry crab dip are yummy appetizers. Kids get their own menu. Daddy Mac's has a full-service bar and refreshing house cocktails like the raspberry margarita. There's a good selection of beer and wine, too. Daddy Mac's is open Tuesday-Sunday for lunch and dinner. Lunch begins at 11 a.m., except on Sundays when Daddy Mac's opens at 10 a.m. and offers brunch service, including eggs benedict, prime rib, blintzes and quiche. Dinner always starts at 5 p.m.

GALLAGHER'S BAR AND GRILL

When it's time to watch the game, big or otherwise, head to Gallagher's on North New River Drive in Surf City. The sports bar and grill has plenty of televisions and a wide-open dining room where it's OK to cheer for your favorite teams.

The family-owned establishment offers a fun-filled experience and great prices on food and drinks. Lots of munchies fit Super Bowl football action or March Madness college basketball gatherings.

Think wings, loaded cheese fries and Irish egg rolls filled with corned beef, sauerkraut and Swiss cheese. Salads are balanced by mondo sandwiches and burgers, including the Royale with Cheese, a half-pound, ground chuck burger topped with cheese, bacon and a fried egg.

Fried shrimp, grilled or blackened salmon, hand-cut steaks and chicken dishes are among entrees. A kids menu satisfies tikes.

A local baker makes desserts, one of them the Southern classic Hummingbird Cake, a banana pineapple pecan layer cake with cream cheese frosting. There's also a 14-layer chocolate cake and a 12-layer chocolate peanut butter cake.

Gallagher's sports a full bar serving beer, wine and cocktails. Hours are 11:30 a.m. to 10 p.m. Sunday-Thursday and 11:30 a.m. to 11 p.m. or later Friday and Saturday.

Gallagher's accommodates large groups, but parties of 12 or more are encouraged to reserve tables, especially during busy summer months.

North Topsail Beach

North Topsail Beach is the baby of the Topsail Island family. The town incorporated in 1990. Just 738 people lived there year-round as of 2012, though it appears that the population is growing again and with many more people staying year-round.

The community has long been a "locals' beach" and quiet getaway. A fishing pier, plenty of free parking, lots of public beach access points and a town park with various amenities make North Topsail worth a visit, even if just for the day.

The town is also active in loggerhead turtle nesting observation and protection. A high-rise bridge connects the town with the mainland, where you'll find Sneads Ferry just across the Intracoastal Waterway. Once a quiet fishing village, the community has blossomed over the past several years.

Old fish houses where shrimp boats

Come Visit Topsail's Best Sports Bar!*

There's no better time to visit Gallagher's Sports Bar & Grill! Gallagher's offers local seasonal seafood and features local breads and desserts in addition to the coldest beer in the area. Great appetizers, great burgers, great selection of wine, spirits and beer, all in a friendly, welcoming environment. Come visit.

GALLAGHER'S BAR AND GRILL
SURF CITY, NC

614 North New River Road, Surf City, NC 28445
910-541-0877
www.gallagherssurfcitybarandgrill.com
Open daily at 11:30 a.m.

* Winner of the Topsail Advertiser Reader's Choice

Many people think that local Stump Sound oysters are among the best bivalves in the world. They are a wonderfully affordable treat.

dock still stand, but shopping and dining options have multiplied, partially thanks to the proximity of the Marine Corps base, Camp LeJeune.

Dining on North Topsail Beach

INLET 790 GRILL & BAR

As you're driving down the beach's main New River Inlet Road, watch for Villa Capriani resort. Inlet 790 centers the complex. The restaurant's Italian garden setting includes the happy sound of water trickling down an enchanting fountain. Tile floors and Roman motifs share décor space with seascape paintings by local artists.

Chef David Longo extends his reach well beyond Italy. However, don't miss his grilled shrimp primavera when it's on special. Longo tosses tender shrimp with mushrooms, spinach and tomatoes in silky pesto cream sauce. A couple of pasta dishes are part of the menu's eclectic mix. Chicken, chorizo, shrimp and okra plump tomato-rich jambalaya over jasmine rice. Maple Dijon glazes wild Scottish salmon. Steaks are served, too, but fancy tastes are not required.

Taco Tuesday and from-scratch pizzas, traditional and creative, are two customer favorites. Cooks tuck fried fish filets and fresh slaw into soft, warm tortillas. The casual bar is a great place for a craft beer, good old domestic suds, sangria or the signature Ocean Blueberry Lemonade cocktail with citrus vodka, fresh lemon juice, blueberry puree and lemon-lime soda.

The impressive wine list ranges from easy reds and whites to tony Vueve Cliquot champagne. Inlet 790 works for gatherings large and small. Dinner starts at 5 p.m. Tuesday-Saturday but hours are extended during vacation seasons and new specials are added. Call ahead for details.

TOPSAIL SHRIMP HOUSE

Take the elevator to the top floor of the seven-story St. Regis resort on New River Inlet Road for a fine view and some of the area's best casual seafood. Giant windows line at Topsail Shrimp House, affording every table aerial oceanfront views that extend for miles. Binoculars are available to view sea birds and dolphins.

You'll feel like you're sitting on the world's tallest deck as you munch lightly battered fried shrimp, Buffalo shrimp and Firecracker Shrimp, the latter in creamy sauce with spicy Asian seasonings. Get grilled shrimp skewers, grilled shrimp on salads, shrimp tacos, shrimp po' boy sandwiches, shrimp quesadillas or shrimp and grits.

Crab cakes, grilled mahi, fried flounder and steamed oysters are offered, too. Find steaks, burgers and a seared tuna sandwich with mango salsa. Customize grilled seafood or seared scallops with one of four sauces, including pineapple jalapeno.

Don't miss the kitchen's wide-cut, puffed fries, golden outside, fluffy within. Quench your thirst with cider, assorted beers, affordable wines and fun cocktails like Topsail Beach Punch with vodka, peach schnapps, raspberry schnapps and cranberry. Live and DJ music provide opportunities to dance some nights.

The magnificent space is perfect for parties and wedding receptions. Dinner is served 4 to 9 p.m. Tuesday-Sunday. Sunday brunch is scheduled 10 a.m. to 2 p.m. Look for crab cake eggs Benedict and, of course, a shrimp omelet.

Topsail Beach

This tiny community might seem like the N.C. coast's best-kept secret. High-rise development is not allowed. An old-fashioned skating rink with a wooden floor remains in business.

Although 1,200 houses stand here, just 500 people reside year-round. Everyone else comes to claim their vacation homes when summer heat summons thoughts of ocean breezes. When they arrive, many make two favorite stops.

SOUTH END OUTFITTERS

Tony brands such as Tommy Bahama, Vineyard Vines, Southern Tide and Peter Millar stock this store, launched in 2013. Bags, beach hats, belts and towels are all here. Find Sperry Top-Siders, the perfect shoe for boating, fishing and ambling on the island.

Feeling more ambitious? Rent a bicycle for island touring by land or a stand-up paddle board for exploring the sound or riding ocean waves. Top-of-the-line Bōte boards, are in stock, as are surfboards.

The owners of South End Outfitters also operate Beach Shop and Grill, in business since 1952. It has a split personality. Don shorts and flip flops for casual breakfast and lunch times. Around sunset, diners wear upscale casual attire, say sundresses and khakis.

The restaurant staff breaks out linens and candles for dinner tables. Morning eye-openers include classic eggs Benedict, buttermilk pancakes and create-your-own omelets. Lunch might feature a fried chicken Cobb salad or a golden beet salad with organic greens, candied

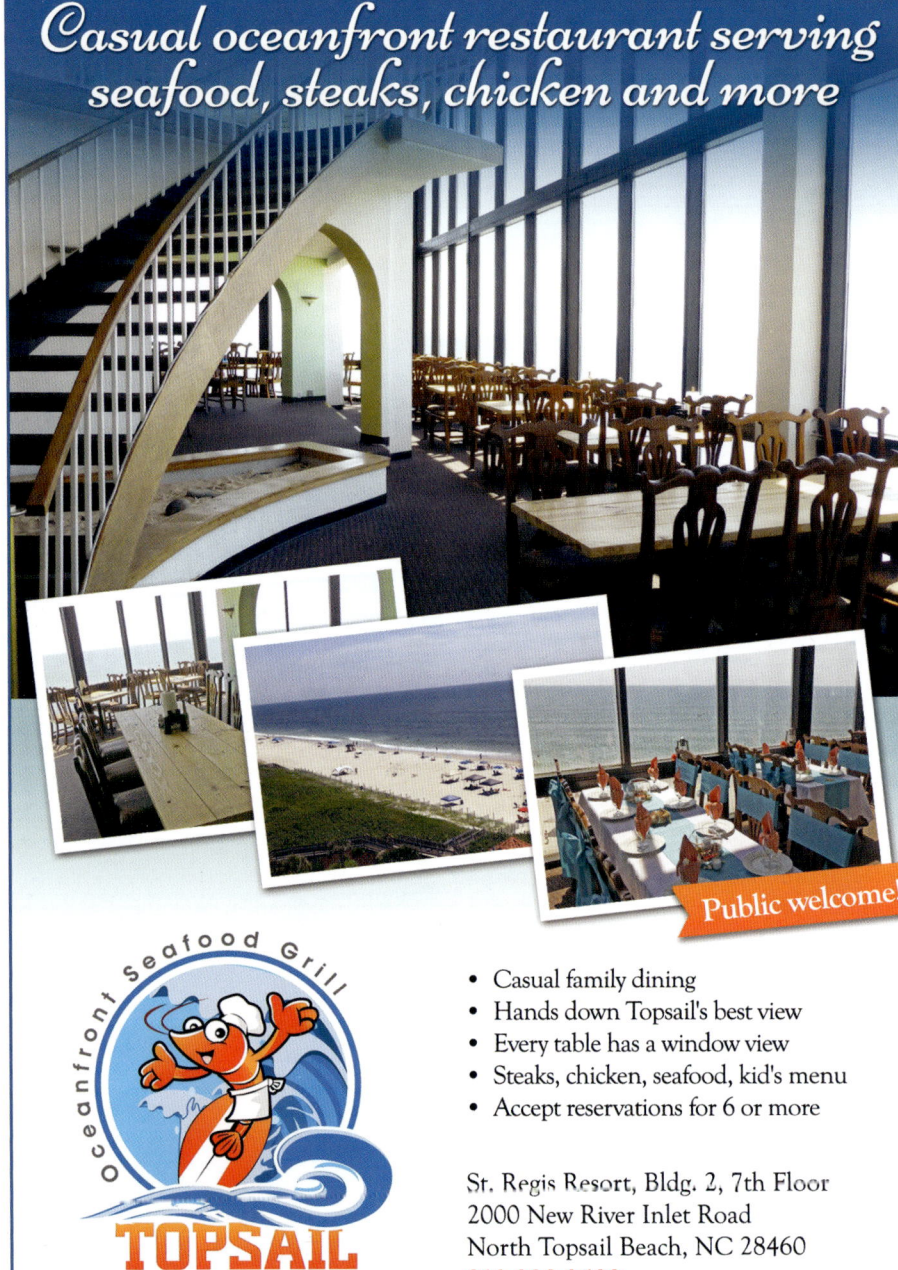

Casual oceanfront restaurant serving seafood, steaks, chicken and more

Public welcome!

- Casual family dining
- Hands down Topsail's best view
- Every table has a window view
- Steaks, chicken, seafood, kid's menu
- Accept reservations for 6 or more

St. Regis Resort, Bldg. 2, 7th Floor
2000 New River Inlet Road
North Topsail Beach, NC 28460
910-328-0582
www.topsailshrimphouse.com

MEET SHOP EAT

AT BEACH SHOP & GRILL and SOUTH END OUTFITTERS

MOUNTAIN KHAKIS • JOHNNIE-O
PETER MILLAR • SPERRY TOP-SIDER
TOMMY BAHAMA • VINEYARD VINES
BOTE • SOUTHERN TIDE
GRETCHEN SCOTT • SOUTHERN MARSH
SMATHERS & BRANSON • COSTA DEL MAR
SMITH OPTICS • PENN REELS
YETI COOLERS • HAVIANAS • MUD PIE

BREAKFAST, LUNCH AND DINNER
SEVEN DAYS A WEEK
FRESH LOCAL SEAFOOD
BLACK ANGUS BEEF
LOCAL FARM FRESH PRODUCE
SUPERB WINE AND CRAFT BEER LIST
HOMEMADE DESSERTS
CATERING AVAILABLE
LIVE MUSIC, WEEKENDS, ON THE PATIO BAR

South End Outfitters | 627 South Anderson Blvd., Topsail Beach, NC | (910) 541.0832
Beach Shop & Grill | 701 South Anderson Blvd. | Topsail Beach, NC 28445 | (910) 328.6501 | BEACHSHOPANDGRILL.COM

pecans, English cucumbers, cherry tomatoes and goat cheese, all tossed in vinaigrette. Choose sandwiches or fresh grouper, grilled and tucked inside tacos. Good luck resisting the fan-favorite, hand-pattied, Angus beef burger.

Steaks, fresh local seafood and pasta are dinner highlights at the restaurant that many beach-goers consider Topsail's best. Specialties include shrimp and grits, jumbo lump crab cakes with lemon aioli and Shellfish Mac 'n' Cheese with shrimp, scallops, lobster, fresh herbs and romano and parmesan cheeses. Leave room for key lime pie with mile-high meringue. Owner and master pastry chef Cheryl Price is the pie queen.

Wine lovers get the island's best selection of labels. Numerous craft beers and fine cocktails are served, too. Despite the delicious array of food and drink, prices are comparable to other area restaurants.

Breakfast, lunch and dinner are served mid-March-November. Call ahead for hours no matter when you visit. Spend time in the attached gift shop. Beach Dog T-shirts that are fast becoming collectibles make great gifts. New designs land each summer.

Life is Good merchandise and all types of beach sundries, towels, hats and souvenirs are available.

Fishing

QUEEN JEAN CHARTER BOAT

Topsail Beach is home base of charter fishing boat Queen Jean. Book half-day fishing trips Monday through Saturday. Passengers head 10 miles off shore.

Depending on the season, anglers might hook black sea bass, snappers, groupers, cobia, mahi and numerous other fins. The two and one-half hour kid's fishing adventure is fun and educational. All gear is supplied. Children learn about the various types of marine life.

For evening sunset cruises, the Queen Jean departs at 6 p.m. so that passengers can sit back, relax and enjoy start-to-finish sunsets that color the Carolina sky in brilliant shades.

An on-board galley serves deli sandwiches, hamburgers, snacks, soft drinks and beer. Depending on channel conditions and dredging, the Queen Jean launches from various docks. Call ahead for information.

A sea turtle sanctuary

Spotting sea turtles is easy at The Karen Beasley Sea Turtle Rescue and Rehabilitation Center just off Topsail Island on Tortuga Drive. The new facility is a result of fund-raising efforts that were helped along by many residents of Topsail Island and the surrounding area.

The volunteer staff cares for and rehabilitates injured loggerhead and other turtles before releasing them back into the sea. Watching the rehabilitated turtles as they are released is a thrill.

Founder and director, Jean Beasley, was the 2007 recipient of Animal Planet's Hero of the Year award.

Volunteers protect and monitor the many nests sea turtles dig in the sand each year. Some rehabilitated turtles are fitted with tracking devices before being released back into the ocean. That way, researchers can track their movement and learn about their habits.

This description tells just a wee bit about the huge impact this facility has made on sea turtle protection. Learn more, including how you can help, at www.seaturtlehospital.org.

More shopping

ARTEXPOSURE

Love art? Located on U.S. Highway 17 about a 10 minute-drive from the Surf City swing bridge, is ArtExposure. Look for it just south of Lowe's Home Improvement store at the intersection of U.S. 17 and N.C. Highway 210.

The facility promotes local artists and crafters. ArtExposure's 5,000-square-foot building hosts classrooms, studios, gallery exhibits and events including wedding receptions, wine tastings and parties. Studio space is available for lease to chosen artists who must be willing to work in their studios while the public watches. Classes for adults and children in a variety of media and techniques are offered and an art supply store is on site. There also is a shop featuring affordable gifts hand-crafted by local artists.

Custom framing, featuring a full supply of frames, archival matting and backing boards, is done on-site too.

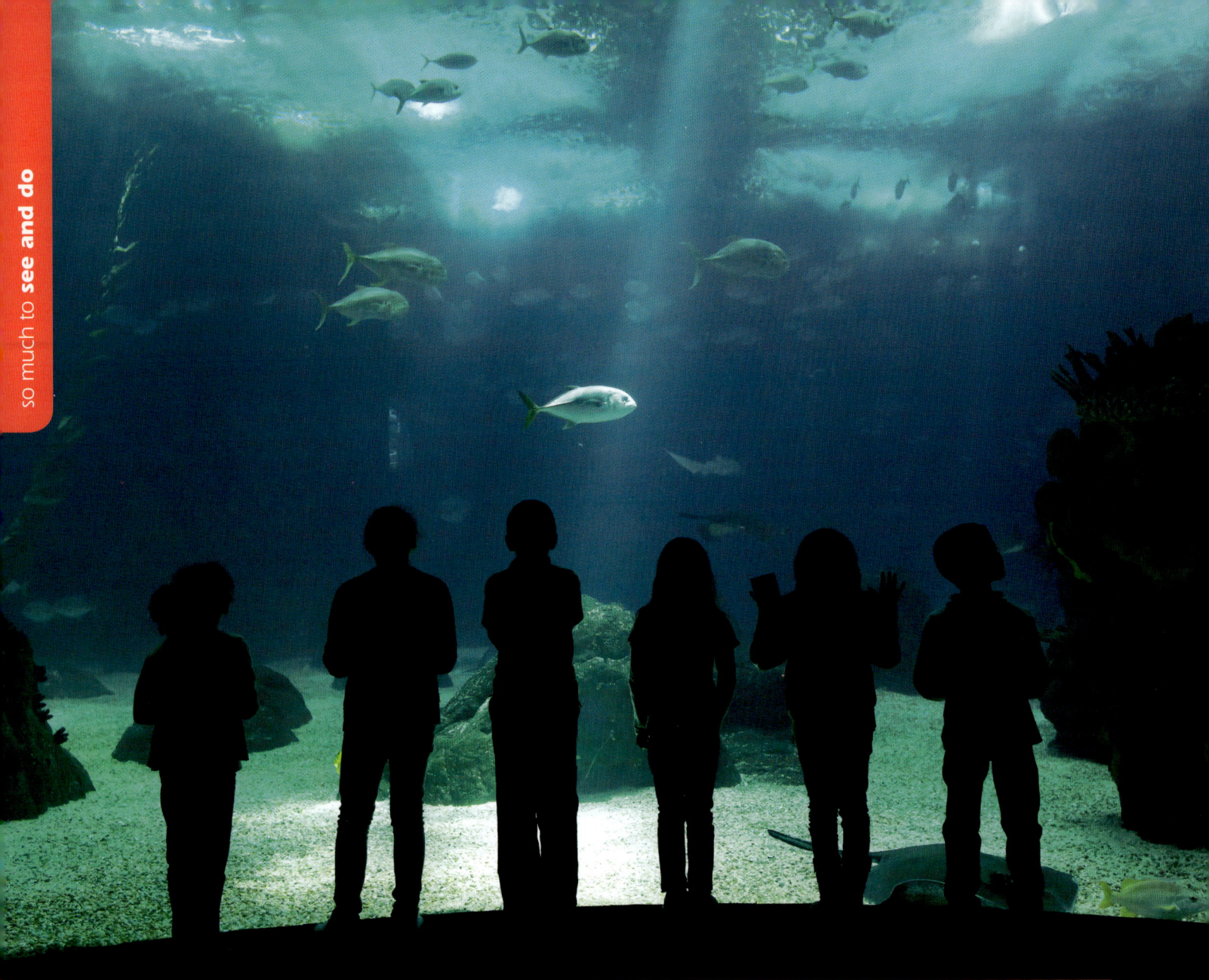

The North Carolina Aquarium at Fort Fisher is one of the area's most popular attractions.

so much to see and do

The North Carolina Aquarium at Fort Fisher was the ninth most-visited tourism site in the state of North Carolina in 2014. Almost 448,000 visitors came to learn about all things aquatic at this outstanding attraction.

Featuring a 235,000-gallon saltwater tank, the theme of the aquarium is "The Waters of the Cape Fear," which showcases both fresh water and salt water aquatic life in a journey down the Cape Fear River to the Atlantic Ocean.

The Aquarium has many beautiful and exotic displays that start with a large tree-filled atrium containing stream, pond and swamp aquatic life, plants and ground cover. Very popular with the kids is the Coquina Outcrop Touch Pool in the Coastal Waters Gallery where the little ones (and big ones too) can reach out and touch whelks, sea urchins, horseshoe crabs and other sea critters.

The focal point of the Aquarium is the Cape Fear Shoals exhibit. The huge, two-story tank displays a vast array of sea life including moray eels, stingrays, sharks and grouper plus a multitude of other varieties of sea life. At feeding time, divers underwater answer questions from the audience as they feed the fish.

The Open Oceans Gallery features creatures found off our coastline, and there are two tanks displaying jellyfish. Another tank contains the beautiful and fascinating sea horses. Other tanks display sea snakes, lionfish, cuttlefish, Pacific Reef fish and an octopus.

In the Shadows on the Sand exhibit, skates and rays endlessly cruise above the sandy bottom. All told, more than 2,500 sea creatures are on display at the North Carolina Aquarium at Fort Fisher, with Luna, a rare albino alligator, perhaps the Aquarium's star attraction.

Key economic role

The Aquarium shows many of the ways that water impacts life in this area. Indeed, water has played perhaps the pivotal role in the Wilmington area's history, development, and continuing growth. We are fortunate that we live in an area where water of all types exists in abundance.

From our spectacular sandy beaches on the Atlantic Ocean to the relatively tranquil Intracoastal Waterway to the majestic Cape Fear River to the lakes and ponds that are ubiquitous in Southeastern North Carolina, we live, work, play, fish, swim, surf, snorkel and relax in close proximity to the water.

There are a number of ways to get a sense of the role water plays in our economy, and several worthwhile options can be found in historic downtown Wilmington.

Battleship North Carolina

One way to understand the role water plays is to visit Wilmington's most noticeable attraction, the Battleship North Carolina, which is moored across the Cape Fear River from downtown's Riverfront Park.

The Battleship is beginning its 54th year here and is even more beautiful than before, having gone through a major restoration to prepare it for the celebration of its 50th anniversary in Wilmington that took place in 2011.

Scheduled by the Navy to be scrapped, a successful statewide campaign to save the North Carolina began in 1958. In 1961, the ship was moved from New Jersey to its present location.

The third in a line of naval vessels dating back to 1820 that were commissioned North Carolina, our proud ship participated in every major battle in the Pacific during World War II, and won 15 battle stars before being decommissioned in 1947. Those who have toured the Battleship are surprised that gunners were able to operate in the cramped quarters in the gun turrets. How anyone could sleep in the stacked bunks is another mystery.

The Battleship serves as both an attraction to be toured and a memorial to North Carolinians who served in the military during WW II, especially the more than 10,000 who died in service to their state and nation. More than 200,000 people visited last year.

A new North Carolina was christened in 2007 and commissioned right here in Wilmington on May 3, 2008. This fourth North Carolina is one of the U.S. Navy's fast-attack nuclear submarines of the Virginia class.

Riverboat cruises

A lovely way to view the riverfront in Wilmington is to take a ride on the Henrietta III, a wonderful riverboat berthed on Water Street at the foot of Dock Street.

The Henrietta III features 1-1/2 hour narrated cruises up and down the Cape Fear River during the daytime. Evening cruises, usually lasting nearly three hours, are popular with locals as well as tourists and are great fun for special occasions.

While aboard visitors will see Wilmington's active port and will travel along the Cape Fear River, which has played a very prominent role throughout

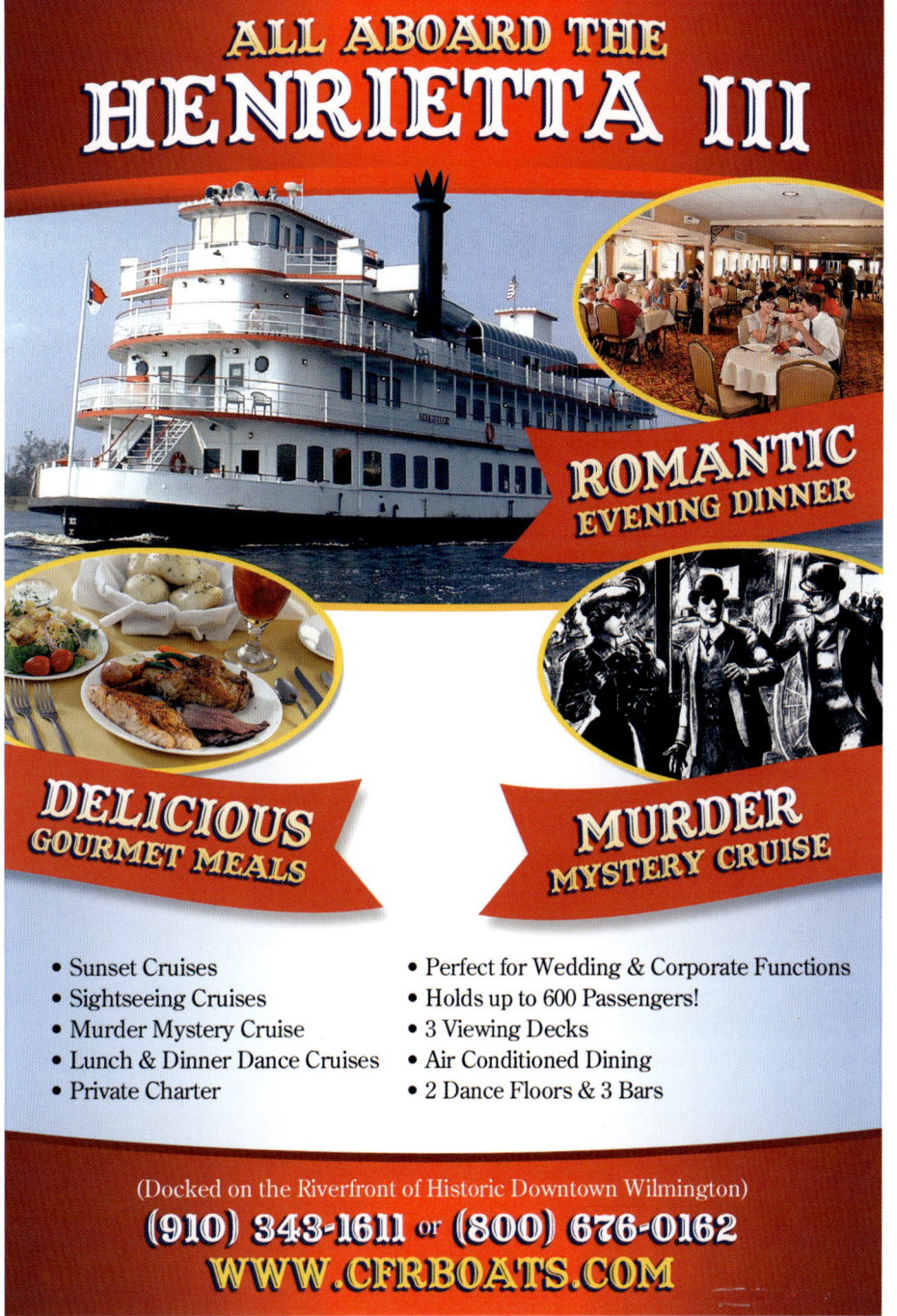

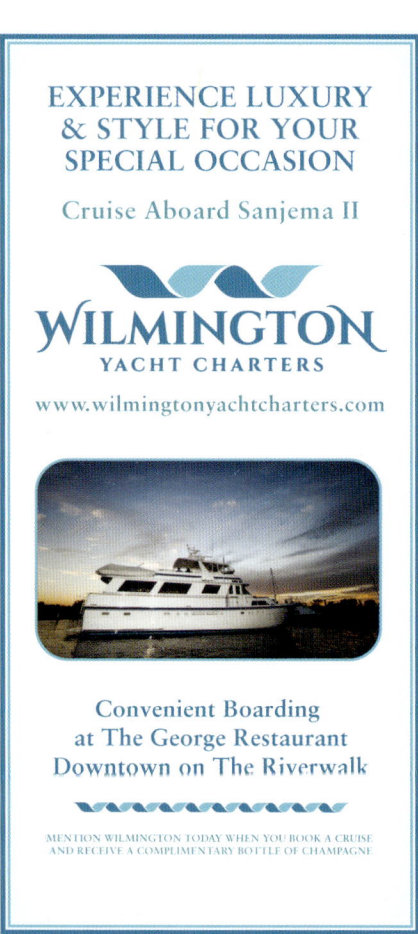

the city's history.

Among the choices are Saturday evening cruises featuring music and great food. There also are Murder Mystery Dinner Cruises and Black Water Sunset Dinner Cruises that feature a captain's narration.

Originally built as a dinner riverboat and later enlarged to be a casino riverboat, Henrietta III has three decks. The two lower decks have dining and dancing facilities while the upper deck has both an enclosed atrium and an open deck.

Railroad buffs must-see

The Wilmington Railroad Museum is situated in Warehouse B, built in 1883, on the north side of downtown at the Coastline Center. For children of all ages, the museum features a variety of historical railroad-related exhibits and extensive displays, a children's area and a gift and bookshop featuring train related items.

Five Lionel layouts plus extensive O scale and HO scale layouts are in operation inside, and a full size locomotive, boxcar and caboose are outside waiting to be explored.

The museum's exhibits tell the story of southeastern North Carolina's railroad transportation history. Visitors can explore the museum on their own or arrange for a guided tour.

The Wilmington Railroad Museum is typically open Monday to Sunday with the exception of major holidays. Hours vary by season, and information is available on their website.

Hop a water taxi

Operating from Water Street at the foot of Market Street, the Capt. J.N. Maffitt, originally a Navy liberty launch, functions as water taxi to the Battleship North Carolina. It also offers 45-minute narrated sightseeing cruises twice per day in season for those whose time is limited.

In addition, the ship offers four-hour nature cruises to the pristine Black River led by a coastal ecologist, where participants will learn all about the diverse ecosystem here. The Maffitt also is available for private charter for parties up to 49.

Yacht available too

The newest way to explore the Cape Fear River is aboard a luxury yacht. Wilmington Yacht Charter's Sanjema II is available by the day or week. Spending time aboard this vessel would be a wonderful way to celebrate such special events as engagements, birthdays, anniversaries or vow renewals.

The Sanjema II was built in 1986 to the highest standards by Hatteras Yachts and has been beautifully maintained since then. Accommodations include a master stateroom, a VIP guest stateroom, an additional guest stateroom, a private bath for guest quarters and crew's quarters.

With either day or overnight charters available, trips to downtown Wilmington or further afield to the Southport area are possible.

The Sanjema II has large open upper decks with U shaped seating perfect for larger groups. The smaller aft deck off the main salon offers a location for more intimate moments aboard. The foredeck with seating and sun pads allows a perfect view while cruising.

Spectacular Thalian Hall

Wilmington's absolute gem, Thalian Hall, is now 154 years old, and looking grander than ever after a much-needed facelift completed in time for the theater's 150th anniversary celebration.

New seats, new lights and a new heating and air conditioning system are among the renovations that make Thalian Hall so much more pleasant to visit and enjoy.

The centerpiece of the renovation is a beautiful chandelier, affectionately named "Alice" in memory of the wife of the person who donated it. It earns an ovation from the appreciative audience when it is raised before each performance begins.

Visitors are invited to take a self-guided tour during the daytime so that they can see why regular theater patrons are so excited about the renovated facility.

Thanks to new exterior lights that were installed in February 2013, the entire building gleams at night. It is a beautiful site.

Everyone should enjoy the experience of dinner and a cruise on the Cape Fear River aboard the Henrietta III.

100+ snakes, reptiles

The Cape Fear Serpentarium is located at the corner of Front and Orange Streets. The Serpentarium has an amazing collection of more that 100 species of snakes, many of them poisonous, in its collection.

Included are the rare and deadly Bushmaster and Black Mamba snakes, a 250-pound 23 foot-long python, a 15 foot-long king cobra, Nile crocodiles, a dragon-sized monitor lizard, Komodo, and many more in this 10,000 square foot living museum.

Kids are fascinated by the displays and by watching reptiles as they are fed.

Wilmington Trolley Tours

Located on Water Street between Market and Dock Streets, the Wilmington Trolley Company offers very informative eight-mile narrated tours of downtown Wilmington in an old-fashioned (except for the rubber tires) trolley car.

a very complete ...ical significance ...ers are available ... have special re... ...edding down... ...beach or vice ...parties can arrive in style on the Wilmington Trolley. The Trolley is a wonderful way to make a birthday or anniversary party memorable too.

Stroll through Wilmywood

Visitors enjoy seeing the real locations and actual sets where some of Wilmington's biggest movies were filmed. *Iron Man 3*, and *We're the Millers* along with a host of others are among the dozens of movies that were shot on location in Wilmington. Following the success of locally filmed *Safe Haven* in 2013, another movie based on a Nicholas Sparks novel, *The Longest Ride*, was filmed in Wilmington in 2014 and released in April 2015.

Fans are also interested in seeing where the cast and crew of *Dawson's Creek* and *One Tree Hill* spent their time. Two television series currently filming in Wilmington, *Under the Dome* and *Secrets and Lies*, are attracting fans too.

Historic downtown buildings

The oldest restored museum house in southeastern North Carolina is the Burgwin-Wright House, which was built in 1770. John Burgwin, a merchant, planter and treasurer of the colony of Carolina, erected the house on the foundation of an old jail. Temporarily occupied by Lord Cornwallis before his fateful departure for Yorktown, this splendid Georgian style house contains authentic furnishings and is surrounded by seven beautifully terraced gardens. Demonstrations of colonial open hearth cooking are presented in the kitchen one Saturday per month.

The largest and most visible house museum is Bellamy Mansion, a spectacular example of antebellum architecture built between 1859 and 1861 by enslaved artisans and carpenters.

The property, occupied by Dr. John Bellamy, his wife and nine children, consists of the 22-room mansion, the beautifully restored gardens and recently reconstructed carriage house. Slave quarters, among the most intact in the South according to architectural historian Catherine Bishir, are scheduled for restoration too. Bellamy Mansion now focuses on history and the design arts, with several changing exhibitions each year.

Any visitor to downtown Wilmington should take the time to stroll through the downtown area. There are historic homes throughout downtown, many with plaques on the front showing when they were built. Take the time to stroll up and down the streets to see the varied architecture. Third, Fourth and Fifth Streets are lined with one interesting home after another.

Hannah Block USO

Opening in December 1941, the USO Club at Second and Orange was built by the Army Corps of Engineers at a cost of $80,000. It operated 24 hours a day, seven days a week and served as the off-duty destination of hundreds of thousands of armed forces personnel that trained in the area. Four charitable organizations affiliated with the USO and a host of volunteers kept it running. At the height of World War II, attendance reached 63,000 per month, with such events as big band dances, plays, music recitals and weekly radio broadcasts featured.

The City of Wilmington purchased the building when the USO ended its full-time operations. Over the years, the buildings use has evolved so that today, it serves as a major cultural resource for New Hanover County.

Classes are offered in a variety of visual and performing arts disciplines and the building is home to the Orange Street Potters. The building also hosts crews for movies, television shows and commercials. In addition, rehearsal space is provided to local nonprofit theater companies and plays are staged in the auditorium.

Managed by the Thalian Association since 1994, the building is listed in the National Register of Historic Places. It is now known as the Hannah Block Historic USO/Community Arts Center and was renamed to honor one of Wilmington's most distinguished civic leaders and World War II veterans.

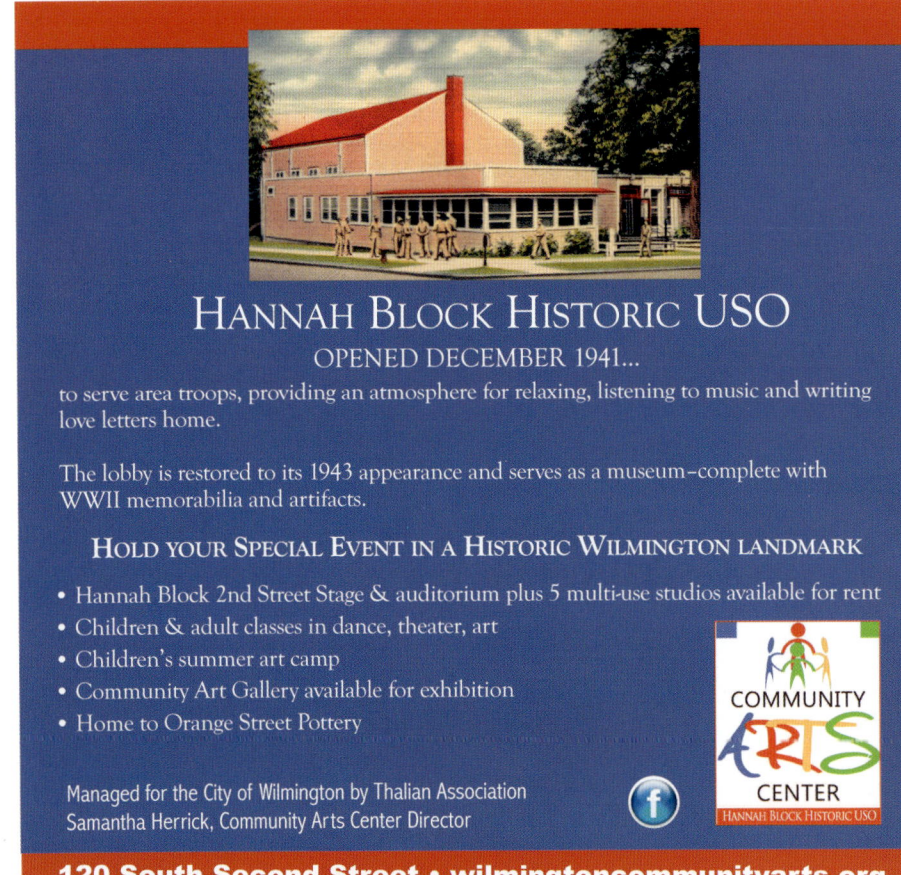

Hannah Block Historic USO
OPENED DECEMBER 1941...
to serve area troops, providing an atmosphere for relaxing, listening to music and writing love letters home.

The lobby is restored to its 1943 appearance and serves as a museum–complete with WWII memorabilia and artifacts.

Hold your Special Event in a Historic Wilmington landmark

- Hannah Block 2nd Street Stage & auditorium plus 5 multi-use studios available for rent
- Children & adult classes in dance, theater, art
- Children's summer art camp
- Community Art Gallery available for exhibition
- Home to Orange Street Pottery

Managed for the City of Wilmington by Thalian Association
Samantha Herrick, Community Arts Center Director

120 South Second Street • wilmingtoncommunityarts.org

Our own microbrewery

Front Street Brewery, located in a beautiful historic building, offers a special tour that provides an opportunity for a rest after spending time taking in all the sites. From 3:00 to 5:00 p.m. each day, Wilmington's original microbrewery will teach you the brewing process. Brewmaster Kevin Kozak and his staff create several award-winning microbrews throughout the year. Two samples are offered during the tour.

After you've had a chance to choose your favorite brew from among the lagers and ales, why not have a seat and enjoy a mug of your selection paired with a bite to eat from the extensive list of appetizers? And in case more incentive is needed, the appetizers are half price from 4:00-6:00 and after 10:00 p.m. every day.

Cameron Art Museum

Few if any other cities the size of Wilmington have a $12.5 million art museum, but Wilmington proudly features the Cameron Art Museum, the only accredited art museum in southeastern North Carolina. Situated on 9.5 acres, the modern structure has 40,000 square feet housing a variety of collections plus a gift shop and cafe.

The mission of the Cameron is to be the cultural gathering place for the community. It is the venue for a monthly series of jazz concerts produced in conjunction with the Cape Fear Jazz Society. The concerts are held on the first Thursday of each month at 6:30 in the evening.

The Museum School at the Cameron Art Museum provides adult and youth art education including a range of beginning and master classes. Programs include instructor-guided access to the museum's exhibitions and select objects in the museum's permanent collection that are not on view. There are weeklong summer arts programs for kids too.

Historic churches downtown

Scattered throughout the downtown area are a number of historically significant churches.

Among these is Chestnut Street United Presbyterian Church. Built in 1858, the church has had a number of

noted African-Americans as members.

Constructed during the 1860s, Saint Paul's Evangelical Lutheran Church also was used by Union forces as a stable. It burned in 1894 and was replaced by the present church.

Saint James Episcopal Church has the most historic congregation in Wilmington; its parish was established in 1729 and the original church was built in 1751. Used by the British as a stable during the Revolutionary War, the original building was razed in 1839. The current structure was built in 1840 and was used as a hospital by the Union forces during the Civil War. On the east and north sides of the church are the old burial grounds where notable persons of the period are interred.

Saint Mark's Episcopal Church, built in 1869, was the first Episcopal church for African-Americans in North Carolina.

Temple of Israel, a unique Moorish style structure, was built in 1876 and is the oldest Jewish synagogue in North Carolina. The Temple is one of fewer than 30 congregations that endure in its original 19th century structure.

Saint Mary's Roman Catholic Church was constructed in 1908 in the Spanish Baroque architectural style.

With a congregation dating back to 1760, the present First Presbyterian Church was built in 1928 replacing three structures built in the 1800s and destroyed by fire.

Having roots tracing back to as early as 1690, the First Baptist Church congregation was organized in 1833 and the church building was completed in 1870. The 197-foot spire was blown down by Hurricane Fran in 1996 and immediately replaced.

Visit Airlie Gardens often

On the east side of Wilmington near Wrightsville Beach, the exquisite Airlie Gardens was established in 1901 and features breathtaking formal gardens, wildlife, historic structures, walking trails, sculptures, lakes and the 467-year-old Airlie live oak. Over 100,000 azaleas and countless camellias bloom throughout the winter and spring, making the gardens a colorful, year-round horticultural delight.

New to Airlie Gardens is the Butterfly House, which should be a must-see for all visitors. Stepping into this fabulous addition is sure to lift the spirits of all who enter it. Airlie Gardens should be seen throughout the year to fully appreciate the beauty of the seasonal changes.

Very near Airlie Gardens is the fascinating New Hanover County Arboretum exhibiting seven acres of plants that grow in our region along with emerging trends in plants for our locale.

With a large staff of trained volunteers, the Arboretum provides suggestions and advice on plants suited for our coastal environment.

Wilmington Hammerheads

The oldest professional sports team in this area is the Wilmington Hammerheads, a team that came here in 1996. The 2015 home opener took place on March 28 with play continuing through September. Home games are played at Legion Stadium.

In 2014, the Hammerheads reached the playoffs for the 12th time in their 17 seasons. Their most successful year came in 2003, when the team captured

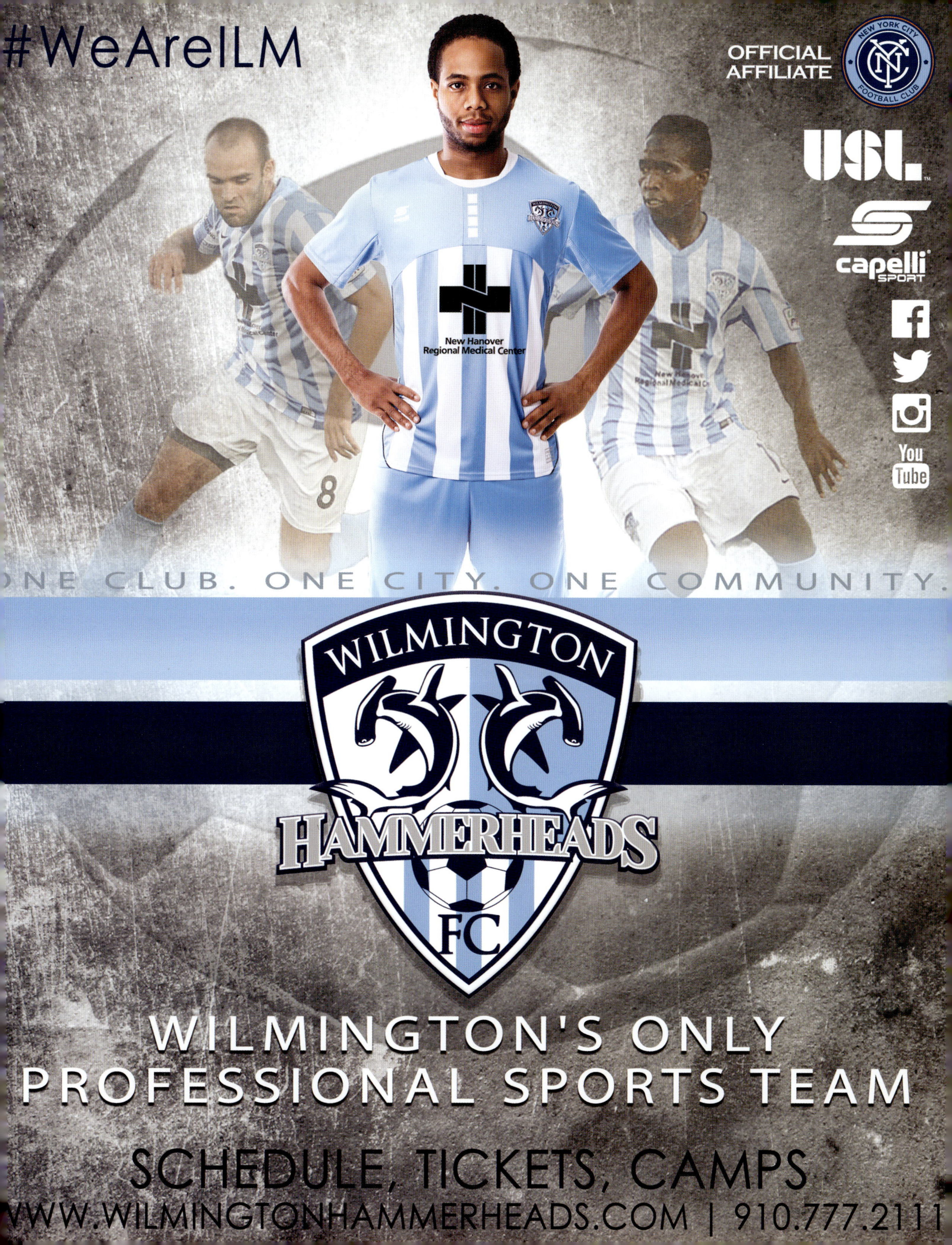
#WeAreILM
OFFICIAL AFFILIATE
NEW YORK CITY FOOTBALL CLUB
USL
capelli SPORT
New Hanover Regional Medical Center
NE CLUB. ONE CITY. ONE COMMUNITY.
WILMINGTON
HAMMERHEADS
FC
WILMINGTON'S ONLY PROFESSIONAL SPORTS TEAM
SCHEDULE, TICKETS, CAMPS
WWW.WILMINGTONHAMMERHEADS.COM | 910.777.2111

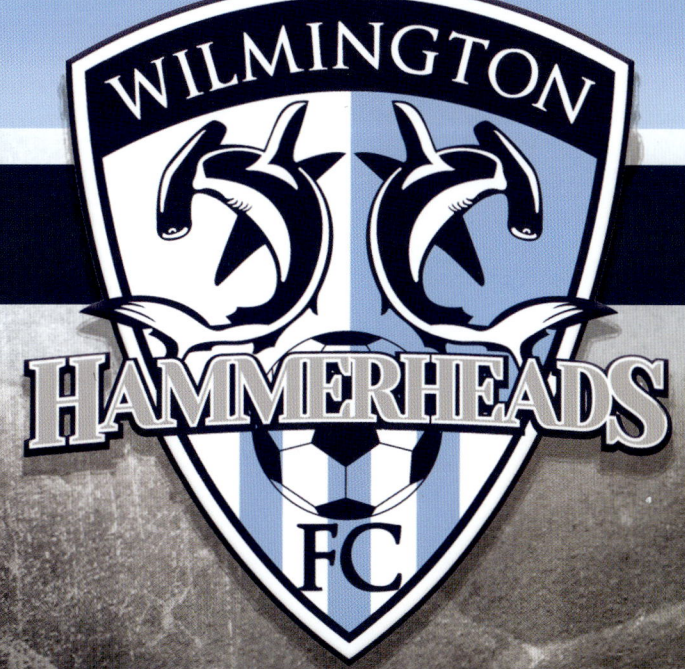

Kids have a great time playing in the water during the summertime.

the USL Second Division title.

George Altirs, bought the team in late 2013. In November 2014, Altiers hired Carson Potter as the coach and technical director for 2015.

Potter replaced David Irving, the coach of the team for 14 seasons who has now moved on to coach the Tulsa Rednecks, a new team in the US Pro Soccer League.

The Hammerheads are active in the community and schedule a number of popular camps for local soccer players.

Fun for kids

Jungle Rapids Family Fun Park, the largest amusement park in southeastern North Carolina, offers such an abundance of fun entertainment that children will beg to go again and again.

During the summer season, visitors can cool off in the Waterpark, which features a half-pipe water slide, a million-gallon ocean-like wave pool, a four-tube slide called the Volcanic Express, the relaxing lazy river, and a Kiddie Splash area with a play structure and child-size water slides. Lifeguards are always on duty, and lockers, tables and umbrellas are available.

When the weather is warm, enjoy a whirl around the go-kart track or challenge your family to a friendly game of miniature golf. The quarter-mile-long Grand Prix Go Kart track features bridge overpasses, banked turns, and

one- and two-passenger cars. Miniature golf enthusiasts will love the 18-hole jungle-themed mini golf course accented with tropical landscaping and waterfalls.

Inside Jungle Rapids you'll find a plethora of other dry activities to keep the family busy, such as Alien Invader Laser Tag, which was recently renovated with a new maze built for team competition or individual play. Additionally, the large, air-conditioned Kid's Jungle indoor playground is the perfect place for kids ages 8 and under to get out some energy. There is also a 30-foot indoor rock-climbing wall offering four different sections ranging in difficulty for the novice to the experienced rock climber. And as if that was not enough, the 100-game arcade will entertain and challenge your game skills.

The water park is open seasonally and dry attractions are open year-round with the exception of major holidays. Check their website for hours and admission prices, which vary by activity.

Tregembo Animal Park

There is another attraction that kids really enjoy. For all the children who love visiting zoos, Tregembo Animal Park should be on the list of attractions to see. The Tregembo family, which for more than 60 years has maintained the only zoo in southeastern North Carolina, has consistently provided local families, children's groups and tourists with a fun, educational place to spend a few hours or a day. The family cares passionately about the animals in its care.

For a very modest admission, visitors can see an amazing variety of more than 100 creatures. Some animals you can feed corn or peanuts, some you can pet. And, of course, you'll want to visit the 4,000 square foot gift shop to take home souvenirs.

Besides the usual zoo animals, the Park boasts many unusual specimens too. If you're curious, go to their website for a preview of the critters that are on display.

Poplar Grove Plantation

Poplar Grove Plantation, one of the oldest existing peanut plantations in North Carolina, is listed on the National Register of Historic Homes and preserved in the North Carolina Coastal Land Trust. It is located five minutes north of Wilmington on US Highway 17 North and is well worth the visit.

The facility, preserved through the efforts of the non-profit Poplar Grove Foundation, opened as a museum in 1980.

The homestead and outbuildings are intact and crafts such as blacksmithing and basket weaving are demonstrated during the year.

Poplar Grove hosts a Farmers Market each Wednesday featuring fruits, vegetables, plants, and pottery grown and made in North Carolina.

One of the events that takes place at Poplar Grove in July each year, the Classy-Chassis Car Show and Country Flea Market, earned distinction as a top 20 event by the Southeast Tourism Society.

Other events held at Poplar Grove are a popular Halloween celebration complete with haunted house and a Christmas tour using traditional displays. Poplar Grove also has become a sought after wedding and special events location.

Pender County Attractions

Pender County is located just north of Wilmington and offers a wealth of opportunities for family vacations as well as interesting day trips.

The large county stretches from the beach to well inland, offering diverse natural beauty and water from the ocean to the Intracoastal Waterway to many lakes, rivers and ponds. The largest attraction in Pender County is beautiful Topsail Island, a barrier island 26 miles long and no more than 1,500 feet wide, bringing thousands of visitors each year to its relatively uncrowded shores.

Boating, paddling in kayaks or canoes, fishing, and water sports including skiing, wind and kite surfing and diving are popular pastimes.

There also are important historic sites in Pender County, from the Burgaw Depot to Poplar Grove to Moores Creek, a Revolutionary War battlefield.

A word of caution - some of the attractions listed above may be closed or have restricted hours during the off-season, so be sure to call first if you're planning a visit during that period.

Daily Tours and Demonstrations

Poplar Grove
PLANTATION

Historic Poplar Grove Plantation
10200 US 17
Wilmington, NC 28411
910.686.9518

Find out what's going on at
www.poplargrove.org

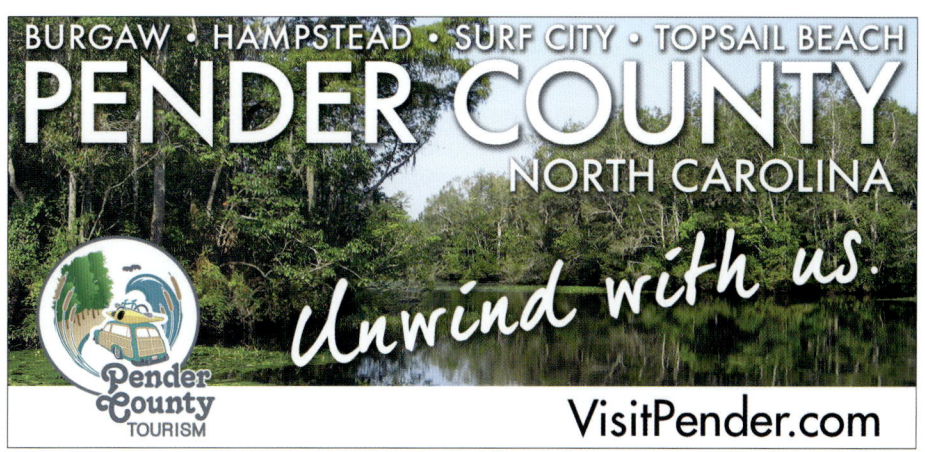

BURGAW • HAMPSTEAD • SURF CITY • TOPSAIL BEACH
PENDER COUNTY
NORTH CAROLINA
Unwind with us.
Pender County TOURISM
VisitPender.com

Seeing what children can do creatively is great fun for adults as well as stimulating for kids.

just for kids

There is no better place to visit or raise your family than the Cape Fear region. Whether you are here on a fun get away, or fortunate enough to live in this beautiful coastal area year-round, you will find much to see and do together. Featuring an abundance of kid-friendly attractions and activities, the area provides many services to keep your kids healthy, happy, educated and entertained.

Aquarium is a must see

The most impressive facility in the area is the North Carolina Aquarium at Fort Fisher. Situated on a wooded oceanfront location complete with lovely gardens and wildlife areas, the aquarium features many beautiful and exotic displays, beginning with a large tree-filled atrium containing stream, pond and swamp aquatic life, plants and ground cover. Very popular with the kids is the Coquina Outcrop Touch Pool in the Coastal Waters Gallery where visitors can reach out and touch whelks, sea urchins, horseshoe crabs and other sea critters.

The focal point of the aquarium is the Cape Fear Shoals exhibit, where visitors can even talk to a scuba diver. The huge, two-story tank displays a vast array of sea life including moray eels, stingrays, sharks and grouper plus a multitude of other varieties of sea life. At feeding time, divers answer questions from the audience as they feed the fish underwater.

All told, more than 2,500 sea creatures, including a rare albino alligator, are on display at the aquarium. Additionally, on sunny days, children will love the new outdoor playground, which is located near the café.

The Aquarium is open from 9 a.m. to 5 p.m. year round (closed Thanksgiving Day and Christmas Day).

Lots of snakes, reptiles

Located on Orange Street is the Cape Fear Serpentarium, exhibiting an amazing collection of more than 100 species of snakes.

The 10,000-square-foot facility features 54 displays, including the rare and deadly Bushmaster and Black Mamba snakes, a 250-pound 23 foot-long python, a 15 foot-long king cobra, Nile crocodiles, a dragon-sized monitor lizard, Komodo, and much more. In addition to the wide range of animals, kids are fascinated by watching as the reptiles are fed.

The Serpentarium is open seven days a week with hours that vary by season.

A favorite spot for kids

Jungle Rapids Family Fun Park, the largest amusement park in southeastern North Carolina, offers such an abundance of fun entertainment that children will beg to go again and again.

During the summer season, visitors can cool off in the Waterpark, which features a half-pipe water slide, a million-gallon ocean-like wave pool, a four-tube slide called the Volcanic Express, the relaxing lazy river, and a Kiddie Splash area with a play structure and child-size water slides. Lifeguards are always on duty, and lockers, tables and umbrellas are available.

When the weather is warm, enjoy a whirl around the go-kart track or challenge your family to a friendly game of miniature golf.

The quarter-mile-long Grand Prix Go Kart track features bridge overpasses, banked turns, and one- and two-passenger cars. Miniature golf enthusiasts will love the 18-hole jungle-themed mini golf course accented with tropical landscaping and waterfalls.

Inside Jungle Rapids you'll find a plethora of other dry activities to keep the family busy, such as Alien Invader Laser Tag, which was recently renovated with a new maze built for team competition or individual play. Additionally, the large, air-conditioned Kid's Jungle indoor playground is the perfect place for kids ages 8 and under to get out some energy.

There is also a 30-foot indoor rock-climbing wall offering four different sections ranging in difficulty from the novice to the experienced rock climber. And as if that was not enough, the 100-game arcade will entertain and challenge your game skills.

The water park is open seasonally and dry attractions are open year-round with the exception of major holidays. Check their website for hours and admission prices, which vary by activity.

Kids love trains

The Wilmington Railroad Museum is a special treat not only for children, but for railroad enthusiasts and history buffs too. On the north side of downtown at the Coastline Center, the Wilmington Railroad Museum is situated in Warehouse B.

For children of all ages, the museum features a variety of historical railroad-related exhibits and extensive displays, a children's area and a gift and book shop featuring train related items..

Five Lionel layouts plus extensive O scale and HO scale layouts are in operation inside, and a full size locomotive, boxcar and caboose are outside waiting to be explored. Built in 1883, the museum's exhibits tell the story of southeastern North Carolina's railroad transportation history. Visitors can explore the museum on their own or arrange for a guided tour.

The Wilmington Railroad Museum is typically open Monday to Sunday with the exception of major holidays. Hours vary by season, and information is available on their website.

Fun and fitness

Both owners and all coaches at Carolina Gymnastics Academy love kids, love gymnastics and love teaching. Their great results are the best testament to those attributes. Children who participate in CGA classes benefit from meticulous training and win accolades at competitions. The school, which opened in 2000, provides a safe environment and a developmentally appropriate curriculum in a modern, very well-equipped 15,000 square foot exercise facility.

Numerous programs are available for boys and girls from crawlers through high school. By incorporating fun physical activities with educational tools, even the very youngest children can pick up gymnastic basics and enjoy learning. CGA emphasizes "what's best" for each child and tailors instruction accordingly.

The Gym & Learn program is an early education program for children ages 3-5. Children learn the important academic, physical and social skills necessary to be prepared for kindergarten. Taught by long-time coach Zoey Zapple, who has a B.A. in Social Work

and a concentration in Early Childhood Education, the program provides age appropriate learning in an active setting. Another feature of the program helps children learn self-discipline, sharing, and taking turns, while developing a healthy self-image through the sport of gymnastics.

Combing academics, physical fitness, and pro-social interaction will help children reach their full potential, enjoy learning, and begin life physically fit. This program provides terrific value and is available with tuition paid weekly in advance.

In addition to these programs, CGA offers an After School Program that includes free gym time and help with homework. Other popular offerings are Watch Me Play, an open gym session for crawlers to 5 years. For parents' convenience, CGA hosts Parents Night Out every Friday and Saturday night from 6 to 10 p.m. for children ages 3 to 10. Parents especially appreciate a chance to have a night out knowing that their children are well cared for and entertained, and the service is open to members, non-members and visitors.

Gorgeous Airlie Gardens

With breathtaking formal gardens, wildlife, historic structures, walking trails, sculptures, lakes and a 467-year-old live oak, Airlie Gardens has something to offer the entire family. Children will especially enjoy the Tranquility Garden, a 2,700-square foot native butterfly house. From April 15 to October 15, hundreds of butterflies can be seen flying around this open-air, screened structure.

During the summer, Airlie hosts a concert series on their beautiful Oak Lawn on the first and third Friday of every month. Visitors can pack a picnic or buy food from the on-site concessions and enjoy live music. Another fun seasonal event is Enchanted Airlie, when the gardens are transformed into a festive holiday light show beginning the Friday after Thanksgiving and running until just before Christmas.

Children's gardens

Very near Airlie Gardens is the fascinating New Hanover County Arboretum exhibiting seven acres of plants that grow in the region. Kids will delight in the Children's Garden, where everything is built on a kid-size scale. The Children's Garden features a cottage, colorful plant and flower garden, and a seating area. Bring plenty of quarters so kids can feed the fish in the koi pond.

The Arboretum is also open daily and year round. Admission to the Arboretum is free.

The shop for babies

Dragonflies Baby, a specialty boutique within Dragonflies, caters to children from infant to school age. Dragonflies Baby features a selection of hand-picked items to beautifully outfit and equip babies and children, from infant christening gowns and raincoats to bathing suits and hair bows, and virtually everything in between.

They carry top boutique brands for clothing and shoes, including Kissy Kissy, Livie and Luca, Johnnie-O, and Aden and Anais. Their clothing section features a selection of casual and dressy items in sizes infant to seven.

Whether you live in Wilmington or are just visiting, Carolina Gymnastics Academy has something for everyone, with programs for children from six months through high school years. Special programs include Watch Me Play for crawlers-5 years and Parents Night Out for children ages 3-10. Summer Half Day Camp is for ages 3-10 and Summer Full Day Camp is for ages 5-10. In addition, Gymnastics Classes for Boys & Girls, After School Programs, Cheerleading, Gym & Learn Preschool and Birthday Parties are available. Visit to meet the talented, caring and responsible staff.

The boutique offers many items for young babies, such as baby carriers, diaper bags, swaddling blankets, and bibs. They even sell a gentle line of baby and children's shampoos, lotions, and soaps.

They also carry unique toys, books, puzzles and dolls. Dragonflies Baby welcomes baby shower gift registries. For added customer convenience, gift wrapping is complimentary.

Theatre for kids

Wilmington is fortunate to have the Thalian Association Children's Theater (TACT) which offers theatrical training and performance opportunities, with most auditions open for children ages seven through high school seniors. TACT remains dedicated to "the enrichment of arts education for our community's youth."

Children may choose to be involved on stage as actors or back stage as part of the technical production team. Five productions each year are held at the Community Arts Center, 120 South 2nd Street, in the Hannah Block Historic USO building. The TACT productions are regularly honored with Wilmington Theater Award for Best Children's Production.

TACT Academy offers an opportunity to create and explore the arts in a non-audition based setting for students ages 4 to high school. Designed to help students better understand theater in all its facets, an array of classes, taught by a large group of talented instructors, enables students to discover their strength, learn new skills and build self-confidence within a nurturing atmosphere. The TACT Academy program is a six-month semester with a showcase for students at the end of each program. The classes are held at the Hannah Block building and at New Hanover Country Public Library Northeast Branch on Military Cutoff Road. The classes are affordable and scholarship opportunities are available.

Places to play

The greater Wilmington area boasts 36 city and county parks and 17 neighborhood parks, plus many green spaces and biking trails. With such a wide variety of parks available, there is no excuse

Our weather allows children to play outdoors most months of the year.

TREGEMBO ANIMAL PARK

Enjoy animals from **AROUND THE WORLD** in a 10-acre park-like setting.

over 100 different types of animals!

5811 Carolina Beach Rd.
Wilmington, NC 28412
910.392.3604

tregemboanimalpark.com

Few things are more fun for children than hand feedng an animal.

to not get outside and stay active. Hugh MacRae Park, one of the oldest and best-known parks in midtown Wilmington, offers two playgrounds catering to younger and older children, several picnic shelters, ball fields, and a tranquil pond. On the north end of town, the 125-acre Ogden Park includes playgrounds, walking/jogging trails and baseball, football and soccer fields. Halyburton Park, on the southwest side of Wilmington, has a 1.3-mile walking and biking trail where undisturbed plant collections can be observed. In addition to playgrounds and picnic shelters, Halyburton has a community building where children can visit reptiles and fish and take fun and educational classes.

Hours vary by park and season. A fee is required to reserve picnic shelters.

Fun-filled annual events

In addition to the many wonderful staples mentioned in this chapter, kids will enjoy a range of one-time events throughout the year. The North Carolina Azalea Festival, the hallmark event of the spring, features a lot of fun activities for kids, including a parade, Cole Brothers Circus, and children's area within the street fair.

In early October, children will love the activities at RiverFest, such as the pirate treasure hunt and costume contest, fireworks, skateboard contest and children's zone. Additionally, Halloween celebrations abound in Wilmington. Two of the most popular are Poplar Grove Plantation's Haunted Halloween over two weekends in October and Battleship North Carolina's Batty Battleship Bash.

Lions, tigers and giraffes

For all the children who love visiting zoos, Tregembo Animal Park should be on the list of attractions to see. The Tregembo family for more than 60 years has maintained the only zoo in southeastern North Carolina. They have consistently provided local families, children's groups and tourists with a fun, educational place to spend a few hours or a day. For a modest admission, you can see an amazing variety of more than 100 creatures. Some animals you can feed corn or peanuts, some you can pet. And, of course, you'll want to visit the 4,000 square foot gift shop to take home souvenirs.

Besides the usual zoo animals, the Park boasts many unusual specimens. If you're curious, go to their website for a preview of the critters that are on display.

The Cape Fear region draws visitors from far and wide who come to enjoy all this area offers.

tourism, strength and growth

Tourism spending continues to be a huge factor in the Wilmington area economy. In New Hanover County in 2013 (the last year available at press time), spending amounted to $477.68 million, an almost four percent increase over 2012. Ranked number eight in tourism expenditures among North Carolina's 100 counties, New Hanover County tourism provided more than 5,460 jobs, supported a payroll of $105.41 million and generated $41.84 million in state and local taxes.

Expenditures in 2013 set an all-time high, exceeding the pre-recession record set in 2007 when visitor expenditures totaled $426.08 million. Tourism revenues are critical to the health of the region since they not only provide jobs in great numbers, but those revenues also help many existing businesses thrive and new businesses form to serve the needs of growing numbers of visitors.

From the River to the Sea has always described the basic theme of Wilmington regional tourism, encompassing the city and its beautiful old downtown along the scenic Cape Fear River coupled with the area's three beach towns on the Atlantic Ocean, Wrightsville Beach, Carolina Beach and Kure Beach.

The entire tri-county area experienced growth in tourism spending. Brunswick County ranked 10th, bringing in $470.58, a 5.54 percent increase. The 5,030 jobs supported a payroll of $85.71 million. Pender County brought in $84.18 million in tourism spending, up four percent from the prior year. A $14.12 million payroll resulted from the 760 jobs that were directly attributable to travel and tourism.

Something for everyone

Visitors from all over the state, the nation and the world travel to the Wilmington area to enjoy our wealth of attractions, festive events and fun-filled activities in a coastal destination rich in history, culture and natural beauty. Many visitors enjoy meandering through the 230-plus blocks of the downtown National Register Historic District with its stately residences and historic buildings, some open for touring, while others opt to venture across the river to board the grand old Battleship North Carolina to get an idea of what life was like on the high seas during World War II.

Many other folks appreciate visiting attractions such as our thriving museums, a new convention center, our fabulous aquarium, great restaurants and tons of shopping. Events such as our spectacular Azalea Festival, Riverfest, Cucalorus Film Festival, Holiday Flotillas, North Carolina Jazz Festival, Pleasure Island Seafood, Blues and Jazz Festival and the East Coast Wahine Championship, among many others, draw throngs of tourists every year.

NORTH CAROLINA'S CENTER OF ATTENTION

We invite you to discover an exciting new perspective on meetings, conventions, and events. The ideal backdrop of historic charm and riverfront views, for conventions, annual meetings and exhibits. Boasting 107,000 square feet of space, Wilmington Convention Center is the largest convention venue on the North Carolina coast, featuring a sophisticated maritime theme and decor, which honors Wilmington as an important port city.

WILMINGTON
NORTH CAROLINA
CONVENTION CENTER

business made casual

www.BusinessMadeCasual.com
910.251.5101

People have opportunities to attend lectures and seminars of all types.

And of course, many tourists come to enjoy the great outdoors. Sunning, swimming, surfing, fishing and just plain relaxing on miles and miles of sandy beaches; all-year golfing on more than 50 area golf courses; boating on the rivers, Intracoastal Waterway and ocean – these are just a few of the multitude of pleasurable activities that bring visitors to this tourism paradise.

Getting here is easy

An easy way for visitors to get here is to fly into our welcoming airport. Whether flying for leisure or business, or a combination of the two, getting into Wilmington International Airport – better known as ILM – is a breeze. After a rough day traveling with flight delays, racing from one concourse to another, or long security lines, arriving at ILM is like coming home and relaxing after a hard day at work. The tensions seem to melt away as one enters the airport's relaxed and hospitable atmosphere, the modern gateway to grand and gracious Wilmington, North Carolina.

More than 700,000 passengers arrived or departed through the airport in 2014. USAirways and Delta, the two major airlines serving ILM, offer several nonstop destinations. Surprisingly, for a city so heavily involved with tourism, traffic at the airport is 71 percent business, a reflection on the city's industrial and technological growth.

The airport has consistently improved its facilities toward greater safety and convenience. One runway and the adjoining taxiway are currently being extended by 750 feet, which offers more distance for takeoff and landing. To better serve the influx of business and pleasure travelers, parking was recently expanded with an additional 300 spaces, and a new on-site rental car service center is being built. Upgraded LED runway lights are brighter and more energy-efficient, saving money.

When you eventually have to tear yourself away from the Wilmington area and fly off, remember that you can come to the airport with family, friends or business acquaintances, get together in some old-fashioned rocking chairs under a replica of the original Wright Flyer and have a relaxed and pleasant farewell.

New business park built

A new addition to the airport grounds, the ILM Business Park, consists of 150 acres of class A office, light industrial and warehouse space. The ILM Business Park offers competitive lease rates and is an approved North Carolina Department of Commerce certified site for business and industry.

Tax credits for job creation, investment tax credits, research and development tax credits and worker training tax credits are offered to qualifying businesses moving to the ILM Business Park.

The new Veterans Administration Outpatient Clinic, part of the ILM Business Park, began treating patients in March 2013, according to Jim Morton, airport finance director. The 102,000 square-foot facility features mental health, women's health, optometric and general practice clinics; a pharmacy; and four surgical suites. The VA Clinic employs 260 health care professionals and support staff.

Convention Center brings visitors

One of the factors that increased tourism in Wilmington is the new Wilmington Convention Center. An advantage of the Center is that it draws visitors to the Wilmington area 12 months a year and allows them to see other parts of our community, potentially enticing future visits at another time. As the largest convention center on the North Carolina coast, the Wilmington Convention Center attracts big conventions previously held in Myrtle Beach and Hilton Head.

The Center is fronted by more than a mile of scenic Riverwalk and is enhancing the beauty of the city on what was once an abandoned and derelict industrial site.

Built with Room Occupancy Tax dollars, the facility has a 30,000 square foot Exhibit Hall and 12,000 square foot Grand Ballroom plus 15,000 square feet of pre-exhibit space, a 12,000 square foot event lawn and 5,784 square feet of meeting space.

With Green Efficiency in mind throughout, the center is an eco-friendly building with LEED (Leadership in Energy and Environmental Design) certification pending.

In fiscal year 2013, the Convention Center held 142 events attended by more than 80,000 visitors. In just its third year of operation, the 26 percent growth in events and 21 percent growth in attendance is noteworthy. The center also generated 5,731 room nights for area hotels, a dramatic 52 percent increase from the prior year. For fiscal year

RELOCATE YOUR BUSINESS
To the ILM Business Park!

MAKE THE BEACH YOUR BACKYARD

The **ILM Business Park** is located at the Wilmington International Airport (ILM). Offering many competitive advantages, it is a perfect home for your business. Accessibility is unparalled with access to air service, rail service, and the Port of Wilmington. The 140 acre business park has shovel-ready sites now available with very competitive lease rates!

CONTACT: JIM MORTON
910.341.4333 X. 1003

WWW.FLYILM.COM
JMORTON@FLYILM.COM

tourism, strength and growth

The Riverfront in Downtown Wilmington draws visitors all year round.

2014, the center has definite commitments from nearly 100 events, including 11 conventions, again an improvement over eight conventions in 2013. The convention center remains a positive factor in Wilmington's economic growth.

Making movie magic

The movie industry also contributes to the number of visitors to the Wilmington area. Now more than 325 movies and television series have been made here during a lengthy filmmaking history.

Beginning with the first movie made at the North 23rd Street location of present-day EUE/Screen Gems Studios, *Firestarter* in 1984, Wilmington has been the locale or headquarters for a number of popular television series including *Dawson's Creek*, *One Tree Hill*, *Eastbound and Down*, and *Matlock*. The series *Sleepy Hollow* completed its filming here in 2015, while *Under the Dome* continues here. A new series starring Ryan Phillippe, *Secrets & Lies*, premiered on ABC on March 1, 2015.

The largest production ever filmed in Wilmington, *Iron Man 3*, shot in several locations over most of the summer of 2012. In 2014, *The Longest Ride*, which is the newest film made from a Nicholas Sparks novel, was filmed here. That film hit movie theaters in early 2015.

EUE/Screen Gems Studios, located on a 50-acre lot, is the largest studio east of California and is capable of handling five separate productions at one time. The facility has 150,000 square feet of column-free production space with ten sound stages and two special-effects water tanks, one of which is among the largest in North America.

With 1,000 Wilmington-area resident technical crew members, in addition to hundreds of business and local support services that depend on its spending, the film industry has been a major factor in economic growth and stability in the Wilmington area.

NHRMC drives growth

As the largest provider of healthcare in Southeastern North Carolina, New Hanover Regional Medical Center (NHRMC) generates a tremendous amount of economic activity, more than $2 billion annually. Operating with a mission to serve all patients, regardless of ability to pay, NHRMC provides more than $145 million in charitable and uncompensated care.

NHRMC consistently makes giant strides in facility upgrades and capital improvements. In 2012, the hospital invested $48 million in medical, operational and information services equipment and facility improvements. On the main campus, the Betty H. Cameron Women's and Children's Hospital and a Surgical Pavilion were completed in 2008, and the Inpatient Tower has been completely renovated. The Atlantic Surgicenter, a $6.6 million, 17,390-square-foot, same-day surgery center opened in Porters Neck in 2008, the result of a partnership between New Hanover Regional Medical Center and a doctor's group called Wilmington Physicians, ASC. Related healthcare providers are building facilities at an almost dizzying rate.

With a team of about 6,000 employees, NHRMC is the largest employer in the area. Their impact on the region's economy is enormous and growing each year.

Small businesses thrive

Not all of the economic drivers here are large employers. The appeal of this area has attracted a growing number of entrepreneurs. Fortunately, many potential customers welcome and support locally owned businesses, making it easier for them to succeed. Retail shops, restaurants, accountants, writers, lawyers, artists, beauticians, architects, engineers, software specialists and website designers are but a few of the many small business owners thriving in this area.

Stating that "Small businesses generate the majority of jobs for workers in this country, and we must do everything we can to help those businesses," Wilmington mayor Bill Saffo has worked with the City Council and city manager to come up with a small business incentives plan and develop a way to make it easier to open new businesses or start a project in the city.

Office space, services

With so many companies being formed, companies serving small and large businesses are expanding, too. The need for executive office space is being met by Landfall Executive Suites, conveniently located just off Military Cutoff and Eastwood Roads.

This extremely well maintained and

LANDFALL EXECUTIVE SUITES
First Class Offices for Professionals • 1213 Culbreth Drive • landfall.biz • 910.509.7250

Furnished Office Packages
Customized to Fit Your Budget

Schedule a tour at one of our two convenient locations

Fully Furnished Office Suites • Short & Long Term Leasing Options • Reception & Waiting Areas
Equipped Conference Rooms • Virtual Offices Starting at $50/mo.

EASTWOOD EXECUTIVE SUITES
Offices for the Coastal Lifestyle • 2018 Eastwood Rd. • eastwoodexecutivesuites.com • 910.509.7100

staffed facility is providing the service that many growing businesses require, from beautifully appointed conference rooms and offices to always-present reception to mail and fax services. Due to economies of scale, all of this is offered at a price far less than business owners would pay on their own. Numerous options for both long and short-term leases are available and the staff is happy to take you through the facility so that you can see what is offered.

Eastwood Executive Suites, located on Eastwood Avenue a short distance from Wrightsville Beach, has opened a facility for those who embrace the coastal lifestyle. Private, furnished offices come complete with telephone and internet services and the complex also has a full time receptionist and conference room. The offices are more casual than those found at Landfall Executive Suites, and will appeal to those who embrace the coastal lifestyle. Rental fees are modest.

Patriotic pride on display

Visitors to this area notice that many of our commercial and residential buildings proudly display the American flag. Perhaps our proximity to major military installations in Jacksonville (home of the Marine Corps Expeditionary Forces) or Fayetteville (home of the Army's Airborne and Special Operations Forces) contributes to local residents' understanding of the sacrifice many have made and continue to make to keep the country safe.

Whatever the reason, All Star Flags keeps busy designing, supplying and installing flags for both businesses and individuals. They have flagpoles and standards of many types and sizes and carry a full range of flags of all types and sizes. They also offer signs and pennants that will meet all your business needs.

Manufacturing, technology

Industry continues to develop, strengthen and prosper in the Wilmington area. The combination of our workforce, temperate climate, financial incentives, readily available space and excellent transportation by water, rail, highway and air make Wilmington a great place to build and expand production and research facilities.

General Electric, with two major segments in the Wilmington area employing about 2,100, is maintaining its growth and success pattern. GE Hitachi Nuclear Energy (GEH), formed in conjunction with Japan's Hitachi Company, operates a 1,600-acre campus including manufacturing, training, simulation and testing facilities. With a demonstration test loop currently under construction, the new uranium enrichment facility using innovative laser isotope separation technology is estimated to cost upwards of a billion dollars and add 900 high paying jobs to the local economy.

At the same Castle Hayne location, GE Aviation continuously grew its 600-person workforce to accommodate record growth in 2011 and 2012. GE Aviation and its joint venture partner, France's Snecma, secured orders and commitments for more than 4,000 CFM56 and LEAP engines worth more than $52 billion.

This, coupled with other orders from airlines, including an increase in GE90 engine orders, will ensure strong production at the Wilmington facility for years to come.

The local plant produces high-pressure turbine disks, shafts, spools and seals for the engines, and much of the production is shipped to GE's Durham, N.C. plant for assembly.

AAIPharma, which filed for bankruptcy in 2006, has rebounded since and enjoyed banner growth recently. The company, which has about 450 employees located mostly at its headquarters near the airport, performs research, material testing, manufacturing and packaging.

The company recently announced the expansion of laboratory service offerings, capabilities and instrumentation at their Wilmington facility.

Additionally, in 2012, the company opened a 40,000-square-foot Technology Center in Wilmington. The Technology Center provides new state-of-the-art labs and equipment, allowing AAIPharma to compete on a global scale.

AAIPharma has announced plans to continue expanding in the area.

PPD LLC, with world headquarters in its sparkling building that is a welcome addition to the downtown Wilmington skyline, is a leading global

Downtown Wilmington, with its stately ships and great buildings, looks wonderful from across the Cape Fear River.

contract research organization providing drug discovery, development and lifecycle management services. PPD is a major local employer with more than 1,700 employees in the area.

On a global level, PPD employs 12,500 professionals in 46 countries and works with 49 of the top 50 pharmaceutical companies. In late 2011, private equity firms The Carlyle Group and Hellman & Friedman purchased PPD, and the company underwent privatization.

Despite recent change, PPD continues to grow, having hired approximately 3,200 new employees globally and adding offices in additional countries around the world.

Port of Wilmington grows

North Carolina's Ports in Wilmington and Morehead City, plus inland terminals in Charlotte and the Piedmont Triad in Greensboro, link the state's consumers, businesses and industry to world markets and serve as magnets to attract new business and industry while receiving no direct taxpayer subsidy. Port activities contribute statewide to 65,000 jobs and $500 million each year in state and local tax revenues.

State-of-the-art Panamax container cranes, more powerful container handling equipment, updated cargo management technology and readily available modern transit and warehouse facilities are making our port an attractive one for international trade. In fiscal year 2014, a total of 4,212,365 tons of goods moved through the Port of Wilmington. Top trading partners for 2014 in order were China, South Korea, Brazil, Belgium and Turkey.

The top five imports in fiscal 2014 were grains, chemicals, fertilizers, machine parts, and metal products. The top five exports were forest products, wood pulp, wood chips, general merchandise and food.

The Port of Wilmington experienced growth in two commodities central to NC's agricultural community with the import of UAN, a liquid fertilizer solution, and the importation of grains used mainly as pork and poultry feed in North Carolina.

N.C. Ports are focused on investing in its facilities for future growth. The Wilmington Harbor Navigation Improvement Study serves as one such project with an immediate need for current and future customers of the Port of Wilmington. There is every reason to believe that the Port of Wilmington will continue to grow and expand.

Construction everywhere

Residential construction in the Cape Fear region continues a strong rebound. With Wilmington's apartment vacancy rate the lowest in both the Southeast and in North Carolina, it seems that major apartment complexes and senior living facilities are under construction all over the area. A huge complex is underway on Eastwood Road near Wrightsville Beach; another is on Market Street near Porters Neck. Housing developments are expanding in the tri-county area too with many of the older communities almost completely built out. A new hotel opened in downtown Wilmington in 2014 and others are planned.

The real estate market is strengthening. The magazine *CNNMoney* named Wilmington as one of the top 10 places to buy in the country. "Nestled between the Cape Fear River and North Carolina's Inner Bank beaches, Wilmington has great golf, mild weather, natural beauty, and a relatively cheap cost of living, all of which make it popular with both permanent residents and second-home vacationers. As the only city of any significant size on the North Carolina coast, Wilmington may be just at the beginning of its boom," the magazine said.

There are few things that are more relaxing and refreshing than a rejuvenating massage.

spas and salons

Keeping fit and fantastic in southeastern North Carolina should be relatively easy since so many activities are available in Southeastern North Carolina. However, most of these activities have consequences that need to be addressed since most take place outdoors under strong sunlight or on and in the water. Swimming, golfing, gardening, fishing, boating, surfing and sightseeing are just a few of the pursuits that many of us enjoy. Unfortunately, all of them create the need for special care for our hair, skin and body.

There is a solution close at hand – after a good workout and time spent outdoors, you'll especially enjoy a massage, sauna or spa treatment. You'll be wise to give your body, mind and spirit the care they deserve.

We're lucky that we have wonderful salons that are uniquely suited to take care of our needs. And in an area with a host of weddings, pageants, proms, parades, festivals, balls and graduation parties, in addition to outdoor activities, women have excellent excuses for frequent salon visits.

Consider spending a few hours to an entire day being fussed over and nurtured. Because spa services are designed to promote relaxation, we recommend that you leave your children, pagers, and cell phones at home. Maybe you'd like to have a relaxation massage, body polish, microdermabrasion, or steam heat therapy. Why not throw in aromatherapy for good measure?

To maximize your experience, try a facility that is widely recognized as among the best places in the area for all your hair and skin care needs.

When you step through the door for

an appointment at Joseph Zell and Company, you'll immediately realize you're in no ordinary salon. You'll instantly notice the antiques and superb Louis XIV reproduction furniture that would not be out of place in a beautiful home. Original artwork on the walls, a gold-domed ceiling, and fabulous accessories complete the opulent space that was decorated by Eve Zell, co-owner of the salon with her husband, Joseph.

The services you'll receive are as spectacular as the surroundings and at prices no higher than at any quality salon. The ambiance is very much in keeping with the clients and staff at Joseph Zell and Company, and many clients feel very much part of a family after just a few visits. The talented staff was handpicked by Joseph, a former featured stylist with Peter Coppola in New York. The staff attends training sessions regularly to stay current with the latest trends.

Among the services offered are all things related to hair care, including fabulous cuts for men and women, color highlights, glossing and dyeing to cover gray or just for a change of pace if the customer prefers. The salon uses European hair products by L'anza, one of the world's preeminent brands. Those interested in having thicker, longer or more voluminous hair can do so with Great Lengths International hair extensions, guaranteed to be made from 100 percent human hair and considered by many the best product available. Kenleigh Register attended classes in 2015 and specializes in Great Lengths extensions. She also is certified in Zuzu makeup, a gluten free, premier product.

Superb facials are a feature at Joseph Zell and Company. A licensed esthetician, Nicole Smith, use Eminence 100 percent organic products to rejuvenate the skin. She also offers microcurrent and LED Light Therapy for the skin, waxing and Xtreme Lash extensions. These treatments are sure to leave customers feeling and looking relaxed and refreshed.

Miranda Raber is a L'anza color specialist. A graduate of CFCC's cosmetology program, Raber tries to take a new class at least once every two months. She is particularly interested in precision coloring and in corrective coloring, which unfortunately is often needed in this area. Erin Cribbs is another graduate of the CFCC Cosmetology program. She is particularly gifted and interest in doing great updos, which many clients prefer for special, elegant occasions.

The services are offered individually or can be combined into a Day of Beauty package that includes a manicure, pedicure, facial, complete hair styling with cut and color and a delicious complimentary lunch. This package would make a wonderful and much appreciated Valentine's Day, Christmas, birthday or anniversary gift for that special someone. The staff also can handle the hair care needs for a wedding party.

Joseph Zell and Company is located in the Arboretum Center on Oleander Drive. The salon is just over the bridge from Wrightsville Beach and is an easy drive from Figure Eight Island as well as from Historic Downtown Wilmington.

Try fitness centers

One of the best things a person can do for their hair and skin is to be physically fit.

A good way to do so is to take advantage of the area's many excellent fitness centers and health clubs.

Don't necessarily join the club that is closest to you. It is much more important that you feel comfortable and confident of the skills of the facility you join. Stop in for tours and meet the personnel who work in them.

Get the feel for a place before committing to membership. We recommend taking advantage of free trial periods when they're available.

Around here you can find a wide variety of facilities, everything from cozy small fitness centers for women only to large, sophisticated, state-of-the-art, freestanding health clubs, with lots of places in between. If you're not into serious strengthening or heavy-duty workouts, you can find less arduous activities on the menus of most fitness centers, but particularly at the area's senior centers, YMCA, YWCA or local recreation centers. With a little effort, you'll find just what you're looking for; after that, it's only a matter of time before you're looking and feeling terrific.

Among the great variety of fitness activities to choose from are the usual and the not-so-usual selections. Depending on your interests and skills, you can exercise in the water, in the gym or

in the great outdoors. Want classes in yoga or Pilates? We've got them. Looking for total body conditioning systems or a personal trainer? We've got lots of them. Need help with prescription exercise or cardiovascular programs? We've got these, too.

Sparkling new gym

Raise the Bar is a new fitness facility that is a welcome addition to Hampstead. It opened early in 2015 and has been popular from day one, perhaps because it is meticulously and constantly cleaned and features state-of-the-art equipment.

Treadmills, elliptical machines, all sorts of leg, chest, arm and back weight training equipment, free weights, and machines in a separate area designed for the abdominal work are available. The owners are both long-term trainers and their friendly, low-key manner makes everyone comfortable regardless of their beginning skill levels.

New classes are being added all the time and visitors are welcome to check out all Raise the Bar offers.

Aveda spa & salon

Mayfaire is home to the area's only Aveda salon. Aveda was founded in 1978 by Horst Rechelbader with this mission: "Our mission at Aveda is to care for the world we live in, from the products we make to the ways in which we give back to society. At Aveda, we strive to set an example for environmental leadership and responsibility – not just in the world of beauty, but around the world."

Van Davis Aveda Salon and Spa, one of fewer than 8,000 Aveda salons worldwide, offers whatever rejuvenation services men, women and children might want. In addition to haircuts and styling, many other hair services are available. Bang trimming, double process color, individual, partial or full foils, flat iron styling and corrective color are just of few of the services offered by the talented staff. Prices are a la carte, so clients can get as much or as little as they would like.

Spa services are extensive too. Aveda Spa offers facial and massage treatments that are designed to benefit each person's specific skin and body care needs. Several different packages are offered, ranging from a refreshing service that requires a bit more than an hour to a full day retreat.

Manicures and pedicures of several types are offered too. The staff at Van Davis Aveda salon and spa will happily consult with you to determine what services best meet your needs.

All hair and skin care products are professionally developed and clinically tested from botanicals and their pure essential oils.

Safe tanning available

Most everyone now recognizes the harmful effects of spending hours tanning in the sun. However, there is a safe and effective way to get that golden glow. Airbrush tanning achieves the same result, but with no damage to the skin.

Twin sisters Kyra and Rachael Skairus are happy to travel to your location for airbrush tanning.

They also are skilled in makeup applications that give their clients the look they want, whether it is bold and dramatic for a special evening out or a more subdued look to enhance a person's natural beauty.

They are happy to provide full makeup services for wedding parties. A trial session is included so that brides and their attendants decide in advance how they would like to look on that special day.

Drink, drink, drink

What keeps skin looking as youthful as possible? Avoiding the sun by wearing sunscreen with a SPF of 15 or higher at all times, including in this area's winter months. If you're outdoors gardening, enjoying the beach, playing golf, eating at one of our great waterfront restaurants, walking downtown or any of the things that take us outdoors, reapply the sunscreen often.

Another thing that helps keep skin healthy is hydration. During the summer's hot and humid months, drink plenty of liquids. If you feel thirsty, you're not drinking enough - thirst is a sign of dehydration. And remember, alcohol is dehydrating. Enjoy your cocktails, but drink plenty of water too.

Makeup Artistry by the Twins!

For expert airbrush tanning done on location and expert makeup artistry to help you look your best, contact Kyra or Rachael Skairus at 910-612-9821 or rachaelmaryskairus@gmail.com

Students have a wide choice of highly regarded schools to attend in the Cape Fear region.

a good **education**

Lifelong learning is pursued by many who live in Southeastern North Carolina. On the Cape Fear coast, educational opportunities are all around us. Whether formal, fun, frantic or fabulous, you'll find an extensive menu of learning experiences here.

We've got swim classes for six-month-old babies and gymnastics for crawlers. We've got tot this and toddler that. We've got public schools, independent or private schools, charter schools, specialty schools, home schools and more. We have incredible and diverse higher education institutions. We have continuing education programs for everyone who wants them – no age limit. We have free or modestly priced lessons for people who want to try painting, photography, woodworking, gardening and a host of other activities. And we have our historic locale, the rivers, the sea, the wildlife and all the lessons they have to offer us… for free.

Excellent higher education

Whatever you're seeking, be it a technology certificate or an advanced academic degree, you may be surprised to find it's probably available in our area. We have one major university, two private colleges and two community colleges that offer hundreds of programs for your choosing.

Cape Fear Community College (CFCC) 411 North Front Street Wilmington, NC 28401
Phone: (910) 362-7000
www.cfcc.edu

Evident in the quality and quantity of its programs and services, Cape Fear Community College is committed to achieving world-class workforce development. Diverse academic, vocational and technical instruction targets primarily adults age 18 or older who want to acquire new skills, expand their career options or keep pace with ever-changing occupational requirements.

Impacted by economic conditions in recent years, more and more people are turning to CFCC for education and job training. The college continues to grow dramatically. A combined curriculum and continuing education student population of roughly 30,000 makes CFCC one of the largest among North Carolina's 58 community colleges. In addition to its main campus in downtown Wilmington and its northern campus in northern New Hanover County, CFCC also offers a campus in Surf City in Pender County.

The implementation of an ambitious Facilities Master Plan 2007 2013 has made the college even more attractive to those who would benefit from its services; consequently, demands have also grown. The influx of students has caused serious classroom and parking concerns, leading to the necessity

108 ■ www.wilmingtontoday.com

CFCC Works!

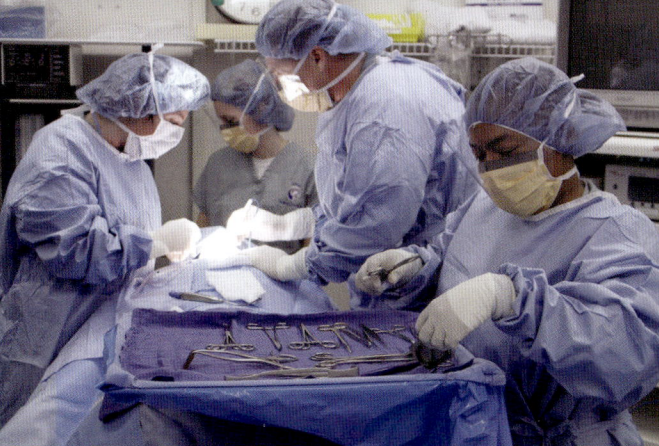
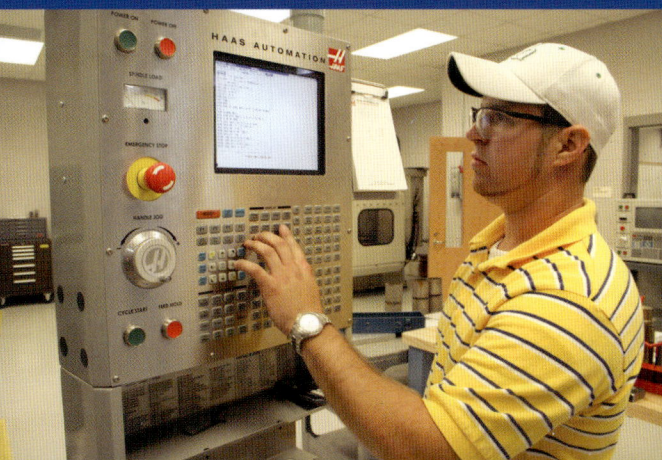

- Over 60 career training programs
- Comprehensive college transfer program
- Continuing education classes
- Small class sizes
- Day and evening classes
- Distance education
- Low tuition

Cape Fear
COMMUNITY COLLEGE®

Wilmington - Castle Hayne - Burgaw - Surf City - (910) 362-7000 - www.cfcc.edu

With all the choices of schools in the local area, students can find programs that will keep them interested and involved in continuing to study and learn.

of leasing building space and increasing online and hybrid classes. A new 1,200 car parking deck opened in 2012 and a 250,000 square-foot classroom building opened in 2013.

Perhaps the largest indicator of growth at CFCC is the new Humanities and Fine Arts Center, which is set to open for classes and performances in fall 2015. The building will include a theatre with more than 1,500 seats, classrooms, studios and offices.

Superb workforce training

Considered the preeminent regional provider of workforce training, CFCC can provide employees with the skills they need, from learning a new software program to understanding how to operate specialized equipment.

According to Bill Kawczynski, CFCC's Workforce Development Coordinator, businesses of all sizes can take advantage of the training the college has to offer. "Whether the company is a multi-million dollar corporation or a small family-owned business, having a highly skilled workforce is the key to staying competitive."

An integral part of this endeavor is CFCC's Center for Business, Industry, and Government that offers seminars and customized industry training for individuals and businesses. Most of these services cost businesses little or nothing at all.

Tuition costs affordable

Over 60 formal courses of study in a wide range of occupations and hundreds of job training opportunities are there for the taking for an amazingly low tuition fee.

Two-year associate degrees are offered in Applied Science, Arts, Fine Arts, General Education and Science. Having fewer requirements than degree programs, diplomas and certificates are available in many disciplines. CFCC also offers a two-year college transfer curriculum that meets requirements for admission to a senior institution in the University of North Carolina (UNC) System.

UNC Wilmington

In the current academic year, the University of North Carolina Wilmington (UNCW) boasted an enrollment of nearly 13,000 undergraduate and more than 1,600 graduate students registered in five distinct schools comprising Arts and Sciences, Nursing, Business, Education, and Graduate studies. Bachelor's degrees are offered in 52 majors, master's degrees in 42 and doctorates in two. Taking advantage of Wilmington's motion picture industry, the university has a dedicated Department of Film Studies.

Also, UNCW's renowned Center for Marine Science includes a state-of-the-art facility on the Intracoastal Waterway at Myrtle Grove.

In February 2015, *US News & World Report* named UNCW one of the country's "most efficient" colleges and universities and one of the top ten best universities in the South. The university also has been consistently ranked by Kiplinger as one of the nation's "Best Value" Public Colleges and Universities for in-state students and out-of-state residents.

University of Mount Olive

Christian faith-based values provide the foundation for the University of Mount Olive's mission, environment and curriculum. One of its seven campuses is located in Wilmington. This private, four-year college offers 40-plus majors; it offers associate's and bachelor's degrees in liberal arts and professional studies as

well as an MBA program. The University of Mount Olive has small classes, flexible scheduling, many online courses, and one-night-a-week academic programs specifically designed for working adults.

Miller-Motte College

Another private institution of higher learning in Wilmington is Miller-Motte College, which is one among a chain of Miller-Motte colleges throughout the Southern United States offering certificates, diplomas, associate and bachelor's degrees in a variety of career-oriented disciplines. The local campus curriculum is known especially for its Massage Therapy, Cosmetology, Esthetics Technology, and Microcomputer Applications Network Administration. Online opportunities are available for Bachelor programs in Allied Health Management, Business Administration, Nursing, and Criminal Justice.

35 courses at Brunswick Community College

A public, two-year school, Brunswick Community College (BCC) is accredited to award associate's degrees, diplomas and certificates. Some 35 formal courses of study are offered, along with a wide array of continuing education and distance learning classes.

Individuals have access to more than 300 online courses through BCC's ed2go.com/brunswick program. Additionally, 14 Associate Degree programs allow students to transfer credits to a four-year college.

Located on the college's main campus, the Brunswick Interagency Program provides comprehensive education and vocational services designed for adults with developmental disabilities.

Also associated with BCC is the Brunswick Educational Transition Center which serves residents whose first language is not English. Through its New and Expanding Industry Program and its Small Business Center, BCC works closely with area business and industry to tailor skills training to their needs.

Continuing education offered

Thanks to our many academic, healthcare and cultural institutions, we have a cornucopia of learning opportunities that go beyond diplomas and degrees. You can find a class on just about anything you desire. Besides an enormous pool of public offerings, plenty of instructional courses are available through private businesses, non-profit and professional organizations.

Both Community Colleges and the University of North Carolina at Wilmington publish catalogs listing their continuing education, public service and personal enrichment studies. In particular, the Osher Lifelong Learning Institute at UNCW has an extensive and diverse menu of educational experiences.

Cape Fear Community College's Continuing Education Department provides a broad range of training programs and classes that prepare individuals for employment, update knowledge and skills of those already employed, and open doors of opportunity to others. For those who want to take college courses for personal development rather than working toward a degree, diploma or certificate, CFCC admits students as Special Credit or Lifelong Learners. Post-secondary transcripts are necessary for admission and students must meet all prerequisites and placement testing requirements.

Also, an amazingly wide variety of activities, programs and classes are available through the New Hanover County Department of Aging's Senior Resource Center, Brunswick Senior Resources and Pender Adult Services. Print and online newsletters contain specifics about each offering.

Pre-K through 12 schools

For parents who wish to send their children to private schools, there are several that offer education pre-K through grade 12 and numerous more which offer pre-K or K through 8. Many are faith-based. Most are located in New Hanover County, Shallotte, Leland and Southport.

Wilmington Christian Academy (WCA) 1401 North College Road Wilmington, NC 28405
Phone: (910) 791-4248
www.wilmingtonchristian.com

The largest private school in Southeastern North Carolina, WCA provides excellence in education in preschool through high school. Total enrollment for 2014-2015 is 814. This coeducational school boasts a positive, nurturing environment that promotes a high standard of academic growth based on conservative Christian values. The Academy, a ministry of Grace Baptist Church, offers a challenging, sequenced curriculum and emphasizes basic academic skills along with a solid foundation of traditional courses.

Three, four and five-year-old children become well-grounded when they participate in WCA's preschool and kindergarten phonics and math programs. By the time these little ones reach first grade, they've got a good grip on the three R's and possess important building blocks of academic success. Besides school subjects and communication skills, the children have daily Bible lessons which help shape their values and relationships with others. Spanish, art, music, physical education and computer skills are taught weekly.

The accelerated elementary curriculum continues to emphasize core subjects using innovative technology, interactive learning and traditional instruction. Added activities such as physical education, Spanish, art and music, and computer applications help broaden the scope of learning for youngsters in grades 1 to 5.

The WCA middle school program is designed to meet the unique needs of young teenagers. Middle school students continue their academic growth by engaging in activities designed to help them develop critical thinking skills, personal responsibility and teamwork in an enjoyable environment designed to challenge their abilities.

High school students follow one of three academic programs: honors, college preparatory or general. A variety of college-credit, Advanced Placement and on-line courses are available. In addition, students can explore programs in robotics, engineering, CAD and electric vehicle technology.

The school's fine arts program includes group and private instruction in vocal and instrumental music, drama, journalism and art. All students can participate in competitive sports and student organizations. WCA graduates have outstanding achievement scores and are accepted into colleges across the nation.

In keeping with its Christian values, WCA encourages students to become involved in community service and to practice giving to others who are less fortunate. WCA offers myriad opportunities for students at all grade levels to give back to their community. The elementary school participates in a Thanksgiving food drive and community service activities benefiting the Yahweh Center and Relay for Life. Organizations in middle school (C.R.E.W.) and in high school (G.O.A.L.) actively support Pretty in Pink, Coats for the Coatless, Work on Wilmington and the Angel Tree, among others.

New Hanover public schools

New Hanover County has the 12th largest public school system in the state and 311th largest in the United States with approximately 25,000 students in grades pre-K through 12. The system includes two pre-K schools, 25 elementary schools, nine middle schools and seven high schools. Over the years, the NHC school system has received numerous national and state awards and has been recognized for its academic programs and professional development.

Not part of the New Hanover Coun-

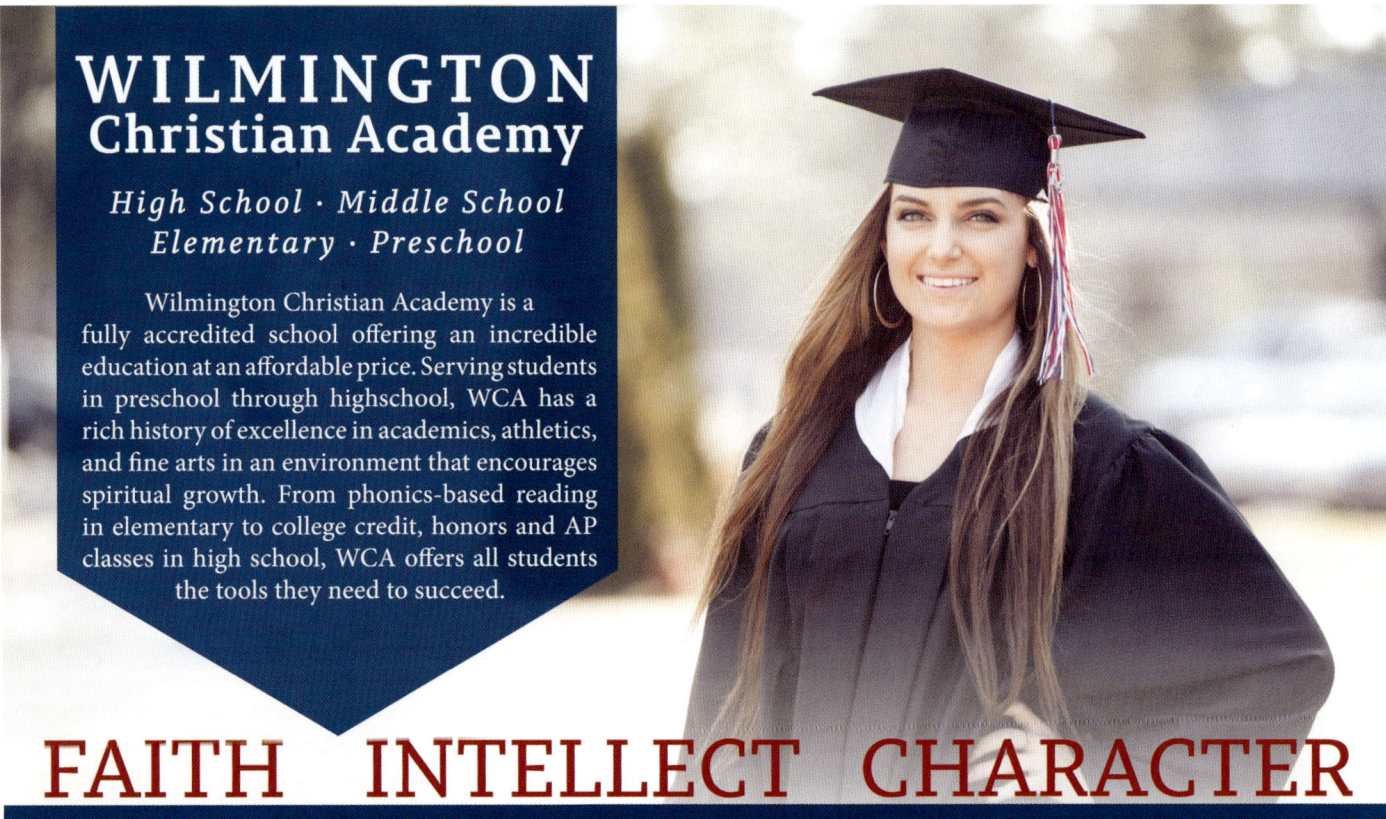

ty School System are two state-funded, tuition-free, public charter schools open to all North Carolina children. The Cape Fear Center for Inquiry in Wilmington (K-8) focuses on promoting a student's abilities to think and create in personally meaningful ways through an inquiry-based, integrated curriculum. The Wilmington Preparatory Academy (K-8) is a year-round, official Core Knowledge School.

The curriculum is highly structured, based on the idea that new knowledge builds on what student's already know, so they are offered a coherent sequence of specific knowledge that builds year by year.

Pender schools succeed

Increasingly, families with growing children have been attracted to Pender County primarily because of its innovative and proactive school system. The district has pioneered in using virtual world technology for staff development and video games in the classroom. The Pender County School District comprises eight elementary schools, four middle schools and four high schools throughout a rapidly growing county with a mix of suburban and rural communities. More than 8,000 students are enrolled in 16 schools.

Pender County residents recognize the importance of a school system that offers opportunities for all children. In November 2014, they overwhelmingly approved a $75 million school building bond that will provide the additional facilities that are required for the growing Pender County population.

Brunswick's public schools

Twenty schools fall under the Brunswick County Schools umbrella encompassing pre-K through grade 12, all running on a traditional school calendar with a total enrollment around 12,200. The official breakdown is ten elementary, five middle and five high schools, although Waccamaw School has students in kindergarten through 8th grade, actually making it a combined elementary and middle school.

The system includes traditional curricula, alternative education programs and an Early College High School where

Children are being taught to use computers at a very early age.

students have the opportunity to graduate with both a high school diploma and an Associate degree in Art/Science in 4-5 years.

Home schooling continues to grow at rapid pace

In North Carolina, homeschooling is a legal option for a parent or other responsible party to provide a child with academic instruction at home or other setting rather than in a formal school. Eligible students are children (ages 6-17) in a grade equivalent to at least kindergarten and not higher than 12th grade. The number of students has grown each year for many years.

New Hanover County in 2014-15 reported 1,113 schools serving more than 1,500 students. Pender County had 460 home schools with nearly 700 students. Brunswick County had 772 schools educating more than 1,000 students.

Requirements and other information are available through the North Carolina Division of Non-Public Education (DNPE).

Learning can be fun, too

The Cape Fear area offers various kinds of educational activities for children as young as one year old through high school age. A host of enrichment programs supplement the activities taught in our schools and are especially helpful at a time when so many school arts and science activities have been eliminated or dramatically curtailed. Learning is fun at the following facilities.

Tregembo Animal Park
5811 Carolina Beach Road
Wilmington, NC 28412
Phone (910) 392-3604
www.tregemboanimalpark.com

Old timers hereabouts remember Tote-Em-In Zoo, now called Tregembo Animal Park, which for more than 60 years has been the only zoo in southeastern North Carolina. During that time, the Tregembo family has consistently provided local families, children's groups and tourists with a fun, educational place to spend a few hours or a day. For a modest admission, you can see an amazing variety of creatures. Some animals you can feed corn or peanuts, some you can pet. And, of course, you'll want to visit the 4,000 square foot gift shop to take home souvenirs.

Besides the usual zoo animals such as a lion, tigers, monkeys and a giraffe, the Park boasts many unusual specimens including a two-toed sloth, a prehensile tailed porcupine, and an East African crown crane. If you're curious, go to the website and view more than 100 photos of critters that are on display.

**Thalian Association Children's Theater (TACT) Thalian Association
Box 1111, Wilmington, NC 28402
Phone (910) 251-1788
www.thalian.org**

Wilmington is extremely fortunate to have the Thalian Association Children's Theater (TACT) which offers theatrical training and performance opportunities, with most auditions open for children ages seven through high school seniors. TACT remains dedicated to "the enrichment of arts education for our community's youth." And what a great place for talented kids to grow – right in the heart of "Wilmywood" with its thriving film industry and nurturing arts community.

Children may choose to be involved on stage as actors or back stage as part of the technical production team. Five productions each year are held at the Community Arts Center, 120 South 2nd Street, in the Hannah Block Historic USO building. For information and class reservations, call (910) 341-7860. The TACT productions are regularly honored with a Wilmington Theater Award for Best Children's Production.

TACT Academy offers an opportunity to create and explore the arts in a non-audition based setting for students ages 4 to high school. Designed to help students better understand theater in all its facets, an array of classes, taught by a large group of talented instructors, enable students to discover their strength, learn new skills and build self-confidence within a nurturing atmosphere. The TACT Academy program is a six-month semester with a showcase for students at the end of each program. The classes are held at the Hannah Block building and at New Hanover County Public Library Northeast Branch on Military Cutoff Road. The classes are affordable and scholarship opportunities are available.

**Carolina Gymnastics Academy (CGA) 3529 Carolina Beach Road Wilmington, NC 28412
Phone (910) 796-1896
www.carolinagymnasticsacademy.com**

Both owners and all coaches at Carolina Gymnastics Academy love kids, love gymnastics and love teaching. Their great results are the best testament to those attributes. Children who participate in CGA classes and win accolades at competitions benefit from meticulous training. The school, which opened in 2000, provides a safe environment and a developmentally appropriate curriculum in a modern, very well-equipped 15,000 square foot exercise facility.

A wide variety of programs is available for boys and girls from crawlers through high school. By incorporating fun physical activities with educational tools, even the very youngest kiddos can pick up gymnastic basics and enjoy learning.

Their Gym & Learn program is an early education program which provides children ages 3-5 the opportunity to get a "jump start" on learning the important academic, physical, and social skills necessary to be prepared for kindergarten. Taught by long time coach Zoey Zapple, who has a B.A. in Social Work and a concentration in Early Childhood Education, the program provides age appropriate learning in an active setting. Another feature of the program helps children learn self-discipline, sharing, and taking turns, while developing a healthy self image through the sport of gymnastics. Combining academics, physical fitness, and pro-social interaction will help each child reach his or her full potential, enjoy learning, and begin life physically fit! This best value program offers gymnastics class, developmental approach to academics, and free play every day. Tuition is weekly, paid in advance.

CGA emphasizes "what's best" for each child and tailors instruction accordingly, with classes, camps, teams and more. There's an After School Program that includes free gym time and help with homework. Other popular offerings are Watch Me Play, open gym, and "Par-

ent's Night Out," when parents can leave youngsters for supervised play. This is a busy place!

Cameron Art Museum
3201 South 17th Street
Wilmington, NC 28412
Phone (910) 395-5999
www.cameronartmuseum.org

Cameron Art Museum offers a number of summer camps for children ages 5-8 in one group and ages 9-12 in another. The instructors encourage students to use their imagination and be creative when practicing various forms of art. Cameron has after school art programs too, again with classes for those 5-8 and 9-12. Classes include an introduction to painting techniques and hand-building with clay. Additionally, children from infant to age 4 and their parents can participate in the weekly Story Explorers program, which emphasizes literacy through the arts and experiential learning.

Airlie Gardens
300 Airlie Road
Wilmington, NC 28403
Phone (910) 798-7700
www.airliegardens.org

Airlie Gardens invites school groups to experience the wonders of their gardens through a variety of field trips catered to ages preschool through eighth grade. During the summer break, Airlie Gardens hosts summer camps for the young naturalist. The lessons are taught by certified North Carolina environmental educator Matt Collogan, and are designed to keep kids active and learning through the summer.

Kids who enjoy the outdoors and want to understand nature surely will benefit from the week-long morning "Wild Adventures Nature Camp" that demonstrates the diversity of life found in the local environment.

North Carolina Aquarium at Fort Fisher
900 Loggerhead Road
Kure Beach, NC, 28449,
Phone 1-800-832-3474 ext. 2
www.ncaquariums.com

We have a really wonderful aquarium here that is one of the outstanding attractions in southeastern North Carolina. Not only that, it's fun and educational as well as entertaining. Besides the usual family visits, plenty of child-oriented programs and events are available. Everything from staff-conducted group tours to birthday parties, sleepovers and holiday festivities are available. How about an Alligator Egg Hunt in the spring? Kids create their own egg baskets and search for candy-filled "alligator eggs" to put in them.

At Halloween, an aquatically-themed festival, "Trick or Treat Under the Sea," is a big winner with the young set.

School field trips are free and extremely popular, largely because Aquarium staffers are very kid friendly, knowledgeable and love what they do. By bringing education alive, children can learn from seeing creatures large and small in their natural environment doing what they do all day. With a truly hands-on approach, children are encouraged to reach into the touch tanks and feel assorted critters or pick them up to look closely at them. For groups, staff may conduct supervised 'show and tell' times and let kids explore exhibits around the Aquarium or in classrooms.

Boy and Girl Scouts can earn merit badges here, too. Aquarium instructors foster creative exploration, teach scientific theory, oversee lab activities and take scouts behind the scenes at the Aquarium to see Aquarists in action. Depending on the badge requirements, scouts may go on hikes through the salt marshes or get experience using seine and dip nets.

Definitely, the Aquarium Gift Shop is a must – it's cool, too. Kids love it!

Host of programs for adults

Many cultural organizations offer programs that enable adults to pursue their interests at reasonable costs. The Cameron Art Museum's Museum School offers several art courses, including art history, drawing, painting, print making/mixed media and photography courses for beginners as well as those who want to improve their skills. Additionally, beginning and experienced writers can learn from local authors through the creative writing workshops. Through the healthy living program, the CAM offers an introduction to T'ai Chi and yoga classes.

Many people who move here from other parts of the country are very interested in learning about the plants that grow well here. New Hanover County offer master gardening programs that are extremely beneficial. New Hanover's program consists of 40 hours of classroom instruction that is given to 40-50 people each year who then agree to 50 hours of volunteer service. This program is based at the New Hanover County Arboretum.

Pender County Extension master gardener programs are offered in January each year. Graduates of the program volunteer to appear periodically in places such as Poplar Grove's Farmers Market and the Blueberry Festival in Burgaw where they help others answer their gardening questions.

Brunswick County has a master gardeners program, too. Their association supplements the educational opportunities provided to master gardeners. Programs in Pender and Brunswick counties are part of the NC State University and A&T State University Cooperative Extension that has been "empowering people and providing solutions" for 100 years.

Many couples choose to exchange their wedding vows at one of our area's exquisite beaches.

time to celebrate

The Cape Fear region's fabulous locations, boundless beauty, and very affordable prices are sure to make any occasion special. No wonder so many couples choose to tie the knot here.

Experience genteel Southern afternoons at an antebellum mansion or a 67-acre garden ablaze with azaleas. Imagine exchanging vows on the deck of an old-fashioned riverboat slowly cruising down historic Cape Fear River. Say your vows on a 67-foot Hatteras Yacht that you've specially chartered for the day.

Thinking something else far from ordinary? No problem. Get married on a golf tee or in the aqua glow of a massive saltwater aquarium full of enchanting underwater life.

The Battleship North Carolina normally is seen guarding Wilmington's downtown, but it also is an awesome, solemn place for a wedding ceremony. Traditionalists find plenty of majestic old churches and little chapels.

And what's more romantic that exchanging vows at sunset by the shore? Just say "I do" to private islands, oceanfront resorts and beach houses large enough to accommodate the entire family.

Special places

Beloved blues define seaside weddings, but dreamy undersea worlds add special magic at Fort Fisher's North Carolina Aquarium. Both ceremonies and receptions are possible – for up to 2,000 people – alongside the aquarium's spectacular sea life, much of it in a 235,000-gallon aquarium.

The complex offers spacious galleries, stunning views and an unforgettable atmosphere, all just steps from the Atlantic Ocean at Kure Beach. Special-events staff tends to every detail, ensuring romantic moments meet or surpass expectations.

From sea to land, the Cape Fear area is awash in vivid color, especially in spring when azaleas, camellias and dogwoods bloom at Wilmington's rambling Airlie Gardens, another gorgeous site for weddings. Spring is lovely but the garden, established in 1886, is always delightful. Settings are diverse. Consider formal grounds, water views, whimsical sculptures or a gigantic 467-year-old live oak draped in silvery moss.

The Minnie Evans Bottle Chapel, a work of art made from hundreds of colorful bottles, is also among event site options. Airlie Gardens is available for afternoon or evening weddings, rehearsal dinners and other special events from March through October.

ENCHANTED *Wedding*
BY THE SEA

South of Wilmington, steps from the ocean.

910.458.8257
ncaff.events@ncaquariums.com
www.ncaquariums.com/fort-fisher

NORTH·CAROLINA
AQUARIUM
at Fort Fisher

time to **celebrate**

MAKE ANY EVENT REALLY SPECIAL!

Come celebrate your wedding, anniversary, birthday, promotion, business anniversary, holiday party, family reunion and so much more aboard our wonderful Riverboat!

HENRIETTA III

Cape Fear Riverboats, Inc.
900-343-1611 • 800-676-0162
www.cfrboats.com

Many couples marry in the late afternoon to take advantage of the light.

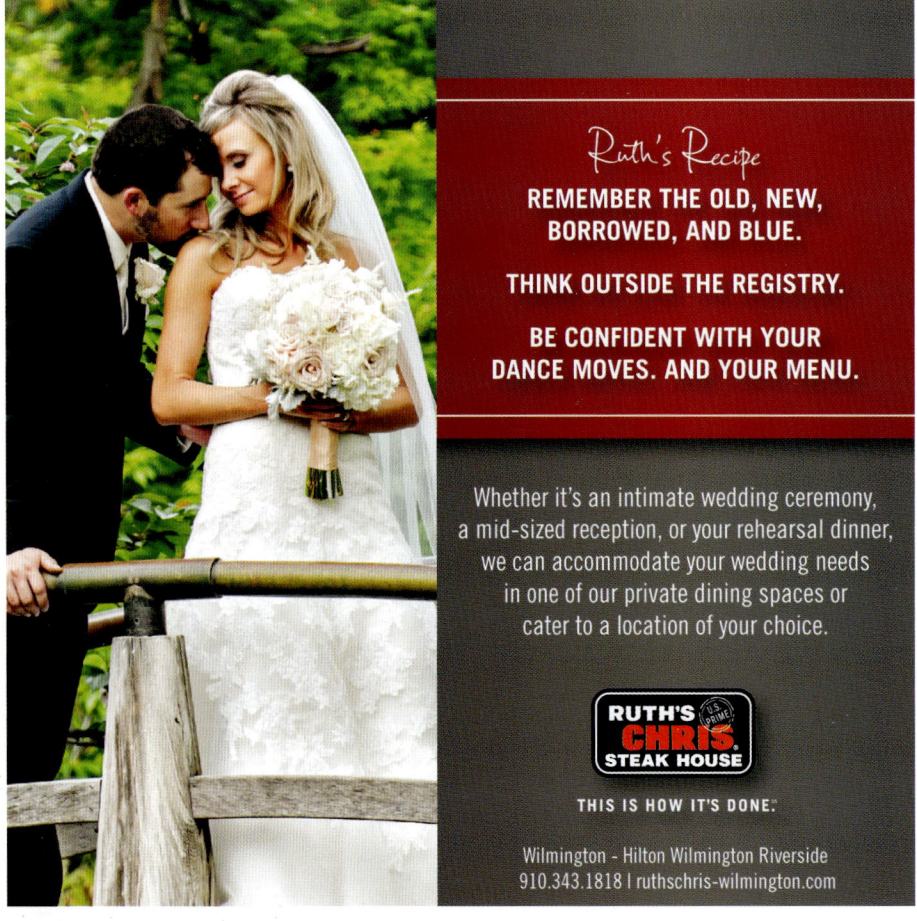

Ruth's Recipe

REMEMBER THE OLD, NEW, BORROWED, AND BLUE.

THINK OUTSIDE THE REGISTRY.

BE CONFIDENT WITH YOUR DANCE MOVES. AND YOUR MENU.

Whether it's an intimate wedding ceremony, a mid-sized reception, or your rehearsal dinner, we can accommodate your wedding needs in one of our private dining spaces or cater to a location of your choice.

RUTH'S CHRIS STEAK HOUSE

THIS IS HOW IT'S DONE.

Wilmington - Hilton Wilmington Riverside
910.343.1818 | ruthschris-wilmington.com

Let the celebration begin

A perfect wedding ceremony deserves a great toast. In the Cape Fear region, revelers may raise glasses everywhere from a down-home, backyard Carolina barbecue to an elegant, formal dinner at a luxurious beach house.

Intimate affairs happen at charming, historic venues. No matter the spot, on-site services and caterers fill the bill of fare.

Plan a sensational party here for any reason: graduations, family reunions, holiday fun, a birthday ice cream social. It's also fine to have a party for no reason at all.

Restaurants, hotels and event spaces, especially those with water views, suit anniversaries and birthdays as well as they do conferences, business meetings and charity events. Outdoor venues are also on the list.

Beautiful wooded parks work for weddings, picnics, children's parties and church activities. Don't forget the deck of mighty Battleship North Carolina.

Floating festivities

The Henrietta III is an old-time riverboat that has been evoking romance and Southern charm for more than 25 years. Day and evening wedding cruises tool along the Cape Fear River like slow boats of yore. Memorable receptions on the decks are a breeze.

Henrietta III staff can make all the arrangements for food, drinks and flowers, letting you relax and enjoy the view. The Henrietta III is docked on the historic downtown Wilmington waterfront and has a staff as accommodating as you could ever hope to meet.

Wilmington Yacht Charters offers a different experience on its state-of-the-art 46-foot catamaran. The ship seats up to 49 guests and can be reserved for any number of special events including weddings, receptions, birthday parties, corporate outings, and anniversaries. Wilmington Water Tours has full ABC permits and can arrange catering too.

The downtown beat

One of downtown Wilmington's most popular restaurants is the brew pub Front Street Brewery. The Beam Room upstairs is a distinctive and affordable event space for both wedding receptions and rehearsal dinners.

Wood tones and tall, sunlit windows highlight 3,000 square feet equipped with a 12-foot digital projection screen and surround-sound audio, making the space equally ideal for seminars, company parties and corporate meetings. All wedding and special event services are provided in-house, but Front Street Brewery provides off-site catering too, all at great prices.

Ruth's Chris Steak House, located at the Hilton Riverside Hotel downtown, is a beautiful location for a wedding reception or other special event. There are several private rooms that are available for events of different sizes. Ruth's Chris is famous for the quality of their steaks; they are the only restaurant in Wilmington that exclusively serves prime beef. The restaurant staff is happy to design whatever menu the clients prefer. All the details are professionally handled so that all the guests need to do is enjoy the party.

A special backdrop: the Cape Fear River

Riverwalk Landing is another complete banquet facility in historic downtown. Various spaces overlooking Cape Fear River accommodate groups of 25 to 200.

Indoor rooms and outdoor spaces afford beautiful views, and the expansive deck at sunset is especially striking.

Elijah's and The Pilot House restaurants provide custom menus. The restaurants have a 30-year record of reliable service.

A pastoral setting

Further north in Wilmington is Poplar Grove Plantation, one of the few surviving plantations in the country.

Brides can chose rustic or elegant weddings, or a blend of the two, as they plan their event at this family home which was built circa 1850 and is listed on the National Register of Historic Places.

The staff at Poplar Grove is happy to help brides with details including catering, photography and music.

Arrive in style

Arrive at receptions in historic style aboard a Wilmington Trolley Company old-school trolley or a modern bus that looks like a trolley.

The company arranges transportation to order for wedding parties and guests, and is happy to take people from the ceremony to the reception site. They will pick the wedding party up at the end of the evening as well.

Lou's Flowers

With more than 30 years of experience, the designers at Lou's Flower World will ensure that your wedding celebration is complemented with personalized, unique and beautiful flowers. Lou's 20,000-square-foot facility is a one-stop shop for all things floral, and they specialize in wedding floral services.

The first step is to set up a complimentary consultation with Lou's wed-

ding floral staff. Bring along your fabric swatches, photos, and ideas for your big day and allow Lou's staff to bring your vision to life.

The staff will help you select flower colors, ribbons and other accents that will complement the motif and style of your wedding.

Lou's offers a wide variety of wedding options and packages to meet the needs of any wedding, from a small, intimate affair for 25 to a grand event for 500, and everything in between. Let Lou's handle your wedding flowers and enjoy their beautiful, affordable and stress-free services.

Food to order

Reliable caterers provide just-right food and ambiance to order. Chefs prepare fine meals, fancy or casual, in any setting, whether home entertaining, beach condo meals or parties of all sizes.

Besides food, caterers decorate, set up, provide bartenders and beverages if requested, serve and clean after the event is over.

Many will arrange outdoor events, including rentals of tents, chairs, tables and other accessories.

Boat lovers may use caterers for onboard parties or club socials (by the way, Cape Fear-area sailing and boating groups accept members).

Once the budget, event space and number of guests are set, consult with caterers.

Even the smallest get-together can be much work; don't hesitate to call on a pro for assistance.

Long-time caterer

Wrightsville Beach has been a popular wedding and party destination for many years. Thanks to Jerry Rouse's Catering, perfect events have been produced for more there and elsewhere throughout the area for more than 40 years.

The catering company is well known for delicious food, and dietary restrictions, whether religious or health related, are no problem. Jerry Rouse's Catering also will handle everything you might need for the special day, including coordinating florists, tents, tableware, location and wine selection.

Rooms with a view

Gatherings large and small are treated to spectacular waterfront views at three Wrightsville Beach locations.

Bluewater Waterfront Grill restaurant stands on the Intracoastal Waterway, and has private rooms large and small. The second-story banquet room's picture windows broadcast breathtaking sunset views.

Oceanic restaurant is an unforgettable beachfront setting on South Lumina Avenue. Dining rooms face Atlantic waves. Outdoor tables line a long wooden pier extending out over the ocean.

A private room with a sea view as well as Oceans restaurant and its outdoor terrace are at Holiday Inn Resort on North Lumina Avenue.

The Melting Pot

The Melting Pot, a fondue restaurant located at Mayfaire Town Center has a private room that would be perfect for intimate wedding receptions or rehearsal dinners. The room has seating

For the perfect wedding reception or other special occasion, contact Jerry's Rouse's Catering. With 38 years experience in creating and executing outstanding events, clients can rest assured that everything will be done as it should be. Any dietary, religious or occasion needs will be met and everything will be prepared using the freshest ingredients from land, sea and vine. Call today.

JERRY ROUSE'S CATERING

7220 Wrightsville Avenue • Wilmington, NC 28405
910.256.8847
jerry@jerrysfoodandwine.com • www.jerrysfoodandwine.com

Come celebrate with us!

We have the perfect room for your special celebration. Receptions, rehearsal dinners, showers, birthday parties or business dinners for 16-32. Audio visual equipment available at no additional charge. Call us today!

The Melting Pot
a fondue restaurant

MAYFAIRE TOWN CENTER | 885 TOWN CENTER DRIVE | WILMINGTON NC 28405
910.256.1187 | WWW.MELTINGPOT.COM/WILMINGTON-NC/WELCOME

BLUE MAINSAIL CATERING

- Weddings & Rehearsal Dinners
- Holiday & Anniversary Parties
- Corporate & Social Events
- Onsite Party Hosting & Offsite Catering Available

Upscale or Casual – Always Reasonable
Serving all of Topsail Island, Surf City, Hampstead, and Sneads Ferry
Surf City, NC • 910-328-0010
www.bluemainsail.com

---

that would be suitable for 16-32 dinner guests. Larger groups could be accommodated for drinks and passed hors' de oeuvre. A number of food choices, including Melting Pot's famous fondue combinations, are available.

Topsail Island choices

On Topsail Island, Mainsail Restaurant in Surf City caters events in two private rooms that can host up to 120 people. They also are happy to provide catering services at any location a client chooses.

The restaurant is a popular spot for wedding receptions, rehearsal dinners, birthday celebrations and family reunions. Fans love Mainsail's seafood selections and chefs will craft formal and informal menus to your taste. A full range of possibilities is available, from Italian-themed dinners with the emphasis on pasta to seafood selections of all types.

Two restaurants that also are popular choices for wedding receptions and other special events are located in North Topsail Beach.

Inlet 790 centers the Villa Capriani resort complex. The restaurant's Italian garden setting, which overlooks a pool with the beach beyond it, is a beautiful site for a wedding and reception.

Chef David Longo is happy to work with clients to be sure that their event is precisely what they would like to have. Any type of food can be ordered and all the details will be taken care of so that everyone will enjoy the event.

Topsail Shrimp House is located on the top floor of the seven-story St. Regis resort with a fine view of the beach from every table.

The magnificent space with panoramic views is available for parties, specail events and wedding receptions. Many couples choose to hold the wedding ceremony on the beach, then go upstairs to the seventh floor for the reception and party. The staff is happy to work with clients on the menu, with whatever type of food they prefer available.

Full service site

Beau Rivage Golf & Resort has a beautiful ballroom that can accommo-

There are numerous caterers who are able to make an event memorable.

date 220 seated guests and 350 standing. There also are several sites for the ceremony itself at Beau Rivage.

The choices include being married under a beautiful live oak adorned with azalea bushes for ceremonies both large and small to a park-like setting on the 16th hole with a view of ponds and a brook for up to 250 guests. Guests reach the colonial-style clubhouse after traveling along a long, winding road lined with beautiful poplars.

Makeup matters

Most brides and attendants look their best with the assistance of professional makeup artists. Makeup By The Twins will arrange appointments at hotels and beach rental cottages.

Twin sisters Kyra and Rachael Skairus offer a trial makeup session so that decisions are made in advance for the bride and the entire wedding party.

Great rings, gifts

The Wilmington area is the place to

commission unique rings or find a special look to remind couples of their loving bond.

Albert F. Rhodes has been providing fine jewelry in Wilmington since 1948. Redesign family heirlooms here or have your personal vision styled into a custom-made piece.

Designers listen closely and are happy to work within your budget. Expect top-notch craftsmanship that has been an Albert F. Rhodes trademark throughout the store's history.

The shop sells a wide variety of rings and bridal jewelry set not only with diamonds, but with other precious stones including rubies, emeralds and sapphires. It's easy to find the product that is geared to your wedding style.

They also resize rings, reset gems, repair necklaces and bracelets and clean and polish precious pieces. Thinking about special keepsakes for attendants? Albert F. Rhodes carries a full line of giftware, too.

At Spectrum Art & Jewelry, in The Forum shopping center, meet award-winning jeweler Star Sosa. After 23 years of designing, she continues to be recognized nationally. In 2012, she received three awards, including the National Recognition Award for Superlative Design and Innovation, presented by the Independent Jewelers Organization. Design consultation is free. Provide your own gems or choose Spectrum's hand-picked diamonds from Belgium. If you have a family ring or gem that you would like reset, the shop can do that, too.

Brighten your smile

Wedding photographs stay with you forever, so you want to be sure to look as perfect as possible on your special day. One of the things that can make a big difference is to be sure that your smile is bright. Fortunately, the dentists at Atlantic Dental Group can help. They can correct flaws in your teeth with veneers or with a type of brace that is invisible. They also can whiten your teeth, and may be able to provide same day service.

Hair and pampering

Prepare for the big day with a great

haircut and style, and some pampering, at Joseph Zell and Company Salon. Joseph Zell came to Wilmington from New York's Madison Avenue and has been credited in major national magazines such as Glamour.

In a luxurious, baroque setting, stylists see to it that everyone in the wedding party looks and feels his or her best. One of the stylists at Joseph Zell is particularly gifted in producing wonderful updos, which many brides and bridal parties prefer. The salon is happy to consult with those interested in finding out more about the available services.

Van Davis Aveda Salon and Spa provides rejuvenating services for the bridal party. A great way to get ready for the special event is to arrange an evening for facials and massages prior to the wedding day.

This full service salon and spa is happy to accommodate groups for facials, body massage, hair styling, manicures and pedicures and more. The staff is happy to consult with clients who are planning their special events.

Get the word out

Occasions…Just Write stationery store at downtown Wilmington's Cotton Exchange shopping complex offers numerous options for letting friends and loved ones know about pending nuptials. Announcements, save-the-date reminders and invitations are among dozens of samples to peruse. The one-stop shop supplies thank-you cards, as well. Choose a pre-designed look or work with consultants to customize a look to your wedding and other event styles. Check the fine gifts here, too. Many items work as gifts for the wedding party.

Bridal style

Finding the perfect wedding veil or headpiece is easy thanks to world-class milliner Jan Wutowski. This talented milliner, who is in demand to teach not only here in this country but around the world too, is available by appointment only.

She happily works directly with clients to create one-of-a-kind looks that will have the bride looking as special as the day she's celebrating.

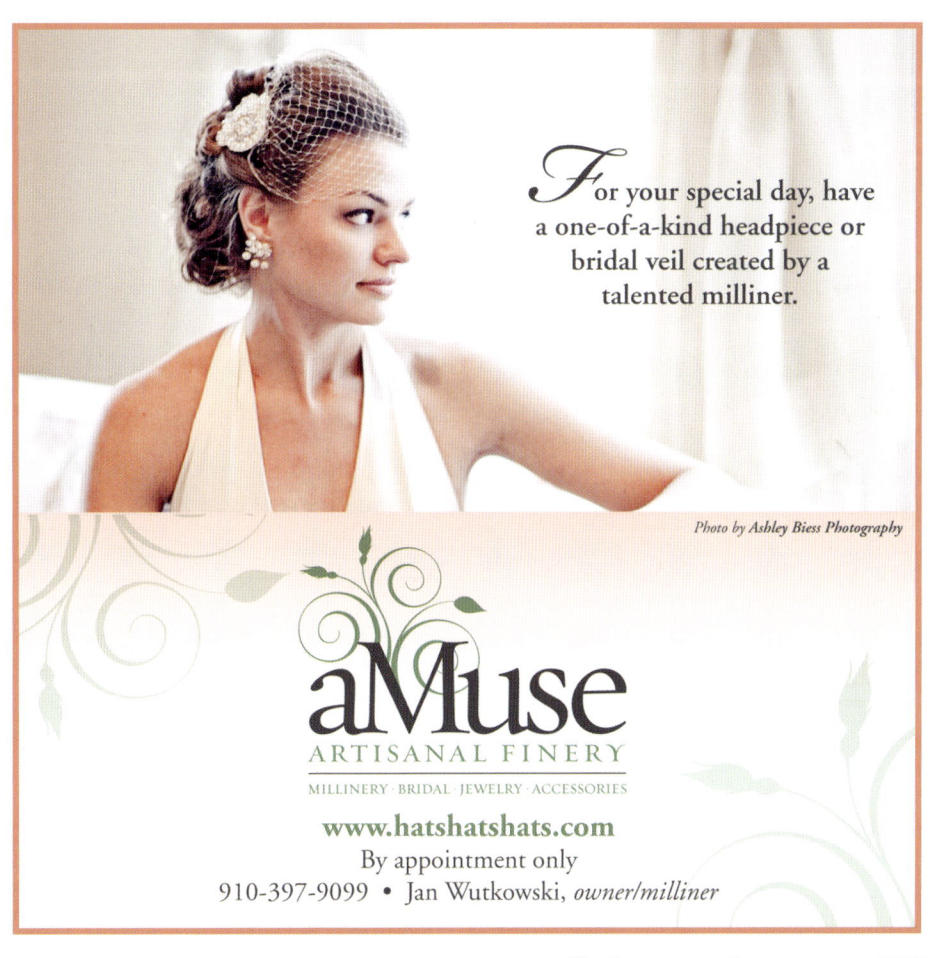

There are a host of good semi-private clubs in the Cape Fear area offering rounds of golf at moderate prices.

play golf year round

One of the advantages of living in Southeastern North Carolina that golfers enjoy is that the warming influence of the Gulf Stream and Atlantic Ocean enables them to play year round. We see sunshine most days, with annual temperatures averaging between 52 and 74 degrees.

Courses remain open so you can play even in January or February, when daytime temperatures average in the mid-50s.

Couple opportunity with more than 50 terrific public and semi-private courses, plus a selection of private ones, and you've got Golf Heaven, right here in the Greater Wilmington area.

Greens fees around these parts vary according to the season, location, exclusivity, course difficulty and desirability, but always represent good value. For 18 holes, you can expect to pay anywhere from $30 to more than $100, plus cart fee; average is $30-$40.

Packages are often a good deal and they're relatively easy to find, as are senior discounts and special group rates.

Feel like a challenge? Head for one of the top-tier courses designed by world-renowned pros. Maybe you're more in the mood for a relaxed round, driving your cart along winding paths through a picturesque plantation. How about navigating the sand dunes and skirting water hazards just for the fun of it? All of these options are available at relatively modest fees.

Regardless of your level of skill, you can find a course to your liking, in your price range, within a reasonable driving distance.

The courses we've detailed here welcome visitors and the normal rules apply: proper attire (no jeans, cutoffs, or T-shirts) is required and metal or ceramic spikes are not allowed.

Some of our favorite public or semi-private courses are characterized below and we've given you yardages from all the tees, as well as details on slope and rating. Enjoy!

BEAU RIVAGE GOLF & RESORT

Beau Rivage Golf and Resort, located on Carolina Beach Road, is a par 72, 18-hole course that earned a 4-star rating from *Golf Digest*. It is the only club in Wilmington with its own resort featuring spacious villas of 900 square feet overlooking the course. The villas are equipped with free wi-fi, wet bar, microwave, mini fridge and cable tv and stay and play packages are offered at moderate prices.

Individuals or groups can enroll in the Golf School that is available year round with either one day or three complete, intensive days of training available. The practice facilities include an elevated driving range, chipping and pitching area with a sand bunker and "rough" grass as well as a putting green.

Beau Rivage is always meticulously maintained, a good thing in a course that can prove challenging with its elevation changes of up to 75 feet, blind spots and water hazards.

PLAY HERE.

STAY HERE.

Wilmington's Premiere Golf Facility

Come test your luck at one of the most dramatically landscaped courses in the Coastal Carolinas. With countless elevation changes, blind shots, narrow fairways, tight doglegs and notoriously slick putting greens, Beau Rivage GC offers even the avid player a fun, yet challenging round.

Whether you're hitting the sticks for a quick nine holes, competing in a tournament match or staying overnight on a group getaway, pristine golf course conditions and first-class hospitality are always guaranteed. You'll feel right at home every time you visit... Make your escape today!

18-Hole Championship Golf Course - Complete Practice Facilities
Dixie's Pro Shop - *The Veranda* Bar & Grill - Swimming & Tennis
PGA Certfied Lessons & Instruction - Group Clinics & Camps
On-Site Guest Suites - Competitive "Stay+Play" Packages
Wide Variety of Club & Resort Memberships Available

Beau Rivage Golf & Resort
649 Rivage Promenade Wilmington, NC 28412
www.BeauRivageGolf.com
910.392.9021

BEAU RIVAGE Golf & Resort

NEVER Cart Path Only

play golf year round

Photo by G. Frank Hart Photography

Women enjoy playing many of the golf courses in our area.

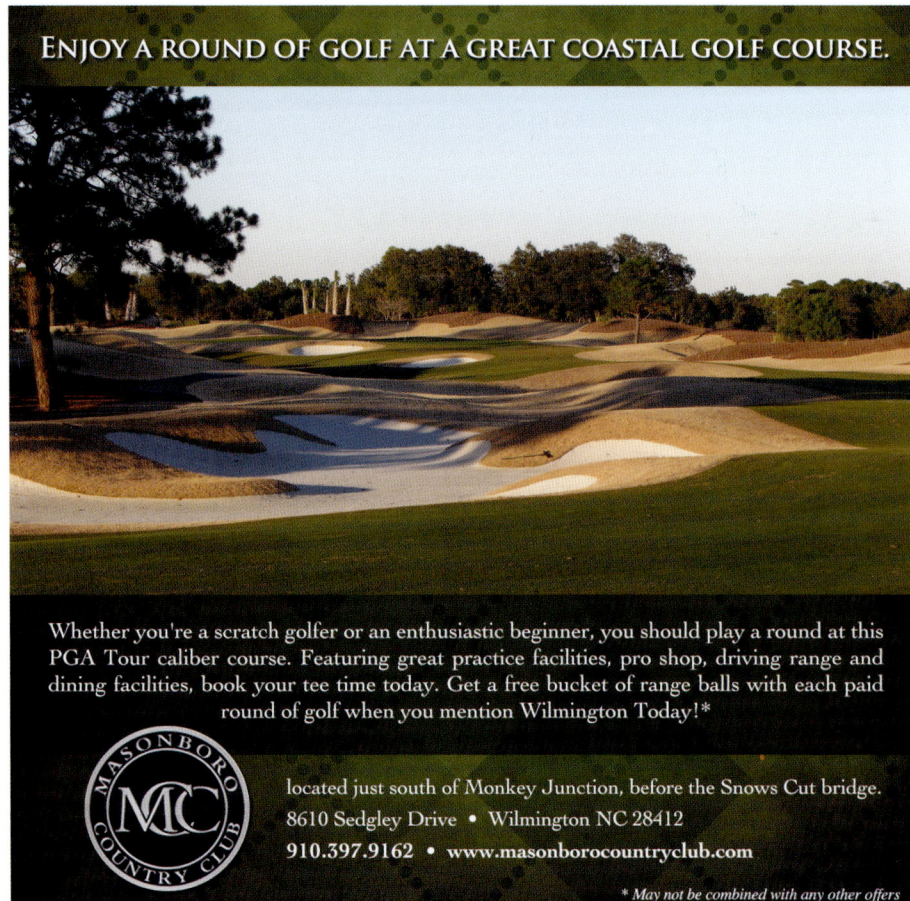

ENJOY A ROUND OF GOLF AT A GREAT COASTAL GOLF COURSE.

Whether you're a scratch golfer or an enthusiastic beginner, you should play a round at this PGA Tour caliber course. Featuring great practice facilities, pro shop, driving range and dining facilities, book your tee time today. Get a free bucket of range balls with each paid round of golf when you mention Wilmington Today!*

located just south of Monkey Junction, before the Snows Cut bridge.
8610 Sedgley Drive • Wilmington NC 28412
910.397.9162 • www.masonborocountryclub.com

*May not be combined with any other offers

128 ■ www.wilmingtontoday.com

The greens are outstanding and are known for their smoothness and speed. The course drains very quickly, which is a blessing in an area that can receive a lot of rainfall in a short period of time.

The Cape Fear River serves as the backdrop on eight different golf holes at Beau Rivage, which creates beautiful vistas throughout the course. The facility is semi-private and has very attractive rates, especially for a course of this caliber.

Beau Rivage has a beautiful clubhouse and dining facility and golf outings also are welcome at Beau Rivage.

649 Rivage Promenade
Wilmington, NC 28412
910-392-9021
800-628-7080

Head Professional: Greg Pitts
Superintendent: Wallace Chavis

Blue Tees: 6709 yards, 72.4/138
White Tees: 6166 yards, 70.1/133
Gold Tees: 5701 yards, 67.7/123
Green Tees: 5087 yards, 69.7/128
Red Tees: 4662 yards, 68.2/115

MASONBORO COUNTRY CLUB

Masonboro Country Club is home to a PGA Tour tournament caliber golf course. The semi-private club features one of the longest courses in the area, measuring 7,041 yards from the tips.

Bob Moore of JMP Golf Design Group, a well-known and highly regarded architect, crafted the course. No expense was spared in creating the facility. Masonboro is the closest golf facility to Carolina and Kure Beaches and is located south of Monkey Junction and north of Snow's Cut.

The immaculately manicured course features Mini-Verde Bermuda greens, 80 acres of turf newly sodded with 419 Bermuda grass, and the same fine white sand found at Augusta National. Unique natural elevation changes, berms and grassy shallows combine to create beautiful vistas.

Masonboro also features superb practice facilities, including a seven-acre driving range, a putting green and a short game practice area. The PGA staff at the club is happy to give lessons that will help golfers improve their games.

The pro shop at the Masonboro Country Club is very well stocked with apparel as well as equipment, including a fine selection of golf clubs and related merchandise.

The Tavern by the Green offers refreshing drinks and food that players enjoy either before or after they play. The restaurant and bar also is available for special events and tournaments are welcome at the club.

8610 Sedgley Drive
Wilmington, NC 28412
910-397-9162

Head Professional: Chad Wiebelhaus, PGA
Superintendent: Trent Venters

Black Tees: 7041, 76/147
Blue Tees: 6511, 73.9/138
Gold Tees: 6012, 71.6/133
Green Tees-Men: 5510, 69.7/124
Green Tees-Women: 5510, 75.2/137

ECHO FARMS GOLF & COUNTRY CLUB

Echo Farms, located just 10 minutes from Historic Downtown Wilmington, opened in 1974 with an 18-hole championship course designed by Gene Hamm. The facility changed dramatically when a major redesign of the course by British architect Ian Scott Taylor in 1998 gave it a more Scottish links feel.

Greens feature Tiff-Eagle Bermuda grass. Echo Farms is adjacent to the Cape Fear River and takes full advantage of the natural features of coastal terrain. Well-placed bunkers and water features provide a challenge for golfers of all skill levels.

The course offers four sets of tees and has a driving range with both grass and artificial tees. There is a practice putting green and separate chipping green surrounded by bunkers suited for all types of short game shots. Both private lessons and clinics are offered for players of all ages.

Echo Farms Golf & Country Club is semi-private. The Club has a very active tennis program with enthusiastic participants and an Olympic-size swimming pool. Membership rates offer a good value for families.

The Echo Farms Clubhouse is located in a renovated bottling barn, a reminder that the facility was built on what had previously been a dairy farm. The pro shop is stocked with equipment and apparel. A grille offering a variety of sandwiches and drinks is available for pre or post-match play.

4114 Echo Farms Boulevard
Wilmington, NC 28412
910-799-0324

Head Professional: Don E. Franklin
Superintendent: Brian Stachowicz

Gold Tees: 7021yards, 74.0/134
Blue Tees: 6629 yards, 72.5/130
White Tees: 5881 yards, 68.5/122
Red Tees: 4986 yards, 69.8/121

CAPE FEAR NATIONAL

The newest golf course in the Wilmington area is Cape Fear National, located in Brunswick Forest, the largest planned community recently started in Brunswick County.

Although the course just opened in April 2010, it is already enjoying great success. Cape Fear National was

Several clubs in Southeastern North Carolina offer excellent instruction by PGA or LPGA professionals.

first named one of *Golfweek's* best new courses in 2010, and then was honored as one of the ten best new courses by *Golf Magazine*.

Tim Cate, who is known for his attention to detail and imaginative routing, designed Cape Fear National. He has built a number of courses in the Carolinas that have won awards, but feels this is his best yet.

The course winds through heavily undulating land and sweeps past large expanses of maple, oak and magnolia trees as well as cypress and pines. There are very picturesque vistas too, with wildflowers in bloom throughout the course, abundant water features including three waterfalls, and several bridges cut through wetlands.

The driving range features grass hitting areas and there are practice putting and chipping areas too.

The large clubhouse at Cape Fear National has a fully stocked pro shop as well as both indoor and outdoor dining and/or bar areas. The club is happy to host golf outings and tournaments. It also is possible to rent the facility for such special events as rehearsal dinners, anniversary or birthday parties and family reunions.

Cape Fear National is easily accessible from downtown Wilmington, since it is located just five miles south on Highway 17 in Leland.

1281 Cape Fear National Drive
Leland, NC 28451
910-383-3283

Head Professional: Ron Thomson
Superintendent: Jim Hahn

Black Tees: 7217 yards, 74.5/143
Blue Tees: 6686 yards, 71.9/134
White Tees: 6195 yards, 69.8/127
Silver Tees: 5603 yards, 67.1/111
Green Tees: 4802 yards, 67.9/114

NORTH SHORE COUNTRY CLUB

You'll find North Shore Country Club located in Sneads Ferry just before the bridge to North Topsail Beach. That location contributes to the natural beauty and challenging play that are the hallmarks of this course.

Several holes are located along the Intracoastal Waterway, which usually brings a prevailing sea breeze into play. Inland holes offer a respite from that breeze and provide a distinctly different look and feel with the holes bordered by large, mature pine trees.

The course is always very well maintained, which definitely adds to its appeal. North Shore earned 4 stars from Golf Digest and was named one of the best places to play in 2008-09.

Among the amenities offered in the large clubhouse are a fully stocked pro shop, bar and restaurant. North Shore is available for such special events as wed-

Cape Fear National

Exclusive By Nature... Open To All

2010 GOLFWEEK'S BEST NEW COURSES

TEE TIMES: 888.342.3622

- The Wilmington Area's Newest Golfing Destination
- "Top 10 BEST NEW COURSES - 2010" - *Golf Magazine*
- 5.7 miles south of Downtown off Hwy 17

Directions: **CapeFearNational.com**
Real Estate: **BrunswickForest.com**

dings and parties too.

A Holiday Inn Express, located adjacent to the facility, works with North Shore Country Club to provide attractive packages for visitors who are interested in lodging and golf.

101 North Shore Drive
Sneads Ferry, NC 28460
910-327-2410

Head Professional: Mark Sorenson
Superintendent: Brian Williams

Blue Tees: 6866 yards, 73.1/135
White Tees: 6358 yards, 70.4/128
Yellow Tees-Men: 5636 yards, 67.4/116
Yellow Tees-Women: 5636 yards, 72.8/132

OLDE POINT GOLF AND COUNTRY CLUB

Located approximately two miles north of Castle Bay on US Highway 17 is Olde Point Golf and County Club. The facility is one of the oldest in eastern North Carolina, opening in 1975 with a design by Jerry Turner.

The course is a challenging layout that offers skilled players as well as beginning golfers a memorable experience. The 18-hole par 72 course winds through mature woodlands, past scenic lakes and ponds, and offers strategically placed fairway and greenside bunkers on every hole. The course is best known for Hole #11, a monster par 5 that requires three of a player's longest and best placed shots to reach the green in regulation, regardless of which of the five sets of tees are used.

Bermuda fairways and large Seashore Paspalum greens are meticulously maintained for year-round enjoyment. A fully stocked pro shop and large practice areas are open to the public and provide a great place to hone skills when there isn't enough time to play a round. Lessons and clinics are available by appointment.

Olde Point is a semi-private club with reasonable daily fees and several types of membership plans available.

513 Country Club Drive
Hampstead, NC 28443
910-270-2403

Head Professional: JoAnn Palazzo, LPGA

Superintendent: Michael McNulty

Blue Tees: 6913 yards, 74.2/136
Gold Tees: 6243 yards, 71.3/132
White Tees: 6008 yards, 69.6/127
Silver Tees: 5522 yards, 67.8/118
Red Tees: 5133 yards, 65.6/111

CASTLE BAY GOLF AND COUNTRY CLUB

Located two miles west of Highway 17 in Hampstead, an unincorporated town just north of Wilmington, you'll find a true Scottish style links course, Castle Bay Country Club. The course is a 20-minute drive from either Wrightsville Beach or Topsail Island and just a 10-minute drive from Figure Eight Island.

Castle Bay's 18-hole, par 72 course features five tee boxes, well placed bunkers, numerous ponds and other hazards that make club selection particularly important. The fairways are reasonably wide, but golfers will be punished for errant shots since the hazards can gobble up stray golf balls. The course also has acres of ever-changing, beautiful wetlands (unless you're in them) and wonderfully true greens, which many consider the best in Pender County.

Castle Bay, a semi-private club, has a fully stocked pro shop. The owner of the facility is an avid golfer himself and, partially as a result of that, sees that the course is in great shape year-round.

Players can hone their skills or warm up for a round on the driving range. They can also sharpen their short games by utilizing the putting green or by hitting to a separate green from the sand trap and chipping areas.

Castle Bay's pro shop is located in a castle, albeit a new one, and there is a shaded patio overlooking the course for relaxing after the round. Golf tournaments and outings are welcome.

107 Links Court
Hampstead, NC 28443
910-270-1978

Superintendent: Allen L. Smith

Gold Tees: 6698 yards, 71.3/130
Blue Tees: 6328 yards, 69.2/125
White Tees: 5793 yards, 67.4/117
Green Tees: 5466 yards, 65.5/107
Red Tees: 4717 yards, 66.6/110

It's never to soon to introduce kids to a game they can enjoy for a lifetime.

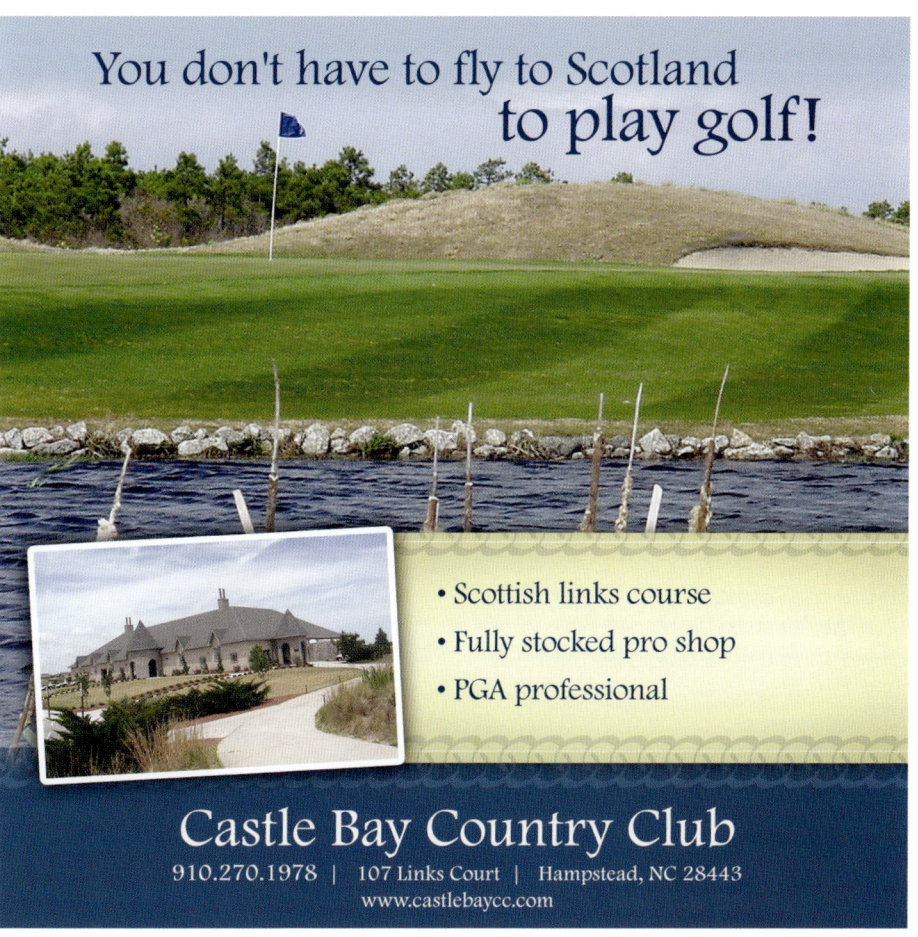

The Wilmington area features numerous restaurants that serve delicious, fresh, local food.

a world of food is available

When you're hungry, you'll find plenty of restaurants where you can indulge your cravings. Southern traditions, world flavors, local ingredients and imaginative chefs season the smorgasbord set before you in the Cape Fear region and surrounding beaches.

The area has been a culinary paradise since the first explorers saw foot-long oysters and wild grapes along the shoreline here some 500 years ago. Wilmington's port city status brought edibles and influences from around the globe. Rich soils and so much fresh seafood provided added bounty that shaped an eclectic cuisine like no other.

The local foods cooperative Feast Down East makes sure chefs have premium ingredients from area farms. Staff and volunteers connect cooks and devoted growers, assuring diners flavorful ingredients – organic and sustainably raised. Can't decide what to eat? Mix it up. Creative chefs are rooted in classics, but they're known for inventing irresistible combinations. And it's not just them. Master bartenders stir the perfect Old Fashioned or unusual martinis. Breweries pour nationally recognized craft beers, and wine flows from award-winning lists. No worries if you're not an oenophile. Seasoned sommeliers guide you. Casual and fine-dining establishments pepper the landscape, but no need to dress up or break the bank at either. The buzz-phrase here is "upscale casual." Khaki pants are fine even at the fanciest restaurants, and affordable prices are everywhere. Beautiful weather most days of the year mean you can dine outdoors in gorgeous settings. Choose sidewalk café tables or a pier extending over the sea. Sit on a riverside deck and watch boats lumber by at sunset. Relax, feel at home and remember to save room for dessert at these restaurants, where the food is always good, the prices are great and you'll leave satisfied.

Ruth's Chris Steak House

Hankering for a USDA Prime steak? Ruth's Chris Steak House in downtown Wilmington's Hilton Wilmington Riverside hotel is the place. Enjoy your favorite cut in the main dining room overlooking the Cape Fear River and the magnificent Battleship North Carolina. Selections include filet, strip, rib-eye, T-bone and a porterhouse for two. The lamb, pork and veal chops are delectable. Seafood, including a huge, three-pound live Maine lobster, is available. Picking just one or two side dishes is difficult with nine vegetable presentations, potatoes prepared eight ways and several delicious salads. Begin the evening with numerous appetizer choices. Pair it all with something from the extensive, award-winning wine list or choose a cocktail or craft beers. Caramelized banana cream pie's white chocolate banana custard is just one of many sweet ways to end a meal. The inviting lounge opens at 3 p.m. daily with dinner beginning at 4 p.m. on Sunday and 5 p.m. all other days. Check the separate lounge menu as well as special offers several days a week on cocktails, wine and the bar menu. A private room for special gatherings affords a beautiful view.

Ruth's Recipe

HOLD THE ELEVATOR.
FORGET INSULTS. REMEMBER COMPLIMENTS.
KEEP DATE NIGHT SACRED.

RUTH'S CHRIS STEAK HOUSE
U.S. PRIME

THIS IS HOW IT'S DONE.℠

Wilmington - Hilton Wilmington Riverside | 910.343.1818 | ruthschris-wilmington.com

a world of food is available

Devoted farmers provide local food

Residents of southeastern North Carolina are lucky to live in a place where the state government not only recognizes the importance of fresh food but also supports it through the North Carolina Department of Agriculture. The agency shows off the state's bounty at events and online via its Goodness Grows in North Carolina and Got to Be NC programs. Visit those websites to find out where to buy local produce at stores, farmers markets, roadside stands and right off the farm. Seafood is part of the North Carolina harvest. Pristine coastal waters provide an abundance of fresh seafood. More than 100 edible species are taken off our shores. Our shellfish aquaculture operations provide fine oysters, too.

Pembroke's

One place that takes advantage of honest farm-to-table fare is Pembroke's, a great restaurant located at The Forum shopping Center.

A native North Carolinian who grew up in the state's coastal plain and worked for top Charleston, S.C., chef Sean Brock, Pembroke's chef James Doss describes his cooking style as "seasonally inspired, ingredient-driven, Southern cuisine." He sources local produce, meat and seafood for the menu, which changes daily. Cooks might fashion boiled peanut hummus with benne crackers. Chowder may showcase fresh clams, roasted potatoes, winter peas and Andouille sausage. Pimento cheese crostini has featured old-fashioned hoop cheese and brown sugar sherry gastrique. Salads might include mixed seasonal greens topped with blue cheese, toasted sesame seeds and duck confit, all dressed with champagne vinaigrette.

Don't miss wood-grilled chicken from the rotisserie, which you can see in action from a seat by the open kitchen. Chefs work behind a Plexiglas partition, and their nightly dance is an engaging show. Watch them craft fine steaks, fresh seafood and some of the city's finest pork dishes. The chef insists on the best produce and meats. His preference is organic, sustainable and humanly raised.

Everything here is made from scratch, and seeing cooks at work and smelling the delicious aromas that rise from the kitchen make this restaurant feel like home. Choose a seat with a kitchen view or tuck into a cozy corner. Honey brown wooden slats, set horizontally, divide the dining room. Dark wood and red brick décor feels somewhere between comfy farmhouse and toasty lodge, all with a just-right level of cool. A private dining area is perfect for groups. A friendly, partially enclosed bar – with truly comfy stools – is perfect for a toasty bourbon apple tart or one of the craft bar's various takes on the Old Fashioned. The Porky blends bacon bourbon, maple syrup, cherry, orange and bitters. Outdoor seating is available on the front patio.

Be sure to make a date for Sunday brunch and bring a strong appetite. Creamy sausage gravy coats fresh buttermilk biscuits. Tender duck confit, sautéed mushrooms and smoked cheddar fill an omelet. You'll find shrimp and grits; fried chicken with waffles, honey and a dash of hot sauce; and pancakes with spiced molasses butter and house cured bacon, but the kitchen turns out a mean hoop cheddar cheeseburger with smoked ham and

Seasonally inspired, locally sourced Southern cuisine

PEMBROKE'S

1125A Military Cutoff Road, Wilmington NC 28405
910-239-9153 ▸ www.pembrokescuisine.com
open Tuesday-Sunday
5:00 p.m. - close
Live music Friday and Saturday night

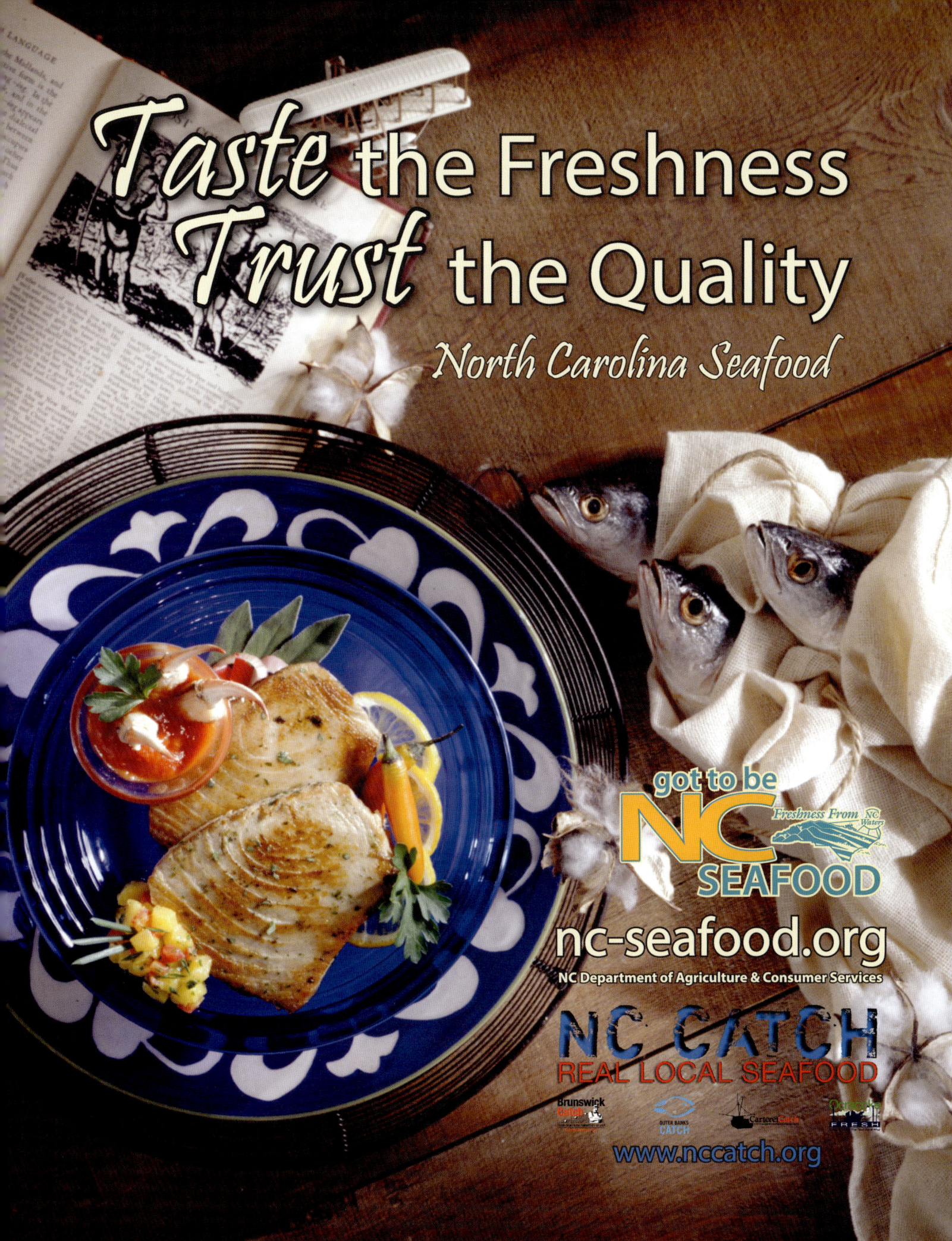

Many diners particularly enjoy sharing a delicious assortment of sushi.

a side of fries, too. Pembroke's is open for dinner Tuesday through Sunday. Friday and Saturday nights may bring live music, never too loud for conversation. Sunday brunch happens 10 a.m. to 3 p.m., usually with a serving of live, soft jazz.

Bento Box

The Forum shopping center on Military Cutoff, near Wrightsville Beach, hosts Bento Box, recognized as Wilmington's premier sushi restaurant. Although, Bento Box is frequently recognized as Wilmington's best sushi restaurant, it's also tops for delectable Asian appetizers, small plates and full-size entrees. The bar's sake selection is outstanding. Everything is prepared with great skill and care from the highest-quality ingredients.

Sit at the sushi bar to watch the masters at work. Consider the signature Delicious Roll, made with either spicy tuna or salmon twirled with avocado, seaweed salad, wasabi tobikko, sesame seeds and crisp tempura crumbles. Two Bento Box signature hot sauces come on the side. The Totally Tuna suits those watching their carbs. Tuna, avocado, wasabi tobikko and sesame soy are wrapped in a thin cucumber sheet, all served with ponzu sauce. The Killer Carrot roll has asparagus, scallions, avocado and shredded carrot with spicy kolchijan, the production drizzled with chili oil. Choose numerous rice less and vegetarian rolls. Gluten-free soy sauce is available. Any roll is delicious, but better yet, ask owner/chef Lee Grossman to customize sushi for you.

Don't miss Thai, Vietnamese, Korean and Japanese specialties. Pork belly lettuce wraps are crispy mother lodes. There's pork belly lo mein, too. Fork-tender Wagyu boneless short ribs are braised with shiitake and ginger and served over wasabi mashed potatoes, all crowned with ginger demi-glace and a wave of tempura-fried fresh kale. Vietnamese ginger beef is a beef tenderloin and vegetable stir-fry in ginger sauce. Pickled sweet red onions and crispy potato straws crown the mix. Banzai chicken is stuffed with sweet potato, asparagus and cheddar cheese and then wrapped in a spring roll, flash fried and served with teriyaki dipping sauce. Oh-so-crispy Japanese fried chicken, marinated in sake, ginger and soy sauce and dusted with potato starch, is gluten-free, as are many items on the menu. Oftentimes, diners choose several dishes and share them to enjoy all the many flavors.

Save room for a chocolate potsticker. Each deep-fried wonton package holds a warm, melty, handmade, Belgian dark chocolate truffle. A delicious caramel dipping sauce comes on the side. You may order just one truffle, but why would you?

The dining room's cool gray and chrome tones lend an exciting urban feel. Hear the trickle of stone waterfalls and, sometimes, live music on the large patio, perfect for warm evenings.

The restaurant is open 11:30 a.m. to 9 p.m. Monday through Wednesday, 11:30 a.m. to 10 p.m. Thursday and Friday and 5 to 10 p.m. Saturday. Chef closes on Sunday so he and the staff can have quality family time.

Mayfaire Town Center

For many people, dinner and a movie are the perfect match. The largest movie complex in Wilmington is at Mayfaire Town Center, on Military Cutoff Road just north of Eastwood Road near Wrightsville Beach. Sixteen screens show first-run movies, and lots of great restaurants are a short walk away.

Tokyo 101

Tokyo 101 is a popular Japanese restaurant in Mayfaire Town Center, just steps away from Cinema 16. An extensive sushi menu and traditional Japanese food are served in a beautiful, serene setting. Be sure to check weekday lunch specials. The prices are fantastic. Tokyo 101's bar showcases different cocktail specials every day. Special sushi prices come Monday through Thursday. Hibachi choices are vegetables, chicken, steak, and five types of seafood, offered either singly or as combinations. Like noodles? The kitchen sends out udon soup and yakisoba creations stir-fried with chicken

Sushi Bar & Asian Kitchen

The Bento Box is the culmination of Asian street food with traditional dishes from Japan, Thailand, Vietnam, China, and Korea. The focal point of The Bento Box is the sushi bar where guests can interact with Chef Lee Grossman and his team of chefs to create a unique dining experience. Knowledgeable food lovers agree that The Bento Box offers the best sushi and sashimi in Southeastern North Carolina.

Enjoy the private dining room for an intimate small group, the outdoor patio with its zen rock garden and water fountains, the sake lounge, or just a quiet corner of the dining room. The Bento Box sources as much organic and sustainably grown product as possible and features salmon from Scotland, hamachi from Kyushu Japan, and free range chicken, organic vegetables, and natural pork from North Carolina.

Monday, Tuesday, Wednesday 11:30 a.m.-9:00 p.m. • Thursday and Friday 11:30 a.m.-10:00 p.m.
Saturday 5:00 p.m.-10:00 p.m. • Closed Sunday to enjoy time with the family.

The Bento Box at the Forum
1121L Military Cutoff Road • Wilmington, NC 28405
910-509-0774 • www.bentoboxsushi.com
http://www.facebook.com/pages/Wilmington-NC/The-Bento-Box/70036701857

or seafood. Deep-fried shrimp-and-crab-stuffed jalapenos are among dishes with a fusion feel. The large menu lists soups and salads, a vast array of appetizers and myriad sushi, some raw, some cooked. The restaurant offers gluten-free choices, too. Portions are generous, and most people wind up taking quite a lot home. Tokyo 101 is available for catering, and they are happy to provide delivery service. There also is a moderately priced children's menu for kids under age 12. A tranquil water wall is among the dining room's lovely features.

An outdoor seating area opens when weather permits. Diners who sit at the sushi bar get to see chefs at work. The restaurant opens at 11:30 a.m. Monday-Saturday and at noon Sunday. Both lunch and dinner are served, but keep in mind that the restaurant is closed 2:30 to 5:30 p.m. on weekdays.

The Melting Pot

The Melting Pot is a fondue restaurant located directly across the street from Tokyo 101 at Mayfaire Town Center. It is a fun place to share a meal with friends and family. Many people come here to celebrate a new romance, a birthday or anniversary, or just a night out while the babysitter is in charge. Often diners choose the four-course experience, which includes cheese fondue, salad, entree and dessert. Others prefer just cheese fondue paired with a glass of wine. Still others find that after a movie (Cinema 16 is a short walk away), cravings can be satisfied with chocolate fondue, which is even better accompanied by a wonderful full-bodied red wine. Cheese fondues include Traditional Swiss (Gruyere and Emmenthaler, white wine, garlic, nutmeg, lemon and Kirschwasser) and zesty Fiesta's cheddar blended with lager beer, jalapeño peppers and salsa. Start meals with one of four fresh salads. Several entree selections range from filet mignon to Atlantic salmon to a seafood trio. Diners may also decide how they would like their dishes prepared. Four cooking styles include Mojo Caribbean-seasoned bouillon with fresh-garlic flavor and citrus flair. Four-course experiences include a cheese fondue, salad, premium entrees and chocolate fondue. The question is which chocolate fondue. Eight are offered, including a create-your-own op-

tion. Perhaps the wisest approach is to start at the top, then work down the list on return visits.

Individual entrees start at $15.50 and four-course combinations begin at $29.95. The Melting Pot has many wines, numerous beers and a full bar. The restaurant opens at 5 p.m. seven days a week and for lunch on Saturday and Sunday. The Melting Pot also has a separate room that would be a perfect spot for a special celebration. Birthday parties, anniversary gatherings, business dinners, rehearsal dinners and small wedding receptions would be suitable in the space that seats from 16-32 guests.

Port Land Grille

Recognized for many years as one of Wilmington's best restaurants, Port Land Grille is a class act from cocktail to dessert. It is known nationally, too, recently receiving a Distinguished Restaurants of North America Award of Excellence. Local, visitors and the famous (Wilmington is home to a busy movie studio) relish well-spaced tables and a warm, stylish ambiance. The restaurant's long-standing reputation is thanks to outstanding service and the extraordinary dishes by chef/owner Shawn Wellersdick. He began offering farm-to-table fare years before it was cool. Some selections are from the "port," for instance pan-seared, wild-caught grouper over blue crab meat, English pea, pancetta risotto, butter-wilted baby organic spinach and a roma tomato, saffron, basil, melted sweet onion "fondue" sauce. Other selections are from the "land," such as the chef's personal favorite: a pork porterhouse chop served alongside roasted butternut squash, balsamic glazed cabbage and "red neck" potato gnocchi with heirloom pork barbecue. Savory bacon jam and sweet and tangy balsamic plum barbecue sauce finish the presentation. Appetizers include the restaurant's famous Red Neck Eggroll filled with housemade pulled pork barbecue and Southern-style local collard greens. A mango and fresh mint dipping sauce comes on the side. Also popular is Shawn's Smooth Pate of Chicken, Duck and Rabbit Liver made with cognac and pistachios and served with quince preserves, crostini, capers, diced red onion, cornichons and wholegrain mustard. Changing seasons and the chef's imagination regularly bring new selections and tweak more regular offerings. Don't miss soft-shell crab season at Port Land Grille. The chef is a master with these fresh delicacies. Port Land Grille also presents snacks, tapas-style plates to share, homemade soups and "not your ordinary salads." The roasted beets, baby organic kale, fennel and gold beet "carpaccio" salad comes with candied walnuts, boursin cheese, fennel pollen and vanilla bean-clover honey-citrus vinaigrette. Find room for dessert, especially the famous and oh-so-tall, caramel-drizzled coconut layer cake filled with mango coulis. Sample classic and signature cocktails from the bar, which has a view of the kitchen. A remarkable wine list, with labels you'll find no place else in the area, enhances meals, and servers really know their stuff when describing, pairing and pouring wine. Port Land Grille opens for dinner at 5:30 p.m. Tuesday-Saturday.

Jerry's Restaurant

The shopping strip where Jerry's restaurant is located won't grab you, but this restaurant's food and service will. Jerry's is nearly hidden at the crossroads of Eastwood Drive and Wrightsville Avenue just before you drive across the drawbridge to Wrightsville Beach. Locals and visitors are loyal to this restaurant, which has been around for years. Chefs are devoted, too, including executive toque Steven Powell, who started his cooking career at Jerry's when he was just 17. He left for culinary school and posts at top North Carolina restaurants, but returned here and has stuck around, becoming executive chef in 2010. He and his kitchen crew prepare scrumptious from-scratch soups and chalkboard specials daily, the offerings blending classic preparations with Southern touches. Starters include quail breasts with sundried cherries over Southern collard greens with crispy smoked bacon and port wine-brown sugar sauce. For dinner, the chateaubriand is the most flavorful and tender in Wilmington. The goat cheese-crusted grilled grouper with roasted tomatoes, buttered asparagus, whipped potatoes and honey-lemon aioli is superb. There's butter-grilled filet mignon, rosemary-dijon grilled rack of lamb and Jerry's popular crab imperial-stuffed flounder with

lemon-caper beurre blanc. If it all seems so rich, don't fret. Half portions are available for diners with smaller appetites, meaning you'll have room for one of the luscious desserts. The restaurant has a full bar and an extensive wine list with prices from moderate to princely. Servers are friendly, knowledgeable, professional and attentive. Jerry's opens at 6 p.m. daily for dinner. Remember that the restaurant's owner, Jerry Rouse, has more than three decades of catering experience. If you need a caterer for a special event, Jerry's is the place to call.

Banks Channel

Part pub, part formal dining room, and serving dinner, late-night eats and weekend brunch, Banks Channel, on Causeway Drive, has something for everyone. Televisions, a friendly bar, traditional pub tables and two pool tables fill the pub and grill in front. Linen-draped tables appoint the separate, more formal dining room. Dishes span casual to upscale, too. Brunch means eggs any way or bacon-wrapped filet with two eggs and fried green tomatoes. Dress down with half-pound burgers, a seafood steamed platter, Caribbean jerk wings, a Philly cheesesteak pizza or signature sandwiches. Don't miss homemade red potato chips and jicama slaw.

Blue jeans are just as welcome when you're craving something fancier, say creamy shrimp and scallop fra diavolo with red peppers, garlic, cilantro and parmesan cheese in creamy tomato sauce. Fried or seared crab cakes come with creamy spinach red pepper orzo. That bacon-wrapped filet is served for dinner, too. Get a surf-and-turf version with shrimp, snow crab legs or a crab cake. Banks Channel offers daily food and drink specials.

Each day brings a different discount for pitchers or buckets of beer as well as specials on individual labels and assorted cocktails. The restaurant is open 4 p.m. to 2 a.m. Monday-Friday and 10 a.m. to 2 a.m. Saturday and Sunday. The kitchen offers after-hours eats until 1:30 a.m. If you're a Burt Reynolds fan, ask about the annual birthday bash in honor of the actor. Banks Channel offers buffet or tableside banquet service, as well, accommodating special occasions and business events.

Bluewater Waterfront Grill

Bluewater Waterfront Grill overlooks a beautiful marina just over Wrightsville Beach's Causeway Bridge, what locals call "the first bridge," as you approach town. The sprawling, two-story restaurant, with both indoor and outdoor seating, offers casual American food and friendly service. Being so close to the shore, seafood is, of course, a specialty. Start meals with classic shrimp cocktail or coconut shrimp with dark rum marmalade dipping sauce. The sandwich menu lists lobster rolls, fish tacos and burgers. When soft shell crabs are in season, look for them deep-fried and in a sandwich. Delicious! Entrees touch land and sea, with baby back ribs, grilled rib-eye steaks, citrus-glazed scallops, seafood lasagna, a fried seafood platter and a mixed grill featuring mahi, salmon and shrimp. Daily specials are other good bets. A full bar serves all sorts of cocktails and beer. Wine is poured by the glass or bottle. Reserve beautiful private rooms with stunning views, especially at sunset, for parties, special occasions or business meetings. Bluewater is open 11 a.m. to 11 p.m. every day of the week.

Oceanic Restaurant

This South Lumina Avenue gem sits three stories high right on the shore. Indoor seating features huge picture windows. Dine right over the ocean on Crystal Pier, an old-fashioned-style wooden length furnished with umbrella tables and room to stroll. Oceanic serves lunch and dinner daily, as well as Sunday brunch. The restaurant is known as a classic seafood house specializing in fresh, local seafood, broiled or lightly breaded and fried, a recipe famously called "Calabash style." Creamy she-crab soup, the Bloody Mary shrimp cocktail or Cajun bacon-wrapped shrimp with fresh corn salsa are some of the wonderful ways to start a meal. Salads, fried flounder, fried seafood baskets, and several types of sandwiches, including a crab melt, are lunch choices. Sunday brunch serves three-egg omelets, French toast and "deluxe scrambled eggs" with bacon, cheddar and spring onions, home-fried potatoes and fresh fruit on the side. Dinner fare includes crab-stuffed shrimp, miso-glazed salmon, seafood paella and

Features the best of the land, sea and vine in a casual bistro atmosphere.
Open seven days from 6 pm.

Jerry Rouse, Owner
7220 Wrightsville Avenue Wilmington, NC 28405
jerry@jerrysfoodandwine.com

Reservations encouraged. 910.256.8847
www.jerrysfoodandwine.com

Feeding Locavores Daily.

Family owned, locally operated, LM Restaurants feeds every craving, from fresh, never frozen burgers, to local seafood & produce. Come check out our culinary creations & relax with our hospitable staff in Leland, Wilmington & Wrightsville Beach.

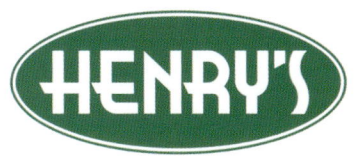  

Crave fresh. Crave LM Restaurants.

LMRest.com

plenty of landlubber fare. New York strip with bourbon pecan butter is among steak, chicken and pasta selections.

A take-out menu, including extensive family-style, to-go selections, is available. A full bar and impressive wine list are offered. Oceans is open 11 a.m. to 11 p.m. Monday-Saturday and 10 a.m. to 10 p.m. Sunday.

South Beach Grill

South Beach Grill is a delightful spot for people and boat watching. The restaurant's location on Lumina Avenue in the center of Wrightsville Beach puts it walking distance to both the beach and boats on Banks Channel. Enjoy the indoor and outdoor seating, both with a water view, for lunch and dinner. The dinner menu, highlighting seafood, meats and pasta, reads fine dining but no need to dress up. Casual attire is fine. Sip a cocktail, beer or wine while chefs carefully craft your meal. One white wine benefits the area's Sea Turtle Conservancy. South Beach Grill features numerous daily specials. Choices depend on what's fresh. Recent suggestions included coconut-crusted local tuna, a shrimp po' boy panini, seafood lasagna, house-smoked salmon and chef James Rivenbark's tender, rib-sticking meatloaf. Check some South Beach traditions, including popular appetizers such as seafood nachos and fried pickles dipped in a secret batter recipe. Grouper Linda has been on the dinner menu for 17 years for good reason. Pan-seared, pecan-crusted grouper is served with backfin crab meat, spring onions and cream sherry beurre blanc. Flounder Francais is a simpler affair with the fresh fish sautéed with a classic lemon parsley butter sauce. Plantation Chicken features sweet tea-marinated chicken breast stuffed with prosciutto, thyme, fresh spinach and Monterey jack cheese. The chicken is coated in panko bread crumbs and pan-fried, then finished with a pan jus and red pepper veloute sauce. South Beach is known for ultra-fresh salads, which may be topped with fried oysters or other seafood. A bowl of the daily soup with a salad is a nice, light lunch. Lots of appetizers, salads and sandwiches are on the lunch menu. Whether you choose a traditional BLT or a crispy fried clam roll with fried Atlantic clams, Monterey jack cheese, cilantro tarter sauce, tomatoes and slaw on a buttered Kaiser, don't forget the house potato chips with chipotle ranch dipping sauce. Vegan and gluten-free plates are available at lunch and dinner. South Beach Grill is open 11 a.m. to 10 p.m. Monday-Saturday and until 9 p.m. on Sunday.

Oceans Restaurant

When the sun splashes its vibrant rays over Wrightsville Beach, Oceans is a great place to be. Perched on the Holiday Inn Resort mezzanine, off North Lumina Avenue, the full bar, dining room and outdoor deck offer a poolside Atlantic Ocean view. Start the day with coffee and breakfast or stop in for lunch, when you can munch various appetizers, tuck into a salad or dig into a grilled burger with pimento cheese, bacon and tomatoes. Open with potato cakes, crab and spinach dip or an appetizer portion of unusual shrimp and grits. Sautéed Carolina shrimp join garlic, tomatoes, bacon and mushroom in parmesan cream sauce over fried cheddar grits cakes. Poached scallop salad features the shellfish over fresh arugula with prosciutto, spiced pecans, fresh strawberries and raspberry vinaigrette. Seafood, steaks, ribs, chicken and pasta are added to the menu at dinner. Chefs crust mahi with macadamia nuts, sauté the fish and then finish it with citrus buerre blanc. Crab-stuffed flounder is roasted before being napped with creamy lobster sauce. Braised short ribs, beef tenderloin, pretzel-crusted chicken and baked penne pasta alfredo with grilled chicken, tomatoes and mushrooms are other options. You can even get a pizza. Choose from a large selection of toppings or a house specialty, say the Moore's Inlet pizza with seasoned shrimp and crab, mozzarella, fresh basil and fresh tomato slices. Oceans is open to the public. Breakfast, lunch and dinner are served daily. Hours are 6:30 a.m. to 10 p.m.

Ogden Tap Room

Beer lovers rejoiced when the craft beer pub Ogden Tap Room opened recently in the north Wilmington community of Ogden. A long, silver pipe behind the handsome stone bar shows off 40 taps, and the Southern-leaning food menu has a compliment for each beer. Suds come from all over the United States, and the list is regularly updated with new selections. Many are from North Carolina, including of-late Weeping Willow Wit from Mother Earth Brewing in Kinston, Peoples Porter from Foothills Brewing Co. in Winston-Salem and Thunderstruck Coffee Porter from Highland Brewing Co. in Asheville. Southern Tier 2X IPA from Southern Tier Brewing Co. in New York pleases "hop heads" who like beer with a bite. Familiar Pabst Blue Ribbon made in Wisconsin and Sam Adams lagers from Boston, Mass., suit drinkers seeking old reliables. The big Ogden Tap Room sign is easy to see from Market Street. On warm days, you'll notice lots of people sitting outside. Just as many are inside the slate and wood dining room/bar. This pub garnered a loyal following quickly. Beer, easy décor and friendly service reeled them in as did the food. Hot salted pretzels, beer-battered Buffalo shrimp and Cajun fried frog legs served with caper aioli are ideal bar snacks to pair with suds. Strawberry jalapeno sauce is on the wings list. Soups include chili, and a few salads populate

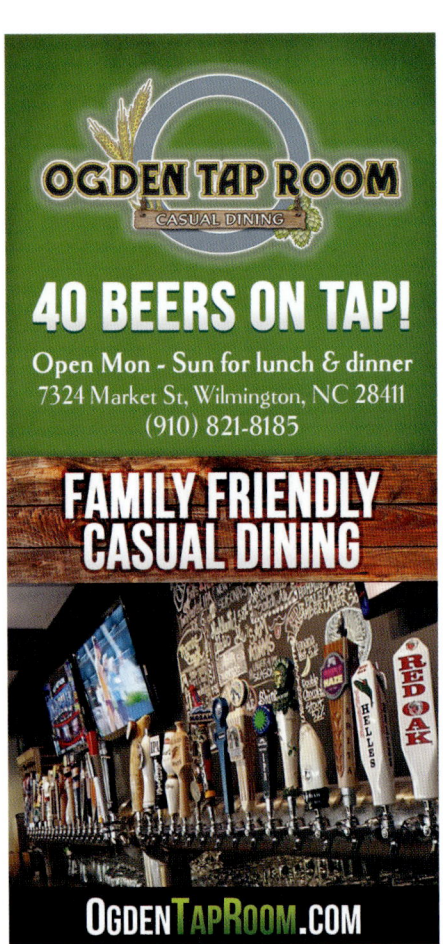

the menu. Numerous sandwiches feature pork loin, curried chicken salad, fried bologna and New Orleans' famous muffuletta jammed with ham, salami, mozzarella and olive tapenade. Brats and beer-seasoned kraut, chicken and waffles and fried fish round out offerings, which the kitchen likes to change up periodically. Beer may be the focus, but Ogden Tap Room feels like a neighborhood restaurant suited to singles, families and groups of friends. No one feels lonely in this welcoming atmosphere, set with booths, tables and televisions for game days. Ogden Tap Room is open 11 a.m. to midnight Monday-Thursday, 11 a.m. to 1 a.m. Friday and Saturday and noon to midnight Sunday.

Catch

In north Wilmington, on Market Street near Gordon Road, find one of not just Wilmington's but the region's most popular restaurants. Catch is a "modern seafood" spot sought by locals, visitors and celebrities. Famous names like Gwyneth Paltrow, Robert Downey Jr. and Gary Cole have dined here.

They come for chef/owner Keith Rhodes' unique take on seafood and more. He has been nominated for a "Best Southeast Chef" James Beard Award, the so-called "Oscars of the food world." Paltrow requested and received a private cooking lesson at Catch. Rhodes also was selected to compete among America's best cooks on the popular Bravo TV show "Top Chef" Season 9.

Local ingredients, including the freshest seafood, American Southern cooking and international influences drive the Catch menu. Asian cuisine especially charms the chef, hence the popular Firecracker Shrimp's plump tempura fried shrimp with spicy cognac cream. Ginger-zested crab cakes were deemed the best at the 2011 N.C. Seafood Festival chef competition in Morehead City, N.C. Another favorite, Angry Lobster, is a nearly two-pound, whole lobster wok-fried in sweet chili basil sauce and served over crunchy, fried rice noodles and soft Israeli couscous blended with wakame slivers.

The menu is subject to change, depending on what seafood and produce are in season and what sparks the chef's imagination.

Seasonally inspired, ingredient driven, Southern cuisine sourced from local farms and fisheries.

Rx Restaurant and Bar
Located in the Historic Hall's Drugstore
421 Castle St.
Wilmington, NC
(910) 399-3080
www.rxwilmington.com

Seafood isn't all you'll find here. Stir-fried bok choy might accompany duck confit and pimento macaroni and cheese. Smoked paprika may season Korean-style baby back ribs served alongside parmesan fries. Catch's famous North Carolina sweet potato salad has recently come with baby spinach, goat cheese, dried cranberries, toasted hemp seeds and honey shallot vinaigrette.

Catch is a truly family affair. Chef Rhodes operates the restaurant with his wife, Angela. Their daughter makes desserts.

The bar serves lovely cocktails, including the Raspberry Sake Kiss and an off-beat margarita brightened by fresh, muddled cucumber and a glass rimmed with salt, black pepper and ancho chili powder.

Sit in the sky blue dining room hung with huge photographs of coastal scenes or enjoy the sunset-hued bar, where fresh herbs used by the kitchen are grown in a hydroponic garden. Catch opens for dinner at 5:30 p.m. Monday-Saturday. Don't forget Catch the food truck. Find it around town for lunch, dinner and late-night and at various festivals. You may also book the truck for private events.

Rx Restaurant

Rx Restaurant in downtown Wilmington, at Castle and Fifth Streets, is a true farm-to-table experience. The name was inspired by the building's former tenant, Hall's Drug Store, one of Wilmington's oldest businesses. A meal here feels and tastes good. Chef James Doss, who grew up in North Carolina's coastal plain, describes the cooking as "seasonally inspired, ingredient-driven, Southern cuisine." He sources local produce, meat and seafood for the menu, which changes daily. You'll see the names of farmers and fishermen in nearly every entrée description. Herbs are grown in the restaurant's windowsills, and the kitchen makes everything from scratch, including biscuits, bacon jam, pimento cheese, Andouille sausage and the popular shrimp and grits with bacon, braised fennel, mushrooms, garlic, peppers and onions. Rx cooks love pork, as evidenced by fine charcuterie; crispy, deep-fried, Buffalo-style pig ears that locals can't resist; and thick pork chops served with assorted local vegetables like tender baby limas Southerners call "butter beans." That's not to say there's no beef. Doss sources the best for New York strip, rib-eye and a tartare that he might serve with fried oysters, nasturtium, tarragon-horseradish aioli and pickled onions. Sunday brunch may bring bacon cinnamon rolls, a triple-decker chili cheeseburger or white sweet potato bisque crowned with duck confit, blue chevre and brown butter crumble. Special touches give homespun desserts a certain sophistication, say bourbon ice cream atop warm, sticky toffee pudding. Friendly staff and impressive bartenders enhance the rustic but stylish honey-wood dining room. Local art hangs on the walls.

The wide bar is a fun place to dine or sip wine, a North Carolina beer or an Rx signature cocktail, perhaps the Crab Apple with Bulliet bourbon, Rx's own honey syrup, Crabbies Ginger Beer and a splash of bitters. At $10, Rx has one of the area's most reasonable corkage fees. Rx dinner hours are 5 to 10 p.m. Tuesday-Thursday, 5 to 10:30 p.m. Friday and Saturday, and 5 to 9 p.m. Sunday. Brunch on Sunday is served from 10 a.m. to 3 p.m.

PinPoint

Two things define Cape Fear cuisine more than anything else: fresh seafood and homegrown produce. Downtown Wilmington's new PinPoint restaurant showcases the combination in delectable seasonal menus with the perfect dash of creativity from a chef who has worked with the best.

Dean Neff ran the kitchen at Five & Ten, one of four Georgia restaurants owned by James Beard Award-winning chef and Bravo "Top Chef" judge Hugh Acheson. Neff was working alongside Acheson when Neff met longtime restauranteur Jeff Duckworth. The chefs were catering Duckworth's wedding reception. Neff and Duckworth kept in touch, finally landing in Wilmington to develop PinPoint.

The restaurant is named after a tiny Chatham County, Ga., community, near Savannah, that's rich in coastal Gullah food and culture. Seafood dominates the menu and influences the decor. Cool greys match a striking oyster shell chandelier over the dining area. The open space features a lounge area that moves from tall tables to a bar along the left

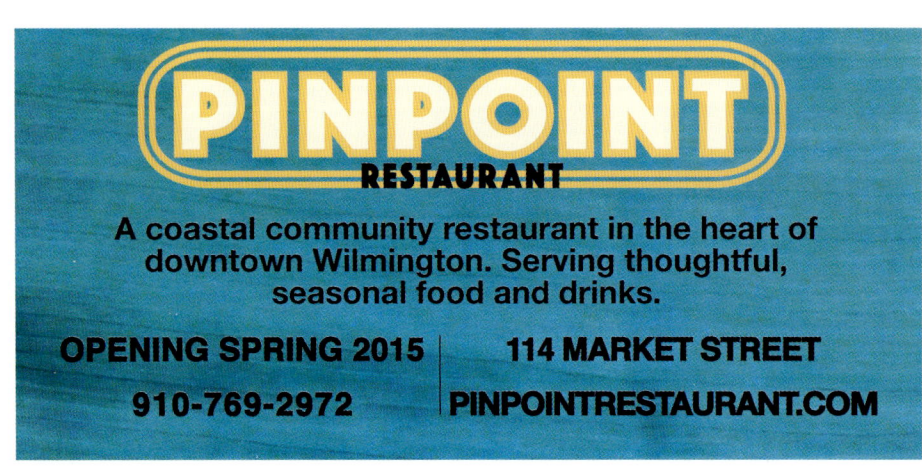

A coastal community restaurant in the heart of downtown Wilmington. Serving thoughtful, seasonal food and drinks.

OPENING SPRING 2015 | 114 MARKET STREET
910-769-2972 | PINPOINTRESTAURANT.COM

side of the room. Tables, some against a long banquette, populate the rest of the room decorated with interesting, repurposed items like the check-out booth serving as maitre' d stand.

The menu opens with oysters on the half-shell, including sweet Kumamotos from Washington and salty Beau Soleils from New Brunswick. Snacks bring blue crab cakes with crisp spiced okra and green goddess dressing or oyster and parsnip stew with bacon. Roasted N.C. tilefish for dinner comes with orange-glazed baby turnips, preserved-lemon farro verde, fennel-green tomato relish and watercress emulsion. Seafood is not the only choice. The pan-roasted, 30-ounce, bone-in, dry-aged ribeye for two people is served with local potato gratin, cast-iron-fried smoked tomatoes and garlic-chili-seared kale and crisp marrow. Vegetarians find the likes of family-style vegetable plates; sweet corn soup with charred ramps, Georgia olives and basil cream; or sorghum and urfa roasted delicata squash with poached fennel, arugula, ricotta, fennel frond, lemon and salsa verde.

Menus change depending on what's in season. When tomatoes are done, you're not likely to find the heirloom tomato salad with lardo, fines herbes, shaved celery, crispy fried field peas and chive buttermilk, but something equally delicious is bound to follow. A full bar serves numerous wines, craft beers, locals included, and craft and classic cocktails.

PinPoint will open in April 2015. Dinner service is planned 5 to around 11 p.m. Wednesday-Sunday. Demand will dictate hours. Look for lunch and brunch menus soon after the opening. Be sure to ask about the grilled cheese of the day.

The Little Dipper fondue

At 138 South Front Street downtown, find The Little Dipper, the first Wilmington restaurant to offer tableside fondue. In 2011, the nationally-acclaimed restaurant website OpenTable.com named The Little Dipper one of America's top 100 restaurants. Six cheese fondues are served. Diners get to choose the beer blended into Cheddar Ale Fondue, rich with sharp cheddar and Emmenthaler cheeses. Stella Artois is light in color and flavor, Yuengling produces a medium body and nutty flavor while Guinness imparts a full-flavored dark beer taste. Classic Swiss fondue also gets a twist. A little parmigiano cheese joins Gruyere and Emmenthaler in a white wine base seasoned with nutmeg, garlic and Kirsch. Enjoy fondue and other dishes a la carte or try a three-course meal, which include a cheese fondue for the table to share, the soup of the day or one of five salads, and a selection from the many entrée choices. Desserts are priced separately. Chefs offer six entrée cooking styles, including the most-popular White Merlot and Vegetable featuring rich vegetable stock blended with merlot wine. It or any of the other styles may be applied to the likes of blackened filet mignon, pork tenderloin or a seafood combination. A la carte dishes include grilled scallops and vegetables, a gourmet grilled cheese sandwich and vegetarian sliders. How could you not at least think about dessert for dinner, considering nut-topped caramel and dark chocolate Turtle fondue; milk chocolate, marshmallow cream and peanut butter Fluffernutter fondue; and white chocolate and mixed berry brandy sauce Berry White fondue? Six liqueurs let you create your own dark, milk or white chocolate fondue. As if 12 chocolate fondues were not enough, you may add a slice of cheesecake and berries to any fondue. Old-fashioned, pane-glass picture windows front the main dining room. The Garden Room deck out back can be set up for private parties. The restaurant has a wide-ranging wine list and a full bar offering classic and signature cocktails such as the wonderful chocolate martini. The Little Dipper opens for dinner at 5 p.m. Tuesday-Sunday. The restaurant is open daily from Memorial Day through October. The Little Dipper offers specials several nights a week. Get half-price bottles of wine on Sunday and a four-course, bargain prix fixe menu on Thursday.

The Pilot House

The Pilot House opened in 1978 and was the first restaurant in then-newly restored Chandler's Wharf, a significant section of Wilmington's port city industrial past. Initially, only salads and sandwiches were dispensed from a service window to customers who sat outdoors. Lots more delicious things have

happened since an on-site kitchen was added in 1988. The restaurant specializes in Southern regional cuisine, traditional and with contemporary flair. From-scratch dishes showcase fresh, local ingredients. Everything from "down home cooking" to Cajun to Lowcountry and other coastal cuisines inspire chefs. For lunch, arugula, goat cheese and roasted red pepper embellish a fried green tomato sandwich on a toasted Mexican telera roll. Shrimp and grits includes kielbasa sausage, mushrooms, scallions and collards on fried grits cakes. Shrimp and grits is on the dinner menu as well as everything from lobster macaroni and cheese to cioppino to filet mignon and herb-crusted rack of lamb. Sweet potato-crusted grouper is served with mushroom ravioli, mixed greens and balsamic vinaigrette. Brown sugar, cider vinegar, toasted pecans, fresh thyme and butter season pan-seared Southern Pecan Chicken Cutlets.

The restaurant has a full bar menu that includes wine, beer and delightful cocktails. Hours are 11 a.m. to 9 p.m. Sunday-Thursday and 11 a.m. to 10 p.m. Friday and Saturday throughout the year. The restaurant, deck and private rooms are available for weddings and other special events for groups of 30 to 300.

Elijah's

Elijah's is an American seafood grill and oyster bar that has been a mainstay in Historic Downtown Wilmington since 1984. Its building on Chandler's Wharf was originally a maritime museum. Ship models, nautical artifacts and paintings depicting maritime history remain on display. A large deck facing the Cape Fear River and the pedestrian boardwalk named The Riverwalk is a wonderful spot for people-watching while enjoying drinks, lunch or dinner. Seafood is the kitchen's primary concentration. The famous creamy, cheesy, hot crab dip was requested for a North Carolina's governor's inauguration. Oysters come on the half shell, steamed, fried and Rockefeller-style. A Carolina Bucket is an abundant mix of steamed clams, mussels, shrimp, crab legs, sausage, new potatoes and corn on the cob. Seafood platters, grilled or fried, are buffets on a plate. Landlubbers find New York strip steaks, vegetable linguine, sesame chicken, stuffed pork chops and filet mignon every day. Friday and Saturday are prime rib nights. For dessert, sorbet flavors depend on seasonal fruit while old-fashioned apple pie is a mainstay year-round. Lowcountry Cheesecake is part bourbon pecan pie, part creamy cheesecake, all finished with luscious ganache. The full bar serves beer, wine and cocktails. The restaurant is open daily for lunch, beginning at 11:30 a.m., and dinner year-round.

Front Street Brewery

Happy faces at sidewalk tables and a tall, vertical, neon sign make Front Street Brewery one of Historic Downtown Wilmington's most recognizable places. Seems everyone flocks to this distinctive, historic building for food, fun and some of the country's finest craft beers as well as more than 70 premium and rare bourbons (in 2014, The American Bourbon Association ranked the pub as one of the United States' "great bourbon bars"). Brewmaster Kevin Kozak and team produce a changing array of micro-beers, some seasonal, some aged in bourbon or wine barrels, that have garnered national attention and gold medals. Flagship beers include light Coastal Kolsch, Port City IPA and the wildly popular Dram Tree Scottish Ale. Deep red and lightly hoppy, the latter is a natural with the kitchen's Scottish ale barbecue ribs or sweet cinnamon doughnut bites. The menu also includes Front Street's popular pulled chicken nachos as well as burgers, sandwiches, slow-roasted brisket, Shepherd's pie, Buffalo shrimp and a bratwurst plate. You won't believe the low prices on daily lunch and dinner prices. Additionally, half-price appetizers are available 4 to 6 p.m. and after 10 p.m. every day. Sitting and sipping is just fine. Order a beer sampler, take advantage of the $1.99 mug of the day or take your favorite beer home in a growler or in one of Front Street Brewery's beer-laced cooking sauces. The bourbon selection is among Front Street Brewery's more than 275 spirits. Rare bourbon tastings and beer dinners are just some of the special events. Front Street Brewery stages events for charity, too. Free brewery tours and free beer tastings happen daily. Front Street Brewery is open 11:30 a.m. to midnight every day, and the kitchen never closes. The brew pub's lovely Beam

A perfectly prepared steak served with a great glass of red wine is a treat.

Room upstairs is perfect for private parties, receptions and business meetings.

Manna

The name of this downtown Wilmington restaurant is fitting. Manna (from Heaven) seems just right to describe the outstanding food, spot-on craft cocktails and swanky urban feel of this Princess Street spot between Front and Second streets. Billed as an American restaurant, chefs here have a wide range. They apply classic French technique to America's melting pot of options in imaginative but not contrived ways. Nearly every ingredient is sourced from the United States, and much of what the kitchen uses is grown or raised locally. Everything is homemade. Chefs even churn the butter. Food and drinks are served in a two-part urbane setting. The dining room's minimalist design plays exposed red brick against simple black, white and a pop of tangerine. The theme carries into the elegant bar, which has a doorway leading to an eclectic, grown-ups' lounge named Bourgie Nights, where gifted musicians perform everything from swing to Americana. The menu changes seasonally and according to the kitchen's creative whims. Fine-dining describes the experience, but Manna doesn't take itself too seriously, as evidenced by amusing names for food selections. There's the Clawed Howell (poached lobster, local braising greens, coconut-creamed butternut squash, sunflower seed pistou and fresh tarragon); the Beets Around the Bush (roasted & glazed North Carolina beets, arugula, fresh oranges, housemade cheese, candied pecans and fig sherry vinaigrette); and the Finger Lickin' Pig Pickin' (marinated and grilled N.C. pork chop, Anasazi bean ragout, maple-glazed N.C. sweet potatoes, arugula and smoked pimenton jus). Manna is known for its perfectly seared scallops, the presentation for which changes regularly. Chef Jameson Chavez is a New Mexico native, so chilies show up in dishes like Out of the Friar Pan and into the Fire (braised local monkfish in "Big Jim" red chili sauce, turnips, sweet potatoes, mussels and red cabbage). Pastry chef Rebeca Alvarado Paredes is considered by foodies to be the city's best. If you swoon for dessert, be prepared to have someone check your pulse after her sweet potato crème caramel or "peach melba" with caramelized peaches, frozen creme brulee and raspberry ice. Selections are seldom the same. Cocktails at Manna are notable. Bartenders take pride in making them exactly right each time, whether it's a classic Sazerac or a house special.

Reservations are a good idea most nights, required most weekends. You may also dine at the bar. Add your email to the restaurant's newsletter list to hear about wine dinners and other special events. Manna opens for dinner at 5 p.m. each day except Monday. The kitchen closes 10 p.m. Sunday-Thursday and at 11 p.m. Friday and Saturday. Manna is available for private events and large parties are fine.

The George

Downtown Wilmington dining is at its best with a waterfront view. The George is one of the most beautiful places to dine along Cape Fear River. The covered deck is wide and cozy, with tables under an awning and in full sunshine, even heaters for chilly days. Watch sailboats breeze by and the most spectacular sunsets you can imagine as you enjoy Southern coastal cuisine featuring steaks, pasta, salads and, of course, fresh local seafood. Sip crisp, cool white wine while nibbling Cajun Angels -- five jumbo shrimp wrapped in applewood smoked bacon and lightly blackened before being served atop jicama-apple slaw and fried rice noodles, all drizzled with red wine reduction. Lunch brings spicy, pan-seared, sliced tuna cooked to order and served on grilled flatbread with baby greens, roasted red peppers, green onions, mixed cheeses and wasabi aioli. Choose land and sea options for dinner, say a pair of bone-in chops, grilled pork chops, spiced apples on top, mashed sweet potatoes and sautéed green beans on the side or pecan-crusted fresh grouper, pan-seared and topped with honey butter, all alongside mashed sweet potatoes and grilled asparagus. Vegetarian meals are served. The chef's daily specials bring more choices, as does Saturday and Sunday brunch. Imagine housemade corned beef hash with eggs or French Toast Foster's sourdough bread dipped in cinnamon vanilla egg batter and grilled until golden brown then topped with fresh bananas, candied walnuts and rum syrup.

manna
123 Princess St. Downtown Wilmington 910.763.5252
www.mannaavenue.com

Kids get their own menus. Adults find lots of libations. The martini list alone features a dozen selections. The George is the only riverfront restaurant in downtown Wilmington that lets you dock and dine, meaning you can pull up in your boat and step out for drinks, a snack or a full meal. If you drive in to dine, free parking is available with a requested pass. Indoor dining is as comfortable as sitting on the deck. The bar is a stylish place to meet friends. Lunch hours are 11 a.m. to 4 p.m. Tuesday-Sunday; dinner, 5 to 9 p.m. Tuesday, Wednesday, Thursday and Sunday; and 5 to 10 p.m. Friday and Saturday. Brunch is served 10 a.m. to 3 p.m. Saturday and Sunday.

Fork 'n' Cork

Chef James Smith first grabbed Wilmington with his wildly popular burger truck named The Patty Wagon. When he traded in the truck for permanent gastropub digs on downtown Wilmington's Market Street, fans got a full taste of his comfort food with a twist. His famous burgers as well as brisket and meatloaf sandwiches still populate the menu (gluten-free buns available), but think gastronomic experience rather than typical pub food at this oh-so-comfy restaurant.

The intimate, 36-seat space is all red brick, dark wood and artsy stained glass wall hangings. Scotch eggs and deep-fried, confit duck legs are famous here. Fans adore the mac 'n' cheese creations. Sometimes short ribs or brisket gets tucked between the cheesy pasta layers. Carbonara mac 'n' cheese with shrimp, peas, mushrooms, pancetta and parmesan cream sauce cushions a warm, runny egg yolk. Mini beef Wellingtons are made in house.

Sunday brunch is a must at Fork 'n' Cork when you consider lobster pot pie that combines tender lobster chunks with corn, baby potatoes and fennel in a champagne cream sauce. For brunch, you also might encounter Texas-style barbecue brisket, two sunny-side-up eggs and Creole mustard cream sauce crowning a hefty buttermilk biscuit alongside home fries. Chef Smith likes surprises.

Polished wood wine racks hold nice but affordable labels. Cocktails might mean bourbon on the rocks, a spiked Bananas Foster milkshake or a Bloody

Mary bar. Find craft beers here, too. Hours are 11 a.m. to 11 p.m. Monday–Thursday, 11 a.m. to midnight Friday and Saturday and noon to 1 p.m. Sunday.

Aubriana's

One of downtown Wilmington's most beautiful and most romantic restaurants, Aubriana's features an American menu with European flair. Lovely as it is, friendly and welcoming defines this Front Street blessing, a couple blocks south of Market Street. It's an out-of-the-way place worth finding. The building has an interesting history (it has been a private residence and a mercantile store). Old brick work remains visible inside. What was once the horse-and-carriage area in back is a beautiful brick patio decorated with fresh herbs and flowers.

Whether you dine inside or out, native North Carolinian chef Tyson Amick and his brigade, one of the city's best kitchen teams, present outstanding fare on a seasonally changing menu and a specials board that always impresses. The regular menu's signature "lamb lollipops" are baby New Zealand lamb chops seasoned with mint-infused salt, lightly blackened and served with grilled orange and jalapeno mint gastrique. Appetizers may range from summertime shrimp, crab and corn chowder with fingerling potatoes, applewood bacon and a petit buttermilk biscuit to a blue lump crab tart with bay-spiced crust, fresh mozzarella, creamy citrus custard and chili-garlic greens. Among entrees is a thick, tender, applewood bacon-wrapped Black Angus filet mignon served with Yukon Gold mashed potatoes, asparagus, wild mushrooms and green peppercorn reduction. In fall, roasted organic chicken might accompany sweet potato bread pudding and sage-infused jus. Specials might showcase jumbo shrimp etouffee with housemade duck boudin.

Dessert is always special. Silky gelato is made in-house. Layer cakes are spectacular, especially the creamy coconut cake. A fall menu may show off spiced butternut squash crème brulee. Aubriana's has a full bar serving classics and fresh twists. The wine list has earned an Award of Excellence from Wine Spectator magazine. The restaurant is open for dinner at 5 p.m. Tuesday-Saturday.

Kilwin's

Follow your nose to this Market Street sweets shop in the heart of downtown Wilmington. Fudge, kettle corn, nut brittles and waffle cones made on the premises emit sugary aromas. Just beyond the fudge factory, visible through the front window, fudge bricks in various flavors greet you near the door. Next is a line of chocolate candies and chocolate-dipped madness. There's chocolate-dipped pretzels, chocolate-dipped sandwich cookies, chocolate-dipped candied orange and chocolate-dipped strawberries, to name a very few. Next up, ice cream freezers full of wonderful flavors are available in cups or in one of those crispy waffle cones you smelled on the way here. Flavors suit every taste, whether you're nuts for classic peanut butter and chocolate or a connoisseur seeking single-origin Peruvian chocolate fudge. Kilwin's has plenty of take-away selections that are pre-bagged and boxed. You can get a gift card for those who envy your place in line. The shop is on Market Street between Water and Front streets. Hours are 10 a.m. to 9 p.m. Sunday-

Aubriana's fine dining

Fine food • Craft cocktails • Extensive wine list • Superb service

115 South Front Street • Wilmington NC 28401
www.aubrianas.com • 910.763.7773
Open at 5 pm for dinner, Tuesday through Saturday
Beautiful courtyard open seasonally

Thursday and 10 a.m. to 11 p.m. Friday and Saturday.

Hell's Kitchen

If you're a fan of the CW Network show *Dawson's Creek*, Hell's Kitchen probably looks familiar. When producers worked a college bar into the program's script, they created Hell's Kitchen. When the show's run ended, the watering hole went up for sale.

A local restaurateur bought the place – *Dawson's Creek* décor and all. Fans of the show still stop by just to see Hell's Kitchen, but don't just come to relish in Hell's Kitchen's famous story. This is a spot for serious pub food, great drinks and good times.

Bar munchies galore include grouper fingers, homemade hummus and wings as well-known as Hell's Kitchen's Hollywood past. Lightly breaded, the crispy numbers get coated with your choice of sauces described as tame, hot, fire and "INFERNO!!" Choose Buffalo garlic, teriyaki, barbecue, honey chipotle, bleu Buffalo or tangy N.C. barbecue sauces.

Certified Angus Beef burgers are equally popular, especially the half-pound The Devil Made Me Do It smothered in homemade bacon barbeque sauce and topped with more crisp bacon plus cheddar, fried red onions, lettuce, tomato, and an over-easy fried egg. "So good it's sinful," is how Hell's Kitchen describes it. There's a vegetarian burger too, as well as salads, sandwiches, tacos, quesadillas and seafood.

Choose fish and chips, a Maryland crab cake sandwich or a smoked salmon BLT. Hell's Kitchen provides a full bar, extensive beer list, free Wi-Fi and a kids menu.

Daily specials bring food and drink discounts like $6.99 burgers and $3 pints on Wednesdays and half-price appetizers 4 to 7 p.m. Monday-Thursday. Put Monday night trivia and live music Friday and Saturday nights on your party agenda.

And bonus: Hell's Kitchen serves a late-night menu until 1:30 a.m. Hell's Kitchen hours are 11 a.m. to 2 a.m. daily. Free downtown food delivery is available 11 a.m. to 3 p.m. weekdays. The pub also hosts private events including corporate gatherings and holiday parties.

Slice of Life

Whether they're seeking pizza for comfort, celebration or a quick something to eat, Wilmingtonians grab Slice of Life. The pizzeria is a Port City institution in business for more than 20 years and with four locations.

Get pies and slices however you like them. Twenty-five toppings include standard pepperoni and Italian sausage along with bacon, chicken, steak, pineapple, spinach, jalapenos, fresh basil, feta cheese and artichoke hearts. Dough made daily in-house produces crisp tender pizzas. Gluten-free crust is available. Don't miss the white pizza. Fresh tomatoes replace the sauce on this cheesy, flavorful pie hosting garlic, ricotta, parmesan, mozzarella and fresh basil.

On the rare occasion someone is not in the mood for pizza, Slice of Life accommodates with soups, salads, subs, wrap sandwiches and wings with various sauces, sweet red chili, tequila lime and garlic parmesan to name a few. There's a Mexican bent here, too. Try nachos, quesadillas and tacos. Draft, craft, domestic and imported beers are served as well as wine and cocktails. No matter which location you choose, the atmosphere is red brick rustic and friendly. Plenty of televisions hang up high so everyone can see the big game. Outdoor seating is especially nice on warm, sunny days.

Find Slice of Life downtown on Market Street, uptown at Eastwood Drive and Military Cutoff and midtown at College Road and 17th Street. A visit to the downtown store is lunch and a historic stop all in one. Slice owner Ray Worrell revitalized the circa 1841 Masonic Lodge to host the pizzeria. Look for historic markers near the front door.

Daniel Webster, 11th U.S. President James Polk and presidential candidate Henry Clay all visited this building in the 1800s. Slice of Life is also at Independence Mall, so you can savor some pizza while you shop. Slice of Life locations are open 11 a.m. to 3 a.m. daily, minus the Independence Mall spot, which is open 10 a.m. to 9 p.m. Monday-Saturday and noon to 6 p.m. Sunday.

Hops Supply Co.

You'll have some decisions to make

at Hops Supply Co. Wheat, lager, IPA, ESB, ale, amber, cider or stout? Bottle or draft? Do you want North Carolina beers, a beer flight or a beer cocktail? Don't forget wine. Four whites and four reds are on tap, a system that protects wine from air and light, assuring each glass will taste as it should. You may order a bottle of wine, or you might consider a craft cocktail, maybe a barrel-aged Manhattan with Elijah Craig 12-year-old bourbon and brandy-soaked cherries. Then there's the food. Hops Supply Co. is billed as an American gastropub. A view of the open kitchen from tables and comfy booths near window walls remind diners of more choices. If guests are in for the Sunday "brunch all day" menu, a few of the considerations include French toast baked with local honey; tender fried chicken on a soft black pepper biscuit with smoked ham gravy; and a BLT with cheddar, pesto aioli and a fried egg tucked between the bacon, lettuce and tomato. Lunch and dinner menus present more delicious choices: pimento cheese and bacon deviled eggs; barbecue braised short rib nachos; creamy macaroni and cheese full of shrimp and Andouille sausage; Grilled Bistro Steak with a dark beer reduction sauce. Soups, salads, sandwiches, burgers and entrees fill the interesting menu.

Not long after it opened, diners voted Hops Wilmington's best new restaurant in 2013. Lunch and dinner are served every day at the Oleander Drive spot in mid-town Wilmington. Brunch is served 11 a.m. to 3 p.m. on Saturday in addition to all day Sunday.

Carolina Ale House

You'll immediately know the Carolina Ale House theme when you walk in the door. Two giant, flat-screen televisions and 46 others broadcast sports throughout the family-friendly restaurant. In between are all manner of sports memorabilia from local and state teams. Watch the games and races at booths, bar tables, a large bar inside and another one outside.

The menu fits the fun, game-day feel at this South College Road restaurant. Munchies range from cheese fries to creamy spinach dip to fried pickles to jumbo chicken wings, which are offered fried, grilled or prepared with a dry rub and baked. Wing sauces include Buffalo, honey Buffalo, hot sweet & sour, spicy habanero and fiery Thai. Chili is available every day as well as other soups, salads, sandwiches, burgers, pizzas, entrees and desserts. The signature Pub Burger is piled high with smoky bacon, American cheese, fried onion strings and secret sauce. Hand-battered chicken tenders, crispy bacon bits, hard-boiled eggs, Monterey Jack and cheddar cheese land on the Southern Fried Chicken Salad. Get a classic Philly cheesesteak sandwich with sautéed onions, mushroom and green peppers or a chargrilled rib-eye with garlic mashed potatoes. The kid's menu is varied, with mac and cheese, grilled cheese and chicken tenders. On Tuesday night, kids meals cost just 99 cents for children under age 12.

Portions are huge and no one goes away hungry. The beer is cold, cocktails are an option and service is efficient. The Carolina Ale House is open, and the full menu is served, 11 a.m. to 2 a.m. daily.

Henry's American Food

When you're in the mood for classic,

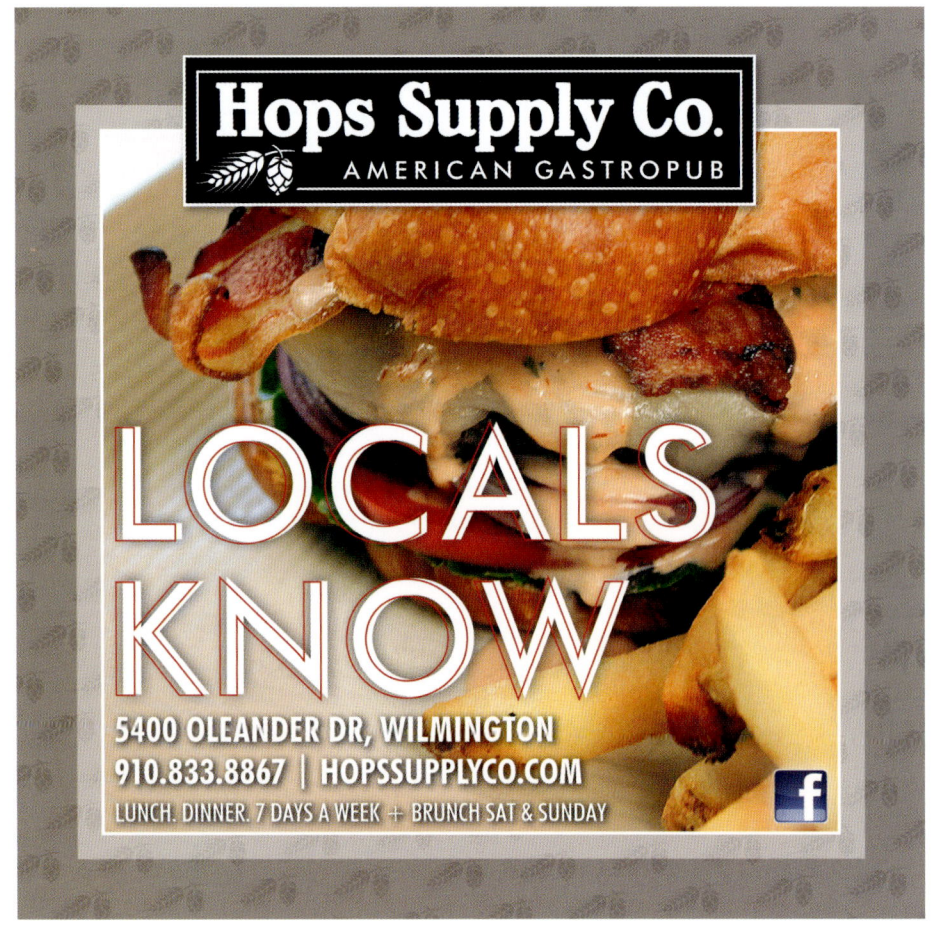

made-from-scratch American fare, treat yourself to lunch or dinner at Henry's, in Wilmington at the corner of Shipyard and Independence Boulevards. Various salads, sandwiches, soups and luncheon plates are offered mid-day. Shrimp and grits and half-pound burgers topped with mushroom gravy are among the favorites. Dinner brings roast chicken breast and homemade meatloaf, each served with mashed potatoes, vegetable of the day and gravy. Seafood choices include coconut shrimp and lump crab cakes. A house salad or soup comes with entrees. Seafood fettuccine, four-cheese penne pasta and fettuccine with grilled chicken, bacon, onions, and mushrooms in parmesan cheese sauce are always in demand. "Two-handed" sandwiches and several entree salads are other choices. Henry's also offers a "crate to plate" special each day that emphasizes local ingredients, an effort recognized by the N.C. Department of Agriculture's Goodness Grows in North Carolina seal. Henry's has a full bar with $5 appetizers starting at 4 p.m. each day. Live music begins at 5:30 p.m. on Friday. Brunch, featuring both breakfast and lunch selections, is offered on Saturday beginning at 11 a.m. Henry's opens at 11 a.m. daily.

The Pine Room at Henry's is a good place for private events such as board meetings, rehearsal dinners, showers and holiday or birthday parties. Henry's also offers a wide selection of party platters for off-site events too.

Umaii

The word umaii in Japanese means "delicious" or "good." It's the perfect name for this Asian hotspot from the owners of Wilmington's popular Japanese restaurant Tokyo 101 at Mayfaire Town Center in north Wilmington. Sushi and Thai food is served at Umaii in north Wilmington's Porters Neck community. Toth Somsnith run the operations with his brother, Lai Somsnith, both from Laos, and Pamuka Holt, a Thailand native. At Umaii, look for Thai classics such as curries, pad thai, drunken noodles, crispy duck with basil and whole fish presentations. You'll find less familiar specialties, as well. Kanon jeeb is a pork, shrimp and water chestnut steamed dumpling. Thai herbs season chaing mai, a housemade pork sausage. Lemongrass dressing naps crispy red snapper finished with fresh cilantro. Also find Japanese fusion dishes and hibachi-style selections. Sushi makers work one end of a bar spanning nearly the full length of the restaurant. Beer, wine and cocktails are served. Sit inside or on the patio. Hours are 11 a.m. to 3 p.m. and 5 to 9 p.m. Monday-Thursday, 11 a.m. to 3 p.m. and 5 to 10 p.m. on Friday, noon to 10 p.m. on Saturday and noon to 9 p.m. on Sunday.

Carolina Beach Restaurants

Saint's Cove Beach Bar & Grill

When Saint's Cove owner Nick Augustine was a Marine Corps pilot, his old pilot call sign was "Saint." "You know, like Saint Nick, Saint Augustine," he says. While stationed in eastern North Carolina for Corps, Augustine fished on a beach pier hosting a little café. The place got him thinking about a seaside business for his future. Enter friendly Saint's Cove Beach Bar & Grill. Tables, some with umbrellas, and pastel wooden chairs furnish the huge deck affording plenty of room for families and friends. Nautical charts under the bartop's clear finish and model sailboats in shadow boxes on the walls provide a maritime feel indoors. Pub appetizers like fried clam strips, bourbon-sauced meatballs, grouper bites and Cheerwine-glazed wings reflect easy beach days. There's a burger piled with onion rings and another with pineapple, bacon, mozzarella and teriyaki sauce. Augustine is from Detroit, so Midwest favorites dot the menu. Look for a fried pork tenderloin sandwich with lettuce and tomato. Cheddar cheese curds are beer-battered and deep-fried.

Of course, much seafood is on the list, everything from grouper bites with spicy mayo to fish tacos to a mixed catch basket with fried clams, shrimp and catfish. Wine, beer and cocktails are available, too. Have an old-fashioned ice cream sundae for dessert or ask about the "chocolate delight of the day." Saint's Cove is open 4 to 10 p.m. Monday-Thursday and noon to 10 p.m. Friday, Saturday and Sunday. Call ahead from late fall to early spring. Off-season hours

Try Thai food at its best!

Authentic Thai food prepared by a truly talented chef is available at Umaii, a new restaurant conveniently located in Porters Neck. Lunch and dinner is served seven days a week. A large sushi bar, seasonal outdoor dining, and full cocktail service contribute to a memorable experience.

Umaii thai cuisine • sushi • bar

8209 Market Street • Wilmington NC 28411
910.821.8474 • www.umaiiportersneck.com

One of the most popular local dishes is fried oysters, which are especially tasty when they come from Stump Sound.

are subject to change.

Shuckin' Shack

Fall and winter oyster roasts and spring and summer shrimp boils are two favorite pastimes on the North Carolina coast. They happen all the time behind the screen door at Shuckin' Shack in Carolina Beach. The restaurant is a cross between backyard seafood feasts and seaside steam shacks. The national magazine *Coastal Living* named Shuckin' Shack one of its favorite seafood dives in 2013. Galvanized buckets serve as drop lights over the bar, which is decorated with newspaper clippings that tell Carolina beach stories about fishing adventures and surfer dudes. Huge photographs of Carolina Beach's famous charter boats serve as "windows." A sign on the wall advises, "It's always 5 o'clock in Carolina Beach." That means settle in and have fun.

Big rich, briny oysters are served raw or steamed. Peel-and-eat shrimp, clam, mussels and snow crab legs and claws come from the steamer, too. Samplers and feasts let you mix and match seafood alongside slaw, hushpuppies and corn on the cob. Get wings, sandwiches – including lobster rolls – and lots of snacks like fried pickles, mini corn dogs and mozzarella sticks. Beer, wine and cocktails are served, including fun specials like the Pleasure Island Pain Killer with rum, orange, coconut, pineapple and nutmeg. Catering is available.

Shuckin' Shack has a downtown Wilmington location, too. Hours are 11 a.m. to 2 a.m. Monday-Saturday and noon to 2 a.m. Sunday. The downtown location may be open past 2 a.m. depending on crowds.

Tavern by the Green

Nothing beats post-links relaxing at Tavern by the Green, overlooking the Masonboro Country Club course. You needn't schedule a day of golf to enjoy this charming restaurant.

Black wrought iron furniture and stylishly cozy interior signal Southern hospitality. There's also a grand outdoor pavilion. Come sit a spell with a refreshing iced tea, craft beer or lovely glass of white zinfandel.

The menu is packed with great nibbles, sandwiches and salads. Munch a basket of fries, refuel with a healthy chef's salad or tuck into hearty sandwiches. Try a BLT, a double cheeseburger or a classic club wrap with turkey, ham, bacon, lettuce, tomato and ranch dressing. The fish and chips plate features beer-battered cod. Planning an event? Call the hospitality experts at Masonboro Country Club. Tavern by the Green and the outdoor pavilion accommodate groups of many sizes. Chefs and event planners arrange menus to suit your tastes, from elegant, full breakfasts to casual barbecue dinners. Participate in various social events and activities that build long-lasting friendships at Masonboro Country Club.

The Crab Shack

Located between Wilmington and Topsail Beach, The Crab Shack is conveniently situated next door to Poplar Grove Plantation on US Highway 17 North. The Crab Shack features whole, steamed blue crabs, messy to eat but a delicacy well worth the effort. The Crab Shack also has a large selection of other seafood including steamed local oysters, assorted steamer pots, seafood platters, crab cakes, grilled scallops and bacon-wrapped shrimp. A terrific list of sides offers crisp onion rings, french fries and fried okra. Not in the mood for seafood? If you love spicy chili, this is the place for a tasty, flavorful and filling bowl. The Crab Shack has hamburgers, club sandwiches, baby-back ribs and barbecued chicken, among many other choices. The restaurant is super casual with a full bar, several draft beers and a patio open when the weather is warm. Prices are modest, especially for the large portions served. The Crab Shack is open 11:30 a.m. to 9 p.m. Sunday-Thursday and 11:30 a.m. to 9:30 p.m. Sunday.

Topsail Island Dining

The beautiful 26-mile long Topsail Island is a narrow band of sand just 500 to 1,500 feet wide. Most of the restaurants there are concentrated in and around Surf City, which is separated from the mainland by an old-fashioned, two-lane swing bridge. However, a restaurant at the south end's Topsail Beach is well worth the drive.

Beach Shop and Grill

Topsail Beach's Beach Shop and Grill is a casual place for breakfast and lunch, and a bit upscale at dinner. Menus for all three meals are extensive. Eggs Benedict, buttermilk pancakes and create-your-own omelets are among morning eye-openers. Lunch features a fried chicken cobb salad and the golden beet salad with organic greens, candied pecans, English cucumbers, cherry tomatoes and goat cheese tossed in vinaigrette. Sandwiches are served, as well as grilled, fresh grouper tacos.

Fans come time and again for the hand-pattied, Angus beef burgers they find to be the best on the beach. Steaks, fresh local seafood and pasta are dinner highlights. Specialties include shrimp and grits, jumbo lump crab cakes with lemon aioli and Shellfish Mac n' Cheese with shrimp, scallops, lobster, romano and parmesan cheeses and fresh herbs. Be sure to save room for key lime pie with mile-high meringue, baked on site by owner Cheryl Price, a master pastry chef.Beach Shop and Grill has been in business since 1952. Each of the more than 90 wines offered earned a rating of 89 points or more, but thanks to the careful selection, both moderate and pricier wines are included. Beach Shop also has numerous craft beers and a wide selection of cocktails. Breakfast, lunch and dinner are served mid-March-November. Call for season and off-season hours.

Mainsail Restaurant

Seafood fans find lots to love at Mainsail Restaurant on North Carolina Highway 50 in Surf City. Popular Calabash seafood platters come with a choice of flounder, shrimp, sea scallops or oysters individually or as combinations. Maryland crab cakes and grilled fish served with a choice of delicious sauces also are popular. A raw bar offers oysters steamed or raw on the half-shell. Steamed snow crab legs are on the menu. Fish and shellfish aren't the only choices. Enjoy the Friday and Saturday night prime rib special. Filet mignon, New York strip and chicken marsala are on the regular menu, along with other meat and pasta dishes. Sandwiches and salads please those who prefer lighter meals. The restaurant serves beer, cocktails and wines that are moderately priced or high-end special bottles. Check the cocktail list for chocolate martinis and fresh fruit daiquiris. Mainsail accommodates large parties, and reservations for larger groups are accepted. A separate room downstairs may be reserved for private parties. The upstairs Commodore Room works for wedding receptions, rehearsal dinners or anniversary parties. Mainsail is open for dinner from 5 to 9 p.m. daily during the summer season. Call for off-season hours.

Daddy Mac's

From fresh seafood accompanied by tasty sauces, to crab cakes done three ways, to the best baby back ribs on Topsail Island, Daddy Macs aims to please every taste. Ribs are slowly roasted, as they should be, so tender the meat falls from the bone. Select sweet Vidalia onion or Cajun beer barbecue sauce. The ribs, fish tacos, fried seafood platters and shrimp and grits are among entrees. Sandwiches are available in the evening, too. They make great lighter fare after a long day on the beach, which is not far away. Daddy Mac's sits oceanfront, and a wide deck set with dining tables affords a beautiful view. Few things are more pleasurable than enjoying a good meal while watching and hearing waves break in the background. Rib-eye, New York strip and tenderloin are ground together for half-pound burgers. Wasabi aioli spikes

SEE WHAT'S IN STORE AT THE CRAB SHACK

You'll find Wilmington's freshest seafood prepared to order with great care in a comfortable, laid-back atmosphere at The Crab Shack. Best known for steamer pots and steamed blue crabs, The Crab Shack has a large additional variety of menu items too. A full bar with all ABC permits and outdoor seating in season makes this the perfect spot to savor some local favorites.

*Open 7 days for lunch and dinner in season,
7 day dinner & limited lunch in the off-season*

55 Scotts Hill Loop Road
conveniently located next door to Poplar Grove Plantation
Wilmington, NC 28411
910-319-0688
www.WilmingtonCrabShack.com

a world of food is available

Enjoying cocktails and a meal at one of many waterside restaurants is fun.

ahi tuna sliders with avocado and fresh cucumber. Backfin crab cakes and Buffalo shrimp are on the appetizer menu. Kids get their own menu of selections. Daddy Mac's has a full-service bar and refreshing house cocktails like the raspberry margarita. There's a good selection of beer and wine, too. Daddy Mac's is open Tuesday-Sunday for lunch and dinner. Lunch begins at 11 a.m., except on Sundays when Daddy Mac's opens at 10 a.m. and offers brunch service, including eggs benedicts, prime ribs, blintzes and quiche. Dinner always starts at 5 p.m.

Gallagher's Bar and Grill

When it's time to watch the game, big or otherwise, head to Gallagher's on North New River Drive in Surf City. The sports bar and grill has plenty of televisions and a wide-open dining room where it's OK to cheer for your favorite teams. The family-owned establishment offers a fun-filled experience and great prices on food and drinks. Lots of munchies are perfect for Super Bowl or March Madness college basketball tournaments. Think wings, loaded cheese fries and Irish egg rolls filled with corned beef, cabbage and Swiss cheese. Salads are balanced by mondo sandwiches and burgers, including the Royale with Cheese, a half-pound, ground chuck burger topped with cheese, bacon and a fried egg. Fried shrimp, grilled or blackened salmon, hand-cut steaks and chicken dishes make up the entrees. A kids menu satisfies tikes.

A local baker makes desserts, one of them the Southern classic Hummingbird Cake, a banana pineapple pecan layer cake with cream cheese frosting. Gallagher's sports a full bar serving beer, wine and cocktails. Hours are 11:30 a.m. to 10 p.m. Sunday-Thursday and 11:30 a.m. to 11 p.m. or later Friday and Saturday. Gallagher's accommodates large groups, but parties of 12 or more are encouraged to reserve tables, especially during busy summer months.

Inlet 790 Grill & Bar

Two new restaurants are located in North Topsail Beach. As you're driving down New River Inlet Road, watch for Villa Capriani resort. Inlet 790 centers the complex. The restaurant's Italian garden setting includes the happy sound of water trickling down an enchanting fountain. Tile floors and Roman motifs share décor space with seascape paintings by local artists.

Chef David Longo extends his reach well beyond Italy. However, don't miss his grilled shrimp primavera when it's on special. Longo tosses tender shrimp with mushrooms, spinach and tomatoes in silky pesto cream sauce.

A couple pasta dishes are part of the menu's eclectic mix. Chicken, chorizo, shrimp and okra plump tomato-rich jambalaya over jasmine rice. Maple Dijon glazes wild Scottish salmon. Steaks are served, too, but fancy tastes are not required.

Taco Tuesday and from-scratch pizzas, traditional and creative, are two customer favorites. Cooks tuck fried fish filets and fresh slaw into soft, warm tortillas.

The casual bar is great place for a craft beer, good old domestic suds, sangria or the signature Ocean Blueberry Lemonade cocktail with citrus vodka, fresh lemon juice, blueberry puree and lemon-lime soda.

The impressive wine list ranges from easy reds and whites to tony Vueve Cliquot champagne. Inlet 790 works for gatherings large and small. Dinner starts at 5 p.m. Tuesday-Saturday but hours are extended during vacation seasons and new specials are added. Call ahead for details.

Topsail Shrimp House

Take the elevator to the top floor of the seven-story St. Regis resort on New River Inlet Road for a fine view and some of the area's best seafood. Giant windows line casual at Topsail Shrimp House, affording every table aerial oceanfront views that extend for miles. Binoculars are available to view sea birds and dolphins.

You'll feel like you sitting on the world's tallest deck as you munch lightly battered fried shrimp, Buffalo shrimp and Firecracker Shrimp, the latter in creamy sauce with spicy Asian seasonings. Get grilled shrimp skewers, grilled shrimp on salads, shrimp tacos, shrimp po' boy sandwiches, shrimp quesadillas or shrimp and grits.

Crab cakes, grilled mahi, fried flounder and steamed oysters are offered, too. Find steaks, burgers and a seared tuna sandwich with mango salsa. Customize grilled seafood or seared scallops with one of four sauces, including pineapple jalapeno.

Don't miss the kitchen's wide-cut, puffed fries, golden outside, fluffy within.

Quench your thirst with cider, assorted beers, affordable wines and fun cocktails like Topsail Beach Punch with vodka, peach schnapps, raspberry schnapps and cranberry. Live and DJ music provide opportunities to dance some nights.

The magnificent space is perfect for parties and wedding receptions. Dinner is served 4 to 9 p.m. Tuesday-Sunday. Sunday brunch is scheduled 10 a.m. to 2 p.m. Look for crab cake eggs Benedict and, of course, a shrimp omelet.

Eddie Romanelli's In Leland

The huge Waterford residential development in Brunswick County, not far south of downtown Wilmington, is home to Eddie Romanelli's. The popular Italian restaurant is known for affordable prices and portions so large doggy bags make up a full meal. Myriad appetizers include hot wings and hot crab dip for two. Among salads, consider the almond chicken salad with sliced chicken, spring onions, pineapple and fresh herbs with a bit of simple mayonnaise, all on a bed of lettuce in a tortilla bowl. Tomatoes, boiled egg and almonds are the garnish.

A large number of sandwiches, pizzas and calzones are featured, too. Italian specialties include eggplant rollatini, chicken marsala, baked ziti and Mama Romanelli's cheesy lasagna. Shrimp Tuscany features sautéed shrimp with mushrooms, basil, tomatoes, scallions and prosciutto in a creamy alfredo sauce tossed with linguini.

Check the family-style, to-go menu for eight to 10 people, perfect for dinners, business lunches and parties. Don't forget curbside to-go service. Eddie Romanell's decadent strawberry cream cake is among family-style menu offerings. The restaurant has a full bar and large wine list. Hours are 11 a.m. to 10 p.m. Sunday-Thursday. Hours are extended to 11 p.m. on Friday and Saturday. Look for drink and food specials on Monday and Tuesday nights. The restaurant's event spaces can host up to 45 people.

Try local wines

The quality of North Carolina wines might surprise you. Early explorers saw wild grapes growing along the shores here as far back as the 1500s. Those vines were tapped to grow some of America's first commercially cultivated grapes. Sweet muscadine wine was the popular choice not just in North Carolina but in many places across the United States. Over time, tastes switched to dry wines. Now, sweet wines are back in vogue. No matter your preference, you'll find a N.C. wine to please your palate. Muscadine wines are better than ever, and lots of wineries along Interstate 40 east of Raleigh and in the Cape Fear region host tastings. Wineries on the coast and mountains use viniferous grapes to make fine wines, too. Two of the Cape Fear region's most popular wineries are Rose Hill's Duplin Winery, known for muscadine wines, and Silver Coast Winery, which viniferous wines, in Ocean Isle Beach.

Craft beer is another hot topic in the Cape Fear region. Front Street Brewery was making beer long before America's current craft beer boom and remains the area's leader of award-winning beers. In the past couple of years, many pubs and breweries have popped up in and around Wilmington, making the Cape Fear region a desirable destination for craft beer lovers.

Beach Portraits

G. FRANK HART
Photography
910.262.8810   gfrankhartphoto.com

There are plenty of places to catch the big one in all the fishing areas near Hampstead.

growth continues in **hampstead**

Hampstead remains the fastest growing community in Pender County, at 933 square miles the ninth largest of the 100 counties in North Carolina. The unincorporated town is located 15 miles north of Wilmington on US Highway 17. It does not have distinct borders but does have a number of attributes people want.

Of paramount importance to the young families who choose Hampstead is the good public school system with supportive parents of the students who attend them. A library in Hampstead that is part of the County system also benefits financially from the dedicated efforts over many years of a group known as the Friends of the Library.

Affordability is another draw for Hampstead residents. Housing prices are relatively low and the types of homes available are diverse too, with everything from modest bungalows to huge multi-story mansions facing the Intracoastal Waterway offered. Compared against New Hanover County and especially against the city of Wilmington, taxes in Pender County are very modest, which adds to the affordability index.

Great beaches nearby

Hampstead is situated between two fabulous beaches, with Topsail Island about 20 minutes north and Wrightsville Beach about 20 minutes south. And thanks to a bypass that was completed just a few years ago, Hampstead residents can easily reach all the attractions in downtown Wilmington in 30 minutes or so.

The community is topographically diverse, stretching as it does from the Intracoastal Waterway to more than five miles inland. There are still farms in Hampstead, though more and more are being sold off for residential development. Nonetheless, you can buy goat cheese on-site from the farmer who makes it. Locally-grown fresh vegetables and fruits are available in season at the nearby Poplar Grove Plantation Farmer's Market.

Fishing and boating are extremely popular in Hampstead. There are several marinas in the area so getting a boat into the water is not a problem.

Fish and seafood can be purchased from those who caught it, and fish is packed, processed and shipped on a daily basis from a processing company located in Hampstead to the major markets on the East Coast, including New York City.

Hampstead, by the way, bills itself as the seafood capital of the Carolinas, and no one has disputed that.

The Crab Shack

Hampstead residents have been traveling a bit south to The Crab Shack since it opened in 2012. Located next door to Poplar Grove Plantation on US Highway 17 North, the restaurant features whole, steamed blue crabs, messy to eat but a delicacy well worth the effort. The Crab Shack also has a large selection of other seafood including steamed local oysters, assorted steamer pots, seafood platters, crab cakes, grilled scallops and bacon-wrapped shrimp. A terrific list of sides offers crisp onion rings, french fries and fried okra.

Not in the mood for seafood? If you love spicy chili, this is the place for a tasty, flavorful and filling bowl. The Crab Shack has hamburgers, club sandwiches, baby-back ribs and barbecued chicken, among many other choices.

The restaurant is super casual with a full bar, several draft beers and a patio open when the weather is warm.

Hampstead residents are delighted to have two services available right in their town that certainly improve their quality of life. No one particularly likes to use medical and dental services, but we're certainly glad we have them here instead of needing a laborious trip into Wilmington.

Pierpan Family Dentistry

An outstanding family practice is Pierpan Family Dentistry located in the Food Lion complex in Hampstead. A husband and wife team, Drs. Henry and Monica Pierpan, who received their D.D.S. degrees from UNC School of

Visit Hampstead's Unique Shops

Hair Care At Affordable Prices
JRs' Barber Shop
15200 US Highway 17N
910-547-1090 • 910-352-1694

Fitness Center, Training, Exercise Classes
Raise the Bar Fitness
16579 US Highway 17 N
910-319-0589
facebook.com/Raise-the-Bar-Fitness

Nail Salon
Passion Nail
17230 US Highway 17N
910-270-9398
facebook.com/Passion-Nail

Dentistry in Chapel Hill, head the facility.

Dr. Henry is passionate about providing his patients with high quality, state-of-the-art dental care. He completed his surgical residency for implant placement in Washington, D.C. in 2007 and is a fellow in the International Congress of Oral Implantologists. He also is a Captain in the U.S. Navy Reserves and serves as a Dental Corps officer at Camp LeJeune.

Dr. Monica's goal in her practice is to treat every patient as family. She strives to be gentle and caring while providing the highest quality of dental care. She is a member of the Port City Study Club, which is committed to dental excellence in all areas.

Since 2006, Pierpan Family Dentistry has provided implant services for their patients, including surgical placement and restoration to help replace missing teeth. They were the first office in this area to use a Cone Beam Dental CatScan to help in diagnosis and placement of implants.

This state-of-the-art technology enables patients to replace missing teeth with a more natural feel, preserving bone and helping patients chew with confidence.

Pierpan Family Dentistry accepts most dental insurance plans and provides a means for patients to apply for credit through a dedicated private dental financing provider.

New businesses open

Two new businesses opened recently in Hampstead. Passion Nails is a full-service nail salon located in the Lowes Food shopping plaza on US Highway 17 North. The spotlessly clean, bright facility is staffed by well-trained people who offer manicures and pedicures at reasonable prices. When those two services are combined, the price is more modest still.

Raise the Bar is a new fitness facility that is a welcome addition to Hampstead. It also is meticulously and constantly cleaned and features state-of-the-art equipment.

Treadmills, elliptical machines, all sorts of leg, chest, arm and back weight training equipment, free weights, and machines in a separate area designed for abdominal work are available. The owners are both long-term trainers and their friendly, low-key manner makes all their clients comfortable regardless of their current fitness levels.

Another business owner, Melvin (June) London, is an in-demand barber at JRs' Barber Shop located on US Highway 17. JR's offers very modestly priced haircuts for people of all ages. They are experts in military cuts too, which is appreciated by the members of the U.S. Marine Corps who live in Hampstead. They also offer senior discounts for the many retirees who've relocated to Hampstead from colder Northern climes. London, whose family has lived in Hampstead for many years, is a beloved volunteer in the area; parents are grateful for the many hours he spends coaching their children.

Quality physical therapy

There has always been a need for rehabilitative physical therapy to help those with broken bones, torn ligaments, and ruptured tendons regain full mobility. And even more therapists are required as the aging population as well as physically intense younger people have hips, knees and other joints repaired or replaced.

Hampstead Physical Therapy is doing wonders with its patients in this location, as well as at the office in Sneads Ferry. Approximately 60 percent of the patients are retirees who are intent on regaining their strength and mobility.

The talented staff, headed and assembled by Rusty Walker, has gained a well-earned reputation for helping their patients get back to normal quickly.

DDT Outlet

A favorite place for Hampstead residents to shop is DDT Outlet, located on US Highway 17 just south of the turnoff for Topsail Island. DDT is a huge store that offers an incredible range of furnishings for the entire home, inside and out. Reflecting its coastal location, DDT has a wide selection of nautically themed furnishings, accessories and gifts.

The showroom has more than 20,000 square feet of constantly changing merchandise, with shipments arriving daily.

Just a few of the brands offered are

Braxton Culler, specializing in a wide range of wicker, rattan and upholstered furniture; solid wood bunk beds by Great American Bunkbed Co.; Flexsteel fine custom upholstered furniture with a patented blue steel frame that comes with a lifetime warranty; and Omnia, a company offering the finest Italian leather furnishings from contemporary to traditional styles. Other lines and products too numerous to mention are available.

Diverse golf courses

Hampstead is home to two very diverse golf courses. When approaching from Wilmington, Castle Bay Country Club. is the first you'll reach; it is located two miles off US Highway 17. Castle Bay is a true Scottish-links course that features lots of protected wetlands and very few trees.

The greens at Castle Bay are kept in very good shape and are among the best around.

Castle Bay has a driving range, putting green, chipping area, and sand trap so that players can work on all parts of their games. The semi-private club also has a fully stocked pro shop.

Located approximately two miles north of Castle Bay on US Highway 17 is Olde Point Golf and County Club. The facility is one of the oldest in eastern North Carolina, opening in 1975 with a design by Jerry Turner.

The course is a challenging layout that offers skilled players as well as beginning golfers a memorable experience. The 18-hole par 72 course winds through mature woodlands, past scenic lakes and ponds, and offers strategically placed fairway and greenside bunkers on every hole.

The course is best known for Hole #11, a monster par 5 that requires three of a player's longest and best placed shots to reach the green in regulation, regardless of which of the five sets of tees are used.

Bermuda fairways and large Seashore Paspalum greens are meticulously maintained for year-round enjoyment. A fully stocked pro shop and large practice areas are open to the public and provide a great place to hone skills when there isn't enough time to play a round.

Lessons and clinics from an LPGA pro are available by appointment.

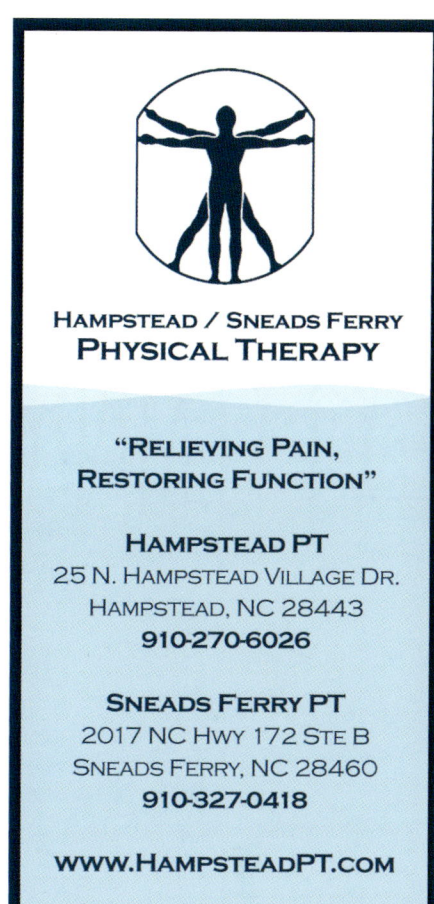

HAMPSTEAD / SNEADS FERRY PHYSICAL THERAPY

"RELIEVING PAIN, RESTORING FUNCTION"

HAMPSTEAD PT
25 N. HAMPSTEAD VILLAGE DR.
HAMPSTEAD, NC 28443
910-270-6026

SNEADS FERRY PT
2017 NC HWY 172 STE B
SNEADS FERRY, NC 28460
910-327-0418

WWW.HAMPSTEADPT.COM

DDT-Outdoor

www.ddtoutdoorwicker.com

ALL YOUR OUTDOOR NEEDS!
5060 New Center Drive, Unit 70
Wilmington NC • 910.686.0338
(Beside DCI Biologicals)

Don't forget our Hampstead location! Indoor and outdoor furniture

Outdoor Wicker • Bronze Statues • Recycled Plastic

Hampstead location: 21740 Hwy 17 • 910-329-0160

The southernmost portion of the Cape Fear peninsula is one of the beautiful parts of this area.

lots to do carolina, kure beach

Pleasure Island is an area comprised of Carolina Beach, Kure Beach and Fort Fisher. Geographically, that area is the southernmost portion of the Cape Fear peninsula, which is cut off from the rest of the peninsula by a narrow band of water called Snow's Cut.

The origin of the name, Pleasure Island, is uncertain, but it aptly attests to the wealth of activities and recreational opportunities available on the island for residents and visitors alike. For a while, some of the more conservative residents of the island objected to the name, feeling it negatively implied a hedonistic lifestyle was prevalent here. However, the State of North Carolina shows Pleasure Island on its maps, and the former Carolina Beach/Kure Beach Chamber of Commerce has become the Pleasure Island Chamber of Commerce, indicating the name is here to stay.

North Carolina Aquarium

One of the perfect places for families is the North Carolina Aquarium at Fort Fisher, listed by the Travel Channel as one of the 20 best aquariums in the country. Featuring a 235,000-gallon saltwater tank, the theme of the aquarium is "The Waters of the Cape Fear," which showcases both fresh water and salt water aquatic life in a journey down the Cape Fear River to the Atlantic Ocean.

Situated on a wooded oceanfront location complete with lovely gardens and wildlife areas, the aquarium features many beautiful and exotic displays beginning with a large tree-filled atrium containing stream, pond and swamp aquatic life, plants and ground cover. Very popular with the kids is the Coquina Outcrop Touch Pool in the Coastal Waters Gallery where the little ones (and the big ones, too) can reach out and touch whelks, sea urchins, horseshoe crabs and other sea critters.

The focal point of the aquarium is the Cape Fear Shoals exhibit, where visitors can even talk to a scuba diver.

The huge, two-story tank displays a vast array of sea life including moray eels, stingrays, sharks and grouper plus a multitude of other varieties of sea life. At feeding time, divers underwater answer questions from the audience as they feed the fish.

The Open Oceans Gallery features creatures found off our coastline, and there are two tanks displaying jellyfish. Another tank contains the beautiful and fascinating sea horses. Five other tanks display sea snakes, lionfish, cuttlefish, Pacific Reef fish and an octopus. In the Shadows on the Sand exhibit, skates and rays endlessly cruise above the sandy bottom. All told, more than 2,500 sea creatures, including a rare albino alligator, are on display at the aquarium.

Located at the southern tip is the Fort Fisher State Recreation Area, which offers visitors unspoiled ocean beaches accessible only by walking from the park offices, bathhouse, nature exhibits and concession area, or by four-wheel drive vehicles on a beach access trail.

Here you'll find the perfect opportunity for swimming, surf fishing, shelling, bird and loggerhead sea turtle watching, hiking and exploring miles of nearly deserted beach and marshes. Lifeguards are on duty during tourist season in the swimming area near the park offices and there is ample parking.

Historic Civil War site

Across US Highway 421 from the recreation area is the Fort Fisher State Historic Site, which attracts more than 600,000 visitors annually. A small portion of the original earthen fortifications at Fort Fisher remains - about 180 yards along the Cape Fear River, and about 70 yards along the ocean. In the Visitor Center, an audiovisual program tells the story of Fort Fisher and guided tours of the outdoor exhibits are conducted along a quarter-mile trail.

During the Civil War, Fort Fisher stood guard over the mouth of the Cape Fear River, keeping the blockading Union ships at a distance, spread out beyond the dangerous shoals, and allowing the famous blockade runners to make their nighttime dashes through the blockades and up river to Wilmington with supplies for the Confederate Army.

The fort withstood several attacks and bombardments from the Union that had amassed more than 40 ships to blockade the river and attack the fort. Finally, in 1865, Union land and sea forces combined to overwhelm the fort and subsequently take the city of Wilmington, cutting off the only supply line to General Lee's Confederate Army. Shortly thereafter, the Confederacy fell.

Just south of the fort at the southern tip of the island, you'll find the dock for the Southport/Fort Fisher Ferry operated by the North Carolina Department of Transportation. The trip across the mouth of the Cape Fear River to historic Southport takes nearly half an hour and costs $15 per car. Pedestrians ride for just $1 and bike riders are charged $3. Kids taking the ferry for the first time should stop at the gift shop for a free sticker.

Many families vacation on Pleasure Island. Two businesses that appeal to kids and their families are located on the way to Carolina Beach. Both offer excellent value for vacationers and residents alike.

Walkways leading over fragile dunes and marshes provide protection.

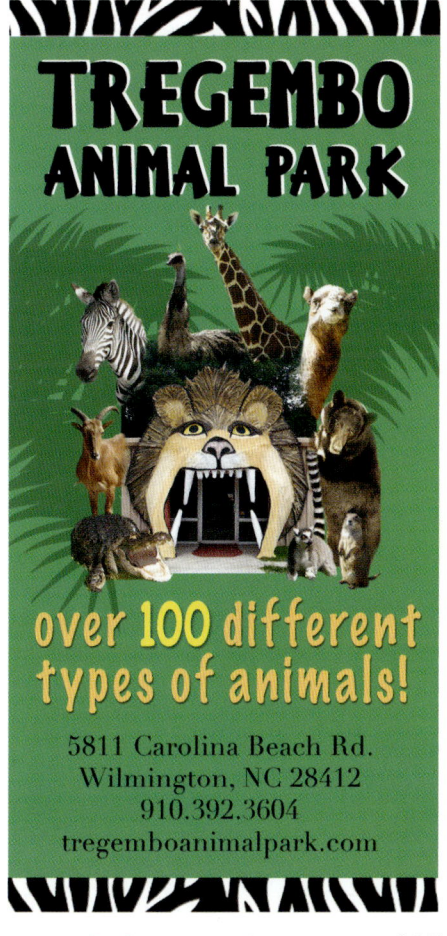

Visit the zoo

The Tregembo Animal Park is the only zoo in southeastern North Carolina. For 60 years, the Tregembo family has consistently provided local families, children's groups and tourists with a fun, educational place to spend a few hours or a day. For a modest admission, you can see an amazing variety of creatures. Some animals you can feed corn or peanuts, some you can pet. And, of course, you'll want to visit the 4,000 square foot gift shop to take home souvenirs.

Besides the usual zoo animals such as a lion, tigers, monkeys and a giraffe, the Park boasts many unusual specimens including a two-toed sloth, a prehensile tailed porcupine, and an East African crown crane. If you're curious, go to the website and view more than 100 photos of critters that are on display.

Kids thrive physically

A great way to promote physical activity is to take children to Carolina Gymnastics Academy. Both owners and all coaches at Carolina Gymnastics Academy love kids, love gymnastics and love teaching. Their great results are the best testament to those attributes. Children who participate in CGA classes benefit from meticulous training and win accolades at competitions. The school, which opened in 2000, provides a safe environment and a developmentally appropriate curriculum in a modern, very well-equipped 15,000 square foot exercise facility.

Numerous programs are available for boys and girls ages 18 months through high school.

By incorporating fun physical activities with educational tools, even the very youngest children can pick up gymnastic basics and enjoy learning. CGA emphasizes "what's best" for each child and tailors instruction accordingly.

There's an After School Program that includes free gym time and help with homework. Other popular offerings are Watch Me Play for crawlers through five years. Parents especially appreciate a chance to have a night out knowing that their children are well cared for and entertained. Members as well as non-members can drop children ages 3-10 off for free play every Friday and Saturday night from 6-10 p.m. Vacationers as well as residents are invited to use this welcome service. Preschool and summer camps are slated too. This is a busy place.

Nearby golf course

An outstanding golf course is the big draw at semi-private Masonboro Country Club. The club features one of the longest courses in the area, measuring 7,041 yards from the tips.

Bob Moore of JMP Golf Design Group, a well-known and highly regarded architect, crafted the course. No expense was spared in creating the facility. Masonboro is the closest golf facility to Carolina and Kure Beaches and is located south of Monkey Junction and north of Snow's Cut.

The immaculately manicured course features Mini-Verde Bermuda greens, 80 acres of turf newly sodded with 419 Bermuda grass, and the same fine white sand found at Augusta National. Unique natural elevation changes, berms and grassy shallows combine to create beautiful vistas.

Carolina Gymnastics Academy
Where Kids Come First and Learning Is Important

Whether you live in Wilmington or are just visiting, Carolina Gymnastics Academy has something for everyone, with programs for children from six months through high school years. Special programs include Watch Me Play for crawlers-5 years and Parents Night Out for children ages 3-10. Summer Half Day Camp is for ages 3-10 and Summer Full Day Camp is for ages 5-10. In addition, Gymnastics Classes for Boys & Girls, After School Programs, Cheerleading, Gym & Learn Preschool and Birthday Parties are available. Visit to meet the talented, caring and responsible staff.

3529 Carolina Beach Road • Wilmington, NC 28412
910-796-1896 • www.carolinagymnasticsacademy.com

There is plenty of room on Pleasure Island to build castles in the sand.

JOIN US TODAY!

Whether you're ready to relax after a round of golf or are just looking for a welcoming sports bar visit us. The public is always welcome.

THE TAVERN BY THE GREEN
Masonboro Country Club
8610 Sedgley Drive
Wilmington NC 28412
910-397-9162
www.masonborocountryclub.com

Masonboro also features superb practice facilities, including a seven-acre driving range, a putting green and a short game practice area. The PGA staff at the club is happy to give lessons that will help golfers improve their games.

The pro shop at the Masonboro Country Club is very well stocked with apparel as well as equipment, including a fine selection of golf clubs and related merchandise.

Restaurants to visit

Nothing beats post-links relaxing at Tavern by the Green, overlooking the Masonboro Country Club course. You needn't schedule a day of golf to enjoy this charming restaurant.

Black wrought iron furniture and stylishly cozy interior signal Southern hospitality. There's also a grand outdoor pavilion. Come sit a spell with a refreshing iced tea, craft beer or lovely glass of white zinfandel. The menu is packed with great nibbles, sandwiches and salads. Munch a basket of fries, refuel with a healthy chef's salad or tuck into

PLAY CAROLINA BEACH'S CLOSEST GOLF COURSE!

A PGA Tour caliber coastal golf course is located just minutes from Carolina Beach. This beautiful course, though challenging enough for talented golfers, is enjoyed by players of all levels. Featuring great practice facilities, pro shop, driving range and dining facilities, book your tee time today. Get a free bucket of range balls with each paid round of golf when you mention Wilmington Today!*

located just south of Monkey Junction, before the Snows Cut bridge.
8610 Sedgley Drive • Wilmington NC 28412
910.397.9162 • www.masonborocountryclub.com

*May not be combined with any other offers

Saint's Cove BEACH BAR & GRILL

Try one of the newest restaurants where the casual beach food is prepared with care. Locally owned since May 2014 by a retired Marine Corps Colonel, Saint's Cove proudly supports the military and first responders.

Full bar, sports bar with NFL package and college football, TVs inside and on the deck.

Monday-Thursday 11 am-10 pm
Friday-Saturday 11 am-11 pm
Sunday Noon-9 pm

Located between Carolina and Kure Beach at 1006 S. Lake Park Blvd.
910-707-1233
www.saintscove.com

---

hearty sandwiches. Try a BLT, a double cheeseburger or a classic club wrap with turkey, ham, bacon, lettuce, tomato and ranch dressing. The fish and chips plate features beer-battered cod. Planning an event? Call the hospitality experts at Masonboro Country Club. Tavern by the Green and the outdoor pavilion accommodate groups of many sizes. Chefs and event planners arrange menus to suit your tastes, from elegant, full breakfasts to casual barbecue dinners. Participate in various social events and activities that build long-lasting friendships at Masonboro Country Club.

When Saint's Cove Beach Bar & Grill owner Nick Augustine was a Marine Corps pilot, his old pilot call sign was "Saint." "You know, like Saint Nick, Saint Augustine," he says. While stationed in eastern North Carolina, Augustine fished on a beach pier hosting a little café. The place got him thinking about a seaside business for his future. Enter friendly Saint's Cove Beach Bar & Grill. Tables, some with umbrellas, and pastel wooden chairs furnish the huge deck affording plenty of room for families and friends. Nautical charts under the bar top's clear finish and model sailboats in shadow boxes on the walls provide a maritime feel indoors.

Pub appetizers like fried clam strips, bourbon-sauced meatballs, grouper bites and Cheerwine-glazed wings reflect easy beach days. There's a burger piled with onion rings and another with pineapple, bacon, mozzarella and teriyaki sauce.

Augustine is from Detroit, so Midwest favorites dot the menu. Look for a fried pork tenderloin sandwich with lettuce and tomato. Cheddar cheese curds are beer-battered and deep-fried. Of course, much seafood is on the list, everything from grouper bites with spicy mayo to fish tacos to a mixed catch basket with fried clams, shrimp and catfish.

Wine, beer and cocktails are available, too. Have an old-fashioned ice cream sundae for dessert or ask about the "chocolate delight of the day." Saint's Cove is opens at 11 a.m. Monday-Thursday they close at 10 p.m.; Friday and Saturday at midnight and Sunday at 9 p.m. Call ahead from late fall to early spring. Off-season hours are subject to change.

Fall and winter oyster roasts and spring and summer shrimp boils are two favorite pastimes on the North Carolina coast. They happen all the time be-

---

NAMED ONE OF COASTAL LIVING'S FAVORITE SEAFOOD DIVES!

OYSTERS • SHRIMP • CLAMS • MUSSELS • CRAB LEGS • WINGS • FISH N' CHIPS • STEAMPOTS

CAROLINA BEACH
6 N. Lake Blvd.
910.458.7380

HISTORIC WILMINGTON
109 Market St.
910.833.8622

SHUCKIN' SHACK OYSTER BAR

WWW.THESHUCKINSHACK.COM

hind the screen door at Shuckin' Shack in Carolina Beach. The restaurant is a cross between backyard seafood feasts and seaside steam shacks. The national magazine *Coastal Living* named Shuckin' Shack one of its favorite seafood dives in 2013. Galvanized buckets serve as drop lights over the bar, which is decorated with newspaper clippings that tell Carolina beach stories about fishing adventures and surfer dudes. Huge photographs of Carolina Beach's famous charter boats serve as "windows." A sign on the wall advises, "It's always 5 o'clock in Carolina Beach." That means settle in and have fun. Big rich, briny oysters are served raw or steamed. Peel-and-eat shrimp, clam, mussels and snow crab legs and claws come from the steamer, too.

Samplers and feasts let you mix and match seafood alongside slaw, hushpuppies and corn on the cob. Get wings, sandwiches – including lobster rolls – and lots of snacks like fried pickles, mini corn dogs and mozzarella sticks. Beer, wine and cocktails are served, including fun specials like the Pleasure Island Pain Killer with rum, orange, coconut, pineapple and nutmeg. Catering is available. Shuckin' Shack has a downtown Wilmington location, too. Hours are 11 a.m. to 2 a.m. Monday-Saturday and noon to 2 a.m. Sunday. The downtown location may be open past 2 a.m. depending on crowds.

Ice cream, treats and more

Squigley's can create and serve more than 4,000 flavors of ice cream within minutes. From Easter through Halloween, this popular Pleasure Island institution offers up hundreds of delectable frozen treats to appreciative guests. Using a secret recipe, Squigley's hand make uniquely flavored waffle cones to hold yummy ice cream creations for kids from a few months to 100 years (or older).

Owner Ann Coen has watched the business grow consistently since 1994. She's assured that Squigley's has premium dairy and in-store made ice cream and she emphasizes high nutritional and hygienic standards. Most summer nights, you'll see people waiting patiently in lines that stretch out the door and down the steps until it's their turn to order. Though the parlor isn't large, it's big enough for several tables with chairs, plus outdoor seating is available. On a warm Thursday evening, people often sit on the grass or curb eating their cones while watching the Boardwalk Fireworks. We love Squigley's.

The house, which is located at the corner of Lake Park Boulevard and Fayetteville Avenue, was originally built in the 1930s as a private residence with separate garage. Over the years, the house experienced a variety of incarnations, including a tourist home and doughnut shop. The ice cream parlor now sits nicely on the ground floor. In 2007 the Coens turned the garage and upstairs apartment into gift shops.

Above the ice cream parlor, Squigley's Gift Gallery boasts four rooms filled with great finds. A Treasure trove of handmade craft items, local art, amazing jewelry, one-of-a-kind specialty items and stained glass is available at prices "ranging from affordable to very high end." One thing is certain; you'll always get value for your money here.

Joe Squigley proudly states "Squigley's will never, has never, raised prices beyond the everyday price in order to advertise a discount sale of 50-70 percent off as some stores do in order to seem-

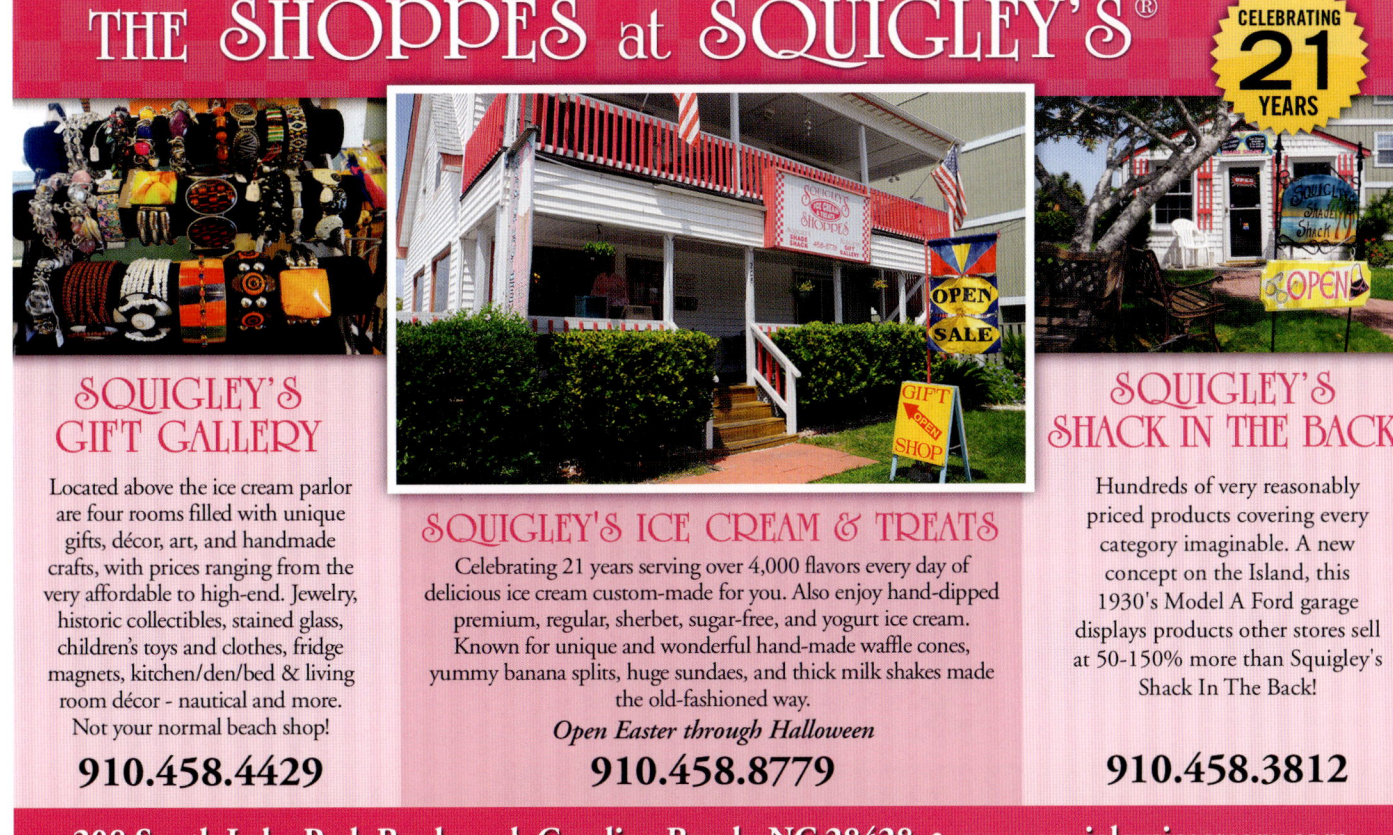

ingly offer a consumer savings."

Fishing draws fans

A major appeal for Pleasure Island is the active fishing community and availability. Fishermen and women flock to the island's waterways to try their luck.

Pleasure Island has two fishing piers, one at the north end of the island in Carolina Beach and one in Kure Beach. The island also is home to a great charter service, Island Tackle.

Island Tackle Fishing Charters has two generations of U.S. Coast Guard licensed charter captains with more than 50 years of combined experience. They cater to families and actively promote youth fishing and junior angling. They offer both in-shore and offshore charters on a half, three-quarter or full-day basis. For the non-fisherman, they have sight-seeing, nature and historic excursions.

Fishermen can find everything they need at Island Tackle and Hardware, a store that began as a small-town fishing tackle store that also sold hardware. But owners Dennis and Wanda Barbour, envisioning robust growth, proceeded to build their current two-story emporium dedicated to supplying an exceptionally complete offering of fishing equipment and supplies coupled with most everything the homeowner or contractor might need in hardware and materials from a True Value dealer.

They now have much more than that too. In addition to apparel ranging from sunglasses and hats to shirts, shorts and shoes, they offer a full selection of rods and reels including electric, boating accessories and trailer supplies, bait for both fishing and crabbing, licenses, official weighing, local nautical art and of course, free advice. And yes, as you would expect, they also make keys.

When you visit the store, be sure to check out the largest Blue Marlin ever caught in North Carolina waters. The behemoth weighed in at 1,228.5 pounds, and is one of several "big fish" photos on display.

Consignment finds

Island Chic is a first class consignment boutique that residents and visitors should visit often since it features designer and boutique clothing and accessories. Owner Regina Scruggs strives to carry "the best designer brand names, the latest styles, at the best prices!" A truly fun place to shop, here you'll find affordable shoes, clothing, handbags, jewelry and seasonal items all either new or just slightly used condition. A big believer in recycling, Scruggs regards her consignment business as an environmental asset. The consigned items are considered to be "recycled" from owner to owner and the store recycles hangers, uses recycled bags and donates unsold items to help those on the island.

Island Chic is also a reputable place to consign your new or gently used items. The shop has a state-of-the-art computer system including bar code scanner for tracking each consigner and all items, pricing and sales for each. Consignees can have itemized printouts at any time and also when they receive their checks.

Island Chic offers new gift items too, including hats, wallets, frames, monogrammed totes and scarves, among many other things. They also carry items such as soaps, lip balms, lotions, oils and bath salts made locally of all natural ingredients. The store carries items for

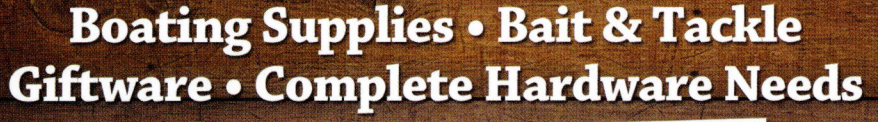

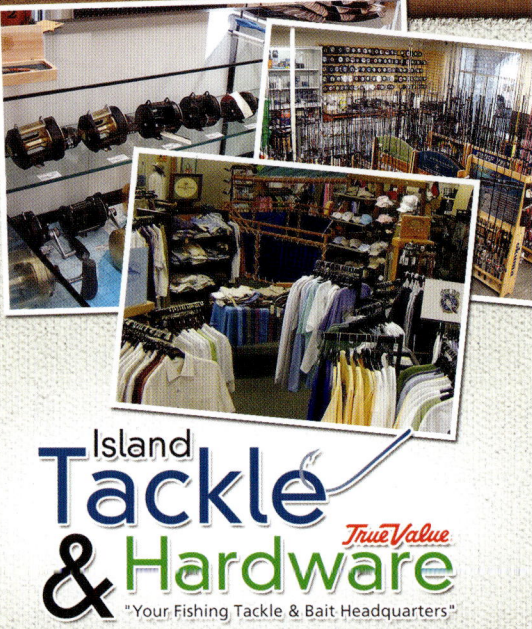

women of all shapes and sizes and has both formal and casual styles.

Catch up on reading

One of the joys of being on vacation is that people have time to catch up on their reading. Whether light hearted beach fare or the latest political tome meets your criteria for a fun read, you'll want to visit Island Book Shop. They have a wide range of both new and used books for adults and for children.

Their knowledgeable and friendly staff of avid readers is happy to recommend a book for you. If what you want is not in stock, they're glad to order it for you.

Island Book Shop also offer business services including fax, color copies and internet. The store has a selection of stationery and a wide selection of materials of local interest.

Carolina Beach history

Many wonder how Carolina Beach was developed. Joseph Winner, who bought beachfront property and laid out plans for a town that subsequently became Carolina Beach, established it in 1857. The first visitors to Pleasure Island were vacationers brought to the island by boat and then conveyed to the beach by a small steam railroad. Shortly thereafter, a Dane named Hans Anderson Kure founded Kure Beach. In 1929, Snow's Cut was dredged to make it part of the Intracoastal Waterway.

Pleasure Island was initially connected to the mainland by a small swing bridge, which eventually was replaced by the current high-rise Snow's Cut Bridge. Carolina Beach developed over the years as the commercial center of the island, a tourism destination and a residential community. Kure Beach evolved as a residential community with relatively little commercial development and limited tourism. In recent years, both communities experienced enormous development as two of the few places along the coast where reasonably priced land near the ocean is still available.

Kure Beach has seen extensive construction of upscale homes and condos while Carolina Beach, spurred by the building of the oceanfront Courtyard

by Marriott resort hotel, saw considerable development of upscale condos and homes. Both towns are thriving and more commercial development, including another high-rise hotel, is on the way.

Marina available

Some vacationers arrive on their boats and want a place to dock. Fortunately, Carolina Beach State Park, located at the northwest corner of the island at the juncture of Snow's Cut and the Cape Fear River, has a marina with more than 40 slips, launch ramps, concessions, hiking trails including the Flytrap trail, an 83-site campground, group camping and an outstanding visitor's center with educational programs and exhibits.

Freeman Park, just past the North End Pier, is owned by New Hanover County but controlled by Carolina Beach, and features about a mile or so of uninhabited beach at the very northeast tip of the island.

The park is accessible only on foot or by four-wheel-drive vehicles with the proper wide tires.

Overnight tent camping on the

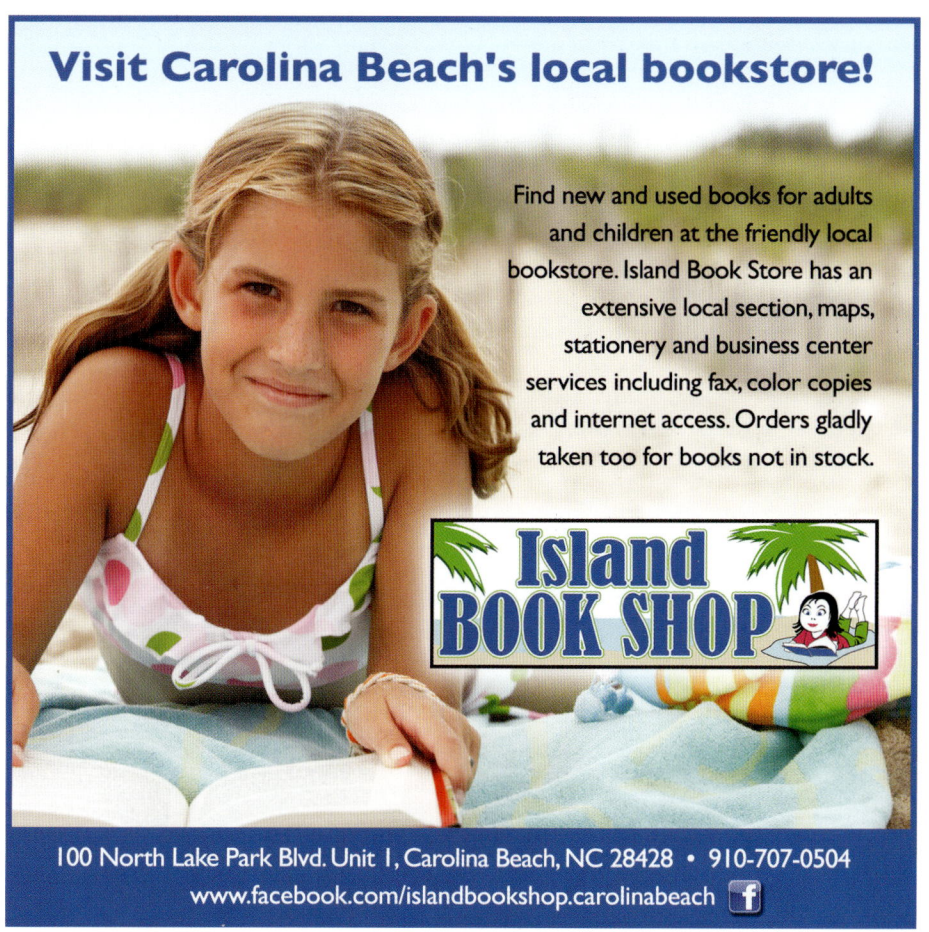

Pleasure Island
2015 SPECIAL EVENTS

April 11	19th Annual Chowder Cook-off
June – August	Free Summer Concerts
June – August	Free Movies every Sunday night at Carolina Beach Lake
June – August	Free Fireworks and Live Entertainment every Thursday night on the beach
June 6	30th Annual Carolina Beach Music Festival on the beach
July 2	Independence Day Fireworks on the Beach and Live Entertainment at the Boardwalk Gazebo
October 10 & 11	22nd Annual Seafood, Blues & Jazz Festival

Hosted by **Pleasure Island** CHAMBER OF COMMERCE
1121 N. Lake Park Blvd. • Carolina Beach
(910) 458-8434
www.pleasureislandnc.org

Pleasure Island is a place where all who visit can enjoy the beach.

strand is permitted, as are campfires. There is an admission charge and Carolina Beach police patrol the area.

And talk about beaches for swimming, the Carolina Beach/Kure Beach strand has about seven miles of them, protected by lifeguards in season and renourished by man if Mother Nature washes the beaches away. Both Carolina Beach and Kure Beach have numerous public beach accesses, many with parking, some with restrooms, and the entire strand is open to the public.

Dogs are not permitted on the beaches during the tourist season.

Rent what you need

Many vacationers find that it's more convenient to rent what they need for a trip rather than to try to bring everything with them. Fortunately, Pleasure Island Rentals has offered the largest inventory and lowest prices since 1996. Whatever a person might need is available.

A wonderful way to traverse the island is on a bicycle, which can be rented by the day or week. It's even possible to rent a 16" kid's bike with training wheels, with a child helmet included at no additional charge.

Pleasure Island Rentals also is a full service bike shop, selling new bikes and repairing damaged ones. Among the items for the water are paddleboards, kayaks, beach chairs including oak ones with a footrest, beach wheelbarrows, umbrellas, and surf boards, all of which can be rented.

Tours on single or tandem kayaks can be arranged with 48-hour notice, and paddles, life jackets and seatbacks are included.

Annual special events

Throughout the year, a variety of events take place. Many of these events are so popular that they have been going for decades, including the Seafood, Blues and Jazz Festival, Beach Music Festival, the Pleasure Island Chowder Cook Off, and the Carolina Beach Music Festival. There are weekly fireworks on Thursday nights and free summer concerts during the tourist season.

The Island of Lights parade and flotilla takes place during Christmas. The year closes with New Year's Eve fireworks and a famous ball drop from the end of a fire department ladder truck.

www.wilmingtontoday.com

Photo by G. Frank Hart Photography

Wrightsville Beach attracts a large number of avid surfers who enjoy the thrill of catching a wave.

what's up at wrightsville beach

Wrightsville Beach, a barrier island wonderland featuring glorious beaches, great restaurants, dream homes, luxurious condos and tony hotels, is located just minutes from the city of Wilmington.

Ranging from 1,000 to 5,000 feet wide, this nearly four-mile stretch features sound-to-sea views and spans Masonboro Inlet north to Mason Inlet. Even better, Wrightsville Beach is a mere ten miles from downtown Wilmington.

The off-season's small-town feel swells when tourists and part-time residents return in spring, summer and early fall. Around 3,000 people live here permanently, but the population hits 30,000 during warmer months. Plenty of accommodations await, everything from by-the-beach motel rooms to oceanfront "sand castles." The island is almost completely developed.

Surf's up – most of the time

Wrightsville Beach is a surfing hotspot for locals. Pros and beginners rush here with surfboards, paddleboards and body boards. Arrive early to find parking, especially on weekends, otherwise you might drive around for hours in search of a space. Don't pull into home driveways or condo lots. Your vehicle will be towed from private spaces.

Sailing through history

Wrightsville Beach was not always the plush vacation and residential area it is today. Early on, when the state of North Carolina owned the island, the area was named New Hanover Banks. Back then, an inlet separated the island into two segments. Shell Island, to the north, kept its name as evidenced by the present-day Shell Island Resort there, which is surrounded by extravagant homes and large condominium communities.

Between 1791 and 1841, the island was private property, uninhabited and visited only by hunters and fishermen. Sailing enthusiasts came, too, and in 1853, the first structure was built, the Carolina Yacht Club headquarters. This is America's third oldest yacht club. Some members were involved in the Civil War, when blockade runners worked nearby waters. Three blockade runners supposedly foundered on the island.

Following the Civil War, an oyster shell-surfaced turnpike linked Wilmington and Wrightsville Sound. Wilmington Seacoast Railroad tracks followed in 1887. They stretched from the city to the Hammocks, a piece of land west of the beach. That land is now named Harbor Island. A footbridge connected the Hammocks with Wrightsville Beach, and development increased. Another yacht club, several hotels and some beach cottages were built.

In 1889, the railroad tracks extended across the Hammocks and Banks Channel to the beach proper. Visitors from Wilmington began to flock to Wrightsville Beach in summer. In 1899, with 40 or 50 residents, most of them seasonal, the Town of Wrightsville Beach was incorporated. Unfortunately, later that year, a hurricane destroyed it.

Surging ahead

The town was soon rebuilt. The rail line became an electric trolley in 1902, and by 1907, 8,700 passengers from Wilmington, New York and other cities rode the "Beach Trolley" to the shore. The stunning Lumina entertainment hall was built at the end of the trolley line in 1905. Costing $7,000, a whopping sum in those days, Lumina comprised 12,500 square feet. Three floors hosted various activities including a ballroom, bowling alley and shooting gallery.

Lumina grew several times. A huge movie screen was erected 50 feet out into the surf. In 1910, 600 electric outdoor lights made Lumina visible from miles away. By 1930, Wrightsville Beach hosted 110 residents, but in 1934 a fire destroyed more than 100 cottages and the Oceanic Hotel. Again, the town rebounded. A year later, a new road linked the mainland to Wrightsville Beach.

The population jumped to 1,500 by 1945. Alas, tragedy struck again. Hurricane Hazel in 1954 blew in winds of 125 to 140 miles per hour and a 12- to 14-foot storm surge. Hazel wiped out upwards of 250 houses and damaged 500 more, but Wrightsville Beach would not be squashed. More homes were constructed in Hazel's wake, and the seven-story Blockade Runner Motor Hotel opened in 1964. Unfortunately, Lumina deteriorated. A special era ended when the hall was demolished in 1973.

Shell Island Resort was built in 1984. Mother Nature, however, did not surrender. Hurricanes Bertha and Fran in the 1990s damaged hundreds of homes and businesses, leveled dunes and destroyed two fishing piers.

Wrightsville Beach rose yet again. Damages were repaired, and the new concrete, hurricane-resistant Johnnie Mercer's pier was built.

Wrightsville Beach Museum of History displays artifacts, photos and exhibits tracing the town's past. A 12-foot model depicts Wrightsville Beach in 1910.

Create a memory

Many vacationers would love to have a personal keepsake of their trip. There's no better way to preserve a memory than with a professional photograph that preserves the occasion for you. G. Frank Hart Photography is happy to work with clients to capture the perfect portrait of a single person or a family group.

Hart is a commercial photographer best known in the area for his architectural and residential photography that has appeared in publications including *Southern Living* and *Professional Builders,* a trade publication.

Although his background includes a degree in forestry and natural resource management, his work with a professor who used field photography in his class work led Hart to what would ultimately become his career.

Hart has photographed the landscapes, people and landmarks of the Carolinas for years and as a result has amassed an extensive collection of outstanding photographs. His keen eye for composition makes his artistic ability readily apparent.

www.wilmingtontoday.com ■ 177

Oceanfront dining

Two beautiful oceanfront restaurants on either end of Wrightsville Beach serve delicious meals with stunning views.

Oceans, on North Lumina Avenue, is perched on the Holiday Inn Resort mezzanine. Open daily for breakfast, lunch and dinner, and hosting a full bar, the dining room and outdoor deck offer a poolside panoramic view of the Atlantic Ocean.

Order seafood, steaks, salads and pasta, or grab a fresh-baked pizza. Choose from a large selection of toppings or a house specialty, say the Moore's Inlet pizza with seasoned shrimp and crab, mozzarella, fresh basil and fresh tomato slices.

Oceanic Restaurant, on South Lumina Avenue, sits three stories high, with seating on each floor. Sip and dine right over the ocean on Crystal Pier, an old-fashioned-style wooden length furnished with umbrella tables and room to stroll. Oceanic serves lunch and dinner daily, as well as Sunday brunch. The restaurant is known as a classic seafood house specializing in fresh, local seafood, broiled or lightly breaded and fried, a recipe famously called "Calabash style." Landlubber dinner fare includes steaks, chicken and pasta.

Lunch brings large salads, sandwiches, seafood baskets and seafood platters. A take-out menu, including extensive family-style, to-go selections, is available. A full bar and extensive wine list are offered.

Watch the world go by

South Beach Grill is a delightful spot for people and boat watching. Located on Lumina Avenue in the heart of Wrightsville Beach's downtown district overlooking Banks Channel, the restaurant has both indoor and outdoor seating.

The menu reads fine dining but no need to dress up. Casual attire is fine. Sip a cocktail, beer or wine while chefs carefully craft your meal. One white wine benefits the area's Sea Turtle Conservancy.

Every day, South Beach Grill features numerous specials. Choices depend on what's fresh. Recent suggestions included coconut-crusted local tuna, a shrimp po' boy panini, seafood lasagna, house-smoked salmon and Chef James Rivenbark's tender, rib-sticking meatloaf.

South Beach is known for ultra-fresh salads, which may be topped with fried oysters or other seafood. A bowl of the daily soup with a salad is a nice, light meal. Vegan and gluten-free plates are available.

Check some South Beach traditions, including seafood nachos and fried pickles dipped in a secret batter recipe. Grouper Linda has been on the menu for 18 years for good reason. Pan-seared, pecan-crusted grouper is served with backfin crab meat, spring onions and cream sherry beurre blanc.

Food and fun

Banks Channel, on Causeway Drive, is part pub, part formal dining room. Televisions, a friendly bar, traditional pub tables and two pool tables fill the pub and grill in front.

Linen-draped tables appoint the separate, more formal dining room.

Having lunch or dinner by the ocean is one of life's great pleasures.

Dishes span casual to upscale, too. Dress down with half-pound burgers, pizza or signature sandwiches. Bacon-wrapped filet mignon and creamy seafood are fancy options. Don't miss homemade red potato chips and jicama slaw.

Banks Channel offers daily food and drink specials. Each day brings a different discount for pitchers or buckets of beer as well as specials on individual labels and assorted cocktails. Dinner is served nightly, and the kitchen offers after-hours eats until 1:30 a.m. Saturday and Sunday brunch is in the mix, as is the restaurant's fun, annual Burt Reynolds Birthday Bash.

Dining on the intracoastal waterway

Bluewater Waterfront Grill overlooks a beautiful marina just over Wrightsville Beach's Causeway Bridge, what locals call "the first bridge," as you approach town. The sprawling, two-story restaurant, with both indoor and outdoor seating, offers casual American food including baby back ribs; thick, creamy

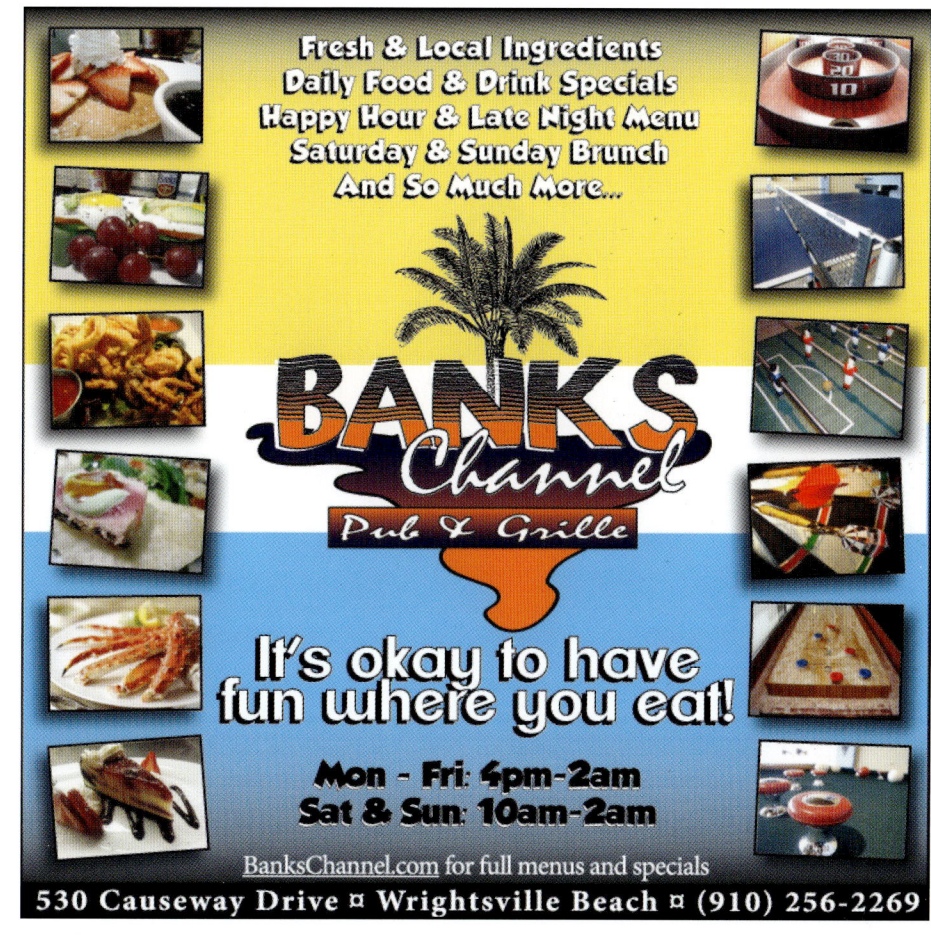

New England clam chowder; grilled rib-eye steaks; and rotisserie chicken, among many other choices.

At lunch, choose appetizers, various sandwiches (consider the fried green tomato club or shrimp salad wrap) and special entrees such as seafood lasagna or coconut shrimp.

Daily specials are other good bets. A full bar serves all sorts of cocktails and beer. Wine is poured by the glass or bottle. Reserve private rooms for parties or special occasions. Bluewater is open every day of the week.

Minutes from the beach

Several outstanding restaurants are a short drive from Wrightsville Beach. Jerry's is tucked into the last strip mall on Eastwood Road before you cross the bridge to Wrightsville Beach. Opening nightly for dinner, the restaurant features steaks, seafood, and pasta dishes, all cooked to order and served by a friendly, knowledgeable staff. Locals and visitors are loyal to this restaurant, which has been around for years. Chefs prepare scrumptious from-scratch soups and specials daily. The chateaubriand is the most flavorful and tender in Wilmington. Half portions are available for diners with smaller appetites. The restaurant has a full bar and an extensive wine list with prices from moderate to princely.

Lumina Station

Lumina Station, on Eastwood Road just beyond the Wrightsville Beach Causeway, features assorted shops, restaurants and a salon, all set in a delightful village atmosphere. Sidewalks wind around a lovely garden and pond. Stores feature fine fashion, art, home décor and other wares.

The shopping village hosts one of Wilmington's premier restaurants, Port Land Grille. Locals, visitors and famous faces relish well-spaced tables and a warm, stylish ambiance. The restaurant's long-standing reputation as among the area's finest eateries is thanks to extraordinary entrees by chef/owner Shawn Wellersdick. He began offering farm-to-table fare years before it was cool. Some selections are from the "port," for instance pan-seared, wild-caught grouper over blue crab meat, English pea, pancetta risotto, butter-wilted baby organic spinach and a roma tomato, saffron, basil, melted sweet onion "fondue" sauce. Other selections are from the "land," such as the chef's personal favorite: a pork porterhouse chop served alongside roasted butternut squash, balsamic glazed cabbage and "red neck" potato gnocchi with heirloom pork barbecue. Savory bacon jam and sweet and tangy balsamic plum barbecue sauce finish the presentation. Changing seasons and the chef's imagination regularly bring new selections. Port Land Grille presents homemade soups, assorted delicious appetizers and salads. Sample classic and signature cocktails from tables in the bar, which has a view of the kitchen. A broad wine list enhances meals. Save room for dessert, especially the famous and oh-so-tall, caramel-drizzled coconut layer cake filled with mango coulis.

Sushi master

The Forum, an upscale shopping center on Military Cutoff Road, is just

Fantastic Carolina skies are always the most dramatic when the colors are seen from a beautiful beach.

five minutes from Wrightsville Beach and home to Bento Box. Frequently recognized as Wilmington's best sushi restaurant, Bento Box does delectable Asian appetizers, small plates and entrees, too. The full bar's sake selection is outstanding. Sushi and sashimi are prepared with great skill and care from the highest-quality seafood. Sit at the sushi bar to watch the masters at work. Consider the signature Delicious Roll, made with either spicy tuna or salmon twirled with avocado, seaweed salad, wasabi tobikko, sesame seeds and crisp tempura crumbles. Two Bento Box signature hot sauces come on the side.

Better yet, let owner/chef Lee Grossman customize sushi for you. He loves to do it and you'll love the result.

Sushi draws a crowd here, but the menu offers much more. Pork belly lettuce wraps are crispy mother lodes. Fork-tender Wagyu boneless short ribs are braised with shiitake and ginger and served over wasabi mashed potatoes, all crowned with ginger demi-glace and a wave of tempura-fried fresh kale.

The restaurant is open Monday through Friday for lunch and dinner and for dinner only on Saturday. Chef closes on Sunday so he and the staff can have quality family time.

Bento Box anchors The Forum's north end. The south end claims a true farm-to-table experience at Pembroke's. Chef James Doss describes his cooking style as "seasonally inspired, ingredient-driven, Southern cuisine." He sources local produce, meat and seafood for the menu, which changes daily.

Cooks might fashion boiled peanut hummus with benne crackers. Chowder may showcase fresh clams, roasted potatoes, winter peas and Andouille sausage. The baby back ribs are so deliciously flavorful and tender that diners have asked that they remain on the menu.

Don't miss wood-grilled chicken from the rotisserie, which you can see in action from a seat by the open kitchen. Chefs work behind a Plexiglass partition, and their nightly dance is an engaging show for foodies.

The wood and red brick décor feels like a cozy lodge, perfect for warm bourbon apple tart or one of the craft bar's various takes on the Old Fashioned. The Porky blends bacon bourbon, ma-

PORTLAND GRILLE

SERVING WILMINGTON'S FINEST - NIGHT AFTER NIGHT

Patio Seating & Private Dining Rooms Available

For reservations call 910-256-6056 or visit our website

www.portlandgrille.com

or www.opentable.com

Located at Lumina Station Near Wrightsville Beach, NC

1908 Eastwood Road, Suite 111
Wilmington, NC 28403
910-256-6056

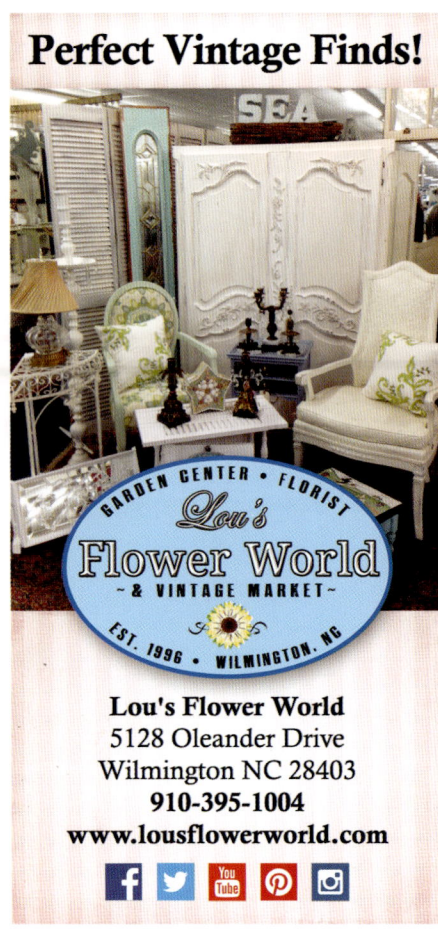

ple syrup, cherry, orange and bitters. Pembroke's is open for dinner Tuesday through Sunday. Friday and Saturday nights may bring live music, never too loud for conversation. Pembroke's recently added brunch on Sundays from 10-3 that usually comes with a serving of live, soft jazz. Be sure to put this on your list of things to do. Creamy sausage gravy with fresh buttermilk biscuits or fried chicken with waffles, honey and a dash of hot sauce are two popular dishes.

Mayfaire menus

Two distinctly different restaurants are opposite each other in Mayfaire Town Center, a shopping center with a downtown feel.

The Melting Pot specializes in fondue, with many different combinations available. Cheese fondues include Traditional Swiss (Gruyère and Emmenthaler, white wine, garlic, nutmeg, lemon and Kirschwasser) and zesty Fiesta's cheddar blended with lager beer, jalapeño peppers and salsa. Start meals with one of four fresh salads.

Several entree selections range from filet mignon to Atlantic salmon to a seafood trio. Diners may also decide how they would like their dishes prepared. Four cooking styles include Mojo Caribbean-seasoned bouillon with fresh-garlic flavor and citrus flair.

Four-course experiences include a cheese fondue, salad, premium entrees and chocolate fondue. The question is which chocolate fondue. Eight are offered, including a Create Your Own option. Perhaps the wisest approach is to start at the top, then work down the list on return visits.

The Melting Pot has many wines, numerous beers and a full bar. The restaurant is open in the evening seven days a week and for lunch on Saturday and Sunday.

Tokyo 101, across the street, serves most every type of Japanese food. Hibachi choices are vegetables, chicken, steak, and five types of seafood, offered either singly or as combinations.

Like noodles? The kitchen sends out udon soup and yakisoba creations stir-fried with chicken or seafood. Deep-fried shrimp-and-crab-stuffed jalapenos are among dishes with a fusion feel. The large menu lists a host of soups and salads, a vast array of appetizers and myriad sushi, some raw and some cooked.

Tokyo 101 is calming and beautiful. A tranquil water wall is among features. An outdoor seating area opens when weather permits. Diners who sit at the sushi bar get to see chefs at work. The restaurant is open seven days a week for both lunch and dinner.

Tokyo 101's bar showcases different cocktail specials every day. Special sushi prices come Monday through Thursday.

Great vintage market

For nearly 20 years, Lou's Flower World has been a one-stop resource for an unmatched selection of flowers, plants, unique furniture and gifts. Lou's 20,000-square-foot facility carries a large selection of gifts for the home and garden, including bird feeders, lawn pagodas and home décor.

As if their flower selection was not enough, Lou's features a large Vintage Market full of unique furniture and accessories that you won't find anywhere else. From beach cottage to shabby chic to antiques and estate pieces, they carry

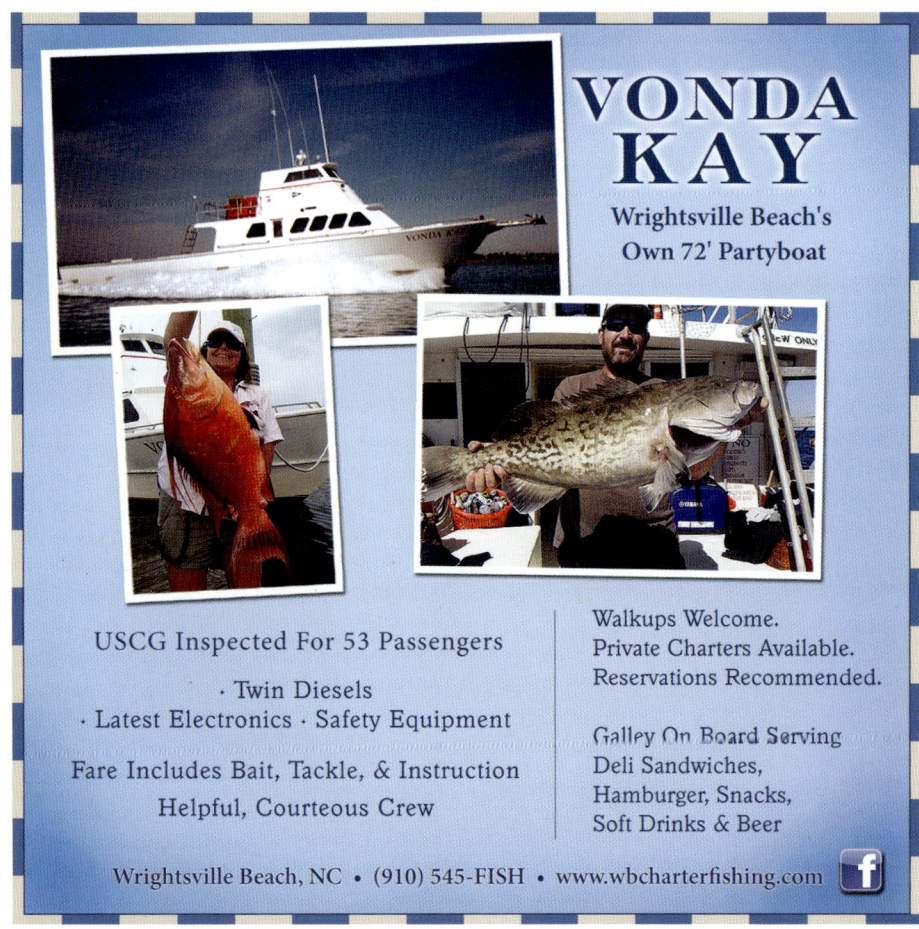

Few things are as exciting as watching sea turtles hatch from their nest.

every style of furniture imaginable. The inventory changes regularly and prices are quite reasonable.

For enhanced customer service, they deliver to the Wilmington, Wrightsville Beach and Carolina Beach areas. Stop by Lou's today to see why they say, "There's something for everyone at Lou's!"

Fishing, boating popular pastimes

After your hunger and thirst are satisfied, relish Wrightsville Beach activities and events, like dropping a line off the charter fishing boat Vonda Kay.

The 72-foot party boat accommodates 72 passengers for full- or half-day Atlantic Ocean fishing trips. Angle for snapper, grouper, triggerfish, amberjack, mackerel, cobia, black sea bass and whatever else grabs the hook. Private charters are available, but walk-ups are welcome, too. Don't worry about packing lunch. The on-board galley serves burgers, sandwiches, snacks and drinks, including beer. Just want to take a boat ride? Evening cruises are part of the line-up.

If you love boats, and certainly many people do, don't miss Wrightsville Beach's annual, November Holiday Flotilla Day in the Park followed by that evening's colorful Holiday Flotilla Boat Parade. Light-festooned boats cruise the waterways around town. This two-day event focuses exclusively on holiday activities.

Wrightsville Beach is not all about boats. Jazz concerts, a Bark in the Park pet day, bocce ball and volleyball tournaments, the Loop fitness trail encircling the inner island, a kayak and canoe trail through the sound and marshes and other events offered by the Wrightsville Beach Parks and Recreation Department keep residents and visitors active and happy.

Remember: sea turtles nest here

As you stroll Wrightsville Beach's white-sand shore, be mindful of an endangered species that lives here. The non-profit Wrightsville Beach Sea Turtle Project educates visitors and residents about sea turtles that visit the island. You may see their tracks during nesting season. Before leaving the beach, fill any holes you dug in the sand and remove all trash. Turn off outdoor lights and keep indoor lights from shining on the beach at night, since lights disturb nesting turtles and hatchlings. Don't use flashlights or flash photography at night on the beach. Call 910-612-3047 to report sea turtle activity, injuries or strandings. If everyone cares, sea turtles will thrive.

"Sleepy Hollow" filmed its two seasons here. Photograph copyright © Brownie Harris/20th. Century Fox

wilmington stars in films

In the more than two decades that Wilmington has emerged as Hollywood East, the Port City has been morphed into several iconic fictional locations for the small screen. Most notably, Wilmington served as Capeside for *Dawson's Creek*, then it was transformed into Tree Hill, N.C. for *One Tree Hill*, then into the eerie *Sleepy Hollow* for FOX's show by the same name.

Now the Port City is home for two additional television series, one in its first season and one now filming its third. *Secrets and Lies*, starring Ryan Phillippe, KaDee Strickland, Juliette Lewis and Dan Fogler, among others, is off to a good start after its premier in March 2015.

Under The Dome, produced by Steven Spielberg's Amblin Televison, has resumed filming for its third season. This was the highest rated series last summer and will air its first show of the new season in late June. Kylie Bunbury and a widely recognized actress not yet announced will join cast regulars Dean Norris, and Rachelle LeFevre.

The second seasons of both *Under the Dome* and *Sleepy Hollow* were filmed in Wilmington in 2014. In addition, a Smithsonian Channel feature film, *Lincoln's Last Day*, filmed here, with Thalian Hall transformed into Ford's Theatre. The film will be broadcast in 2015. Although final figures for 2014 are not yet in, film spending was huge. Just in the first six months of 2014, $268 million was spent in North Carolina.

Television production in Wilmington in 2013 was booming. *Sleepy Hollow* set up production in the area in July and wrapped the first season in late December. The TV series was one of the largest local productions of 2013, employing more than 400 local crew members and often maintaining up to six soundstages at EUE/Screen Gem Studios. The series reimagines the classic Washington Irving story with Ichabod Crane awakening in modern day as a soldier who must defeat his old nemesis, the Headless Horseman.

In addition to *Sleepy Hollow*, CBS's *Under the Dome*, NBC's *Revolution* and HBO's *Eastbound and Down* significantly contributed to the $254 million spent by the film industry in the state in 2013.

The Port City's other post-apocalyptic TV series, *Revolution*, filmed in Wilmington from the summer of 2012 to April 2013, when it moved to Texas.

Eastbound and Down wrapped its show with its fourth season, which was filmed in the area for more than a month over the summer of 2013. Three of the four seasons of *Eastbound* were primarily filmed locally. *Eastbound* and *Under the Dome* together employed 150 base crew members as well as additional second- and third-unit crews as schedules dictated. In addition, several local actors, primarily from the theater community, and many background extras were employed.

The pilot episode of *How & Why*, a new FX comedy, which was filmed locally in April 2014, is waiting to hear if it is picked up for 2015. Michael Cera and John Hawkes are slated to star in the series, which tells the story of a TV show host who understands how and why a nuclear reactor works but is otherwise clueless about life.

Features filmed too

Several feature films were shot in Wilmington in 2014. *Max Steel*, a live action movie based on Mattel's toy line, was directed by Stewart Hendler. Perhaps hoping for lightning in a bottle, this movie follows the monster hit *Ironman 3*, which filmed in Wilmington in 2012 and starred Robert Downey Jr. and Gwyneth Paltrow.

Bolden!, a movie directed by Dan Pritzker and based on a story by him, stars Ian McShane as Judge Perry and Reno Wilson as Louis Armstrong, key figures in Buddy Bolden's life. The title character is played by Gary Carr. Too many people are unfamiliar with Bolden, a great cornet player who is credited with inventing jazz. Perhaps this movie will educate people about his critical contribution to this American art form.

Other 2014 movies filmed in Wilmington include *The Longest Ride*, a romantic drama based on a Nicholas Sparks novel, and starring Scott Eastwood, Britt Robertson and Alan Alda. It was joined by another movie based on a Nicholas Sparks novel, *The Choice*.

Major productions that shot in Wilmington in 2013 include Warner Brother's *Tammy*, featuring Melissa McCarthy, Susan Sarandon, and Dan Aykroyd; *Christmas in Conway*, a Hallmark Hall of Fame production staring Mary-Louise Parker and Andy Garcia; and indie feature film *The Squeeze*.

Dawson's Creek and One Tree Hill

The influx of TV shows such as *Sleepy Hollow* in Wilmington owes its roots to the pioneering series to film in Wilmington, *Dawson's Creek*. Premiering in 1998 and running through 2003, *Dawson's Creek* revolutionized the way TV executives plan scripted series, according to Griffin.

The show created what is known in the industry as the "*Dawson's Creek* model," which involves choosing a filming location, hiring the majority of its crew locally, and giving a mostly unknown cast a one-time relocation fee to offset their move, Griffin said.

Dawson's Creek featured four high school students as they came of age in the small seaside town of Capeside, Mass. The cast included aspiring filmmaker Dawson (James Van Der Beek), tomboy girl-next-door Joey (Katie Holmes), funny and lovable Pacey (Joshua

Julianne Hough shoots a scene in Relativity Media's "Safe Haven." © 2012 Safe Haven Productions. All Rights Reserved. Photo by James Bridges

Jackson) and the new sophisticated girl in town Jen (Michelle Williams).

Following on *Dawson's* heels was its successor, *One Tree Hill*, which filmed locally from 2003 to 2012, making it the longest running TV series produced in North Carolina. The show centered around the lives of five teenagers growing up in fictional small town Tree Hill, N.C., following them from high school to their post-college careers and families. Costing about one million per episode, the series spent more than $180 million in the region throughout its run.

During some of the leaner years for local film production, *One Tree Hill* almost singlehandedly kept Wilmington production alive, allowing the film commission to always point to a successful production during its efforts to market the area to producers, Griffin said.

Tourists visit film locations

Wilmington's history of attracting tourists to film locations goes back to ABC's *Matlock*, which filmed in Wilmington from 1993 to 1995. The U.S. Federal Courthouse on Water Street was prominently featured in the frequent courtroom scenes of the series, and devotees of the show continue to visit the site.

As both *Dawson's Creek* and *One Tree Hill* quickly became popular, cata-

pulting the actors into celebrities, thousands of fans have flocked to the Cape Fear coast to see the locations and sets depicted on TV. The Wilmington and Beaches Convention and Visitors Bureau reported that they have handed out 18,000 locations guides for *Dawson's Creek* over the past 12 years. Even now, about a decade after the show wrapped, tourists still visit famous *Dawson's Creek* locations, such as Hell's Kitchen, which maintains much of the memorabilia from the show, and UNCW's Alderman Hall, which doubled as the outside façade of Capeside High School. Additionally, *One Tree Hill* still brings visitors to the area to tour filming locations such as the EUE/Screen Gems' set, Karen's Café on Front Street, and the Rivercourt beside the USS North Carolina Battleship.

In 2013, Southport hit record tourism numbers due to the popularity of Nicholas Sparks's *Safe Haven*, which opened in theaters in February 2013. Thousands of fans visited Southport's tourism office and visitor center seeking information on film locations.

Millions spent locally

When a film shoots in Wilmington, local businesses ranging from restaurants to hotels to retail stores all benefit. In 2013, approximately $150 million was

wilmington stars in films

Photo by G. Frank Hart Photography

The largest production ever filmed in Wilmington was "Ironman 3", which kept the film community employed and busy for months.

spent in the Wilmington area. Nearly 20 productions spent an estimated $230 million in southeastern North Carolina in 2012, according to the Wilmington Regional Film Commission. That year included huge numbers for *Ironman 3* which skewed the total. The numbers are based on actual dollars spent locally by productions.

With film production booming in our area comes job growth. Film and TV projects created more than 4,000 crew positions throughout North Carolina in 2014. Locally, more than 700 crew members, ranging from production assistants to craft services to grips and electricians, make their home in Wilmington. This large local crew base is another major factor attracting film projects to the area, reports the Wilmington Regional Film Commission. Thousands of background extras also add to those working in Wilmington's film industry.

Southeastern North Carolina's temperate climate and wide variety of locations also make the area especially film-friendly. Popular film locations that were featured in recent productions include the Forest Hills neighborhood (*Stuck in Love, Iron Man 3*), the New Hanover County Courthouse (*Mary and Martha, Community Service*), and Airlie Garden's Lebanon Chapel (*Heart of the Country*) and the wonderful Wrightsville Beach and Carolina Beach areas (*The Perfect Storm, Eastbound and Down*).

Film tax incentives

Since 1983's *Firestarter* put the Port City on the map, more than 300 feature films, miniseries, movies of the week, TV series, commercials and music videos have shot in the greater Wilmington area. But around 2007, film production in the state decreased because North Carolina did not offer attractive tax incentive packages comparable to other states, such as Louisiana, Georgia and Michigan. The situation began to turn around in 2010, when N.C. lawmakers approved a 25-percent refundable tax credit for production companies based on their direct in-state spending on goods, services and labor. Film projects that spend at least $250,000 in the state are eligible. Wilmington Regional Film Commission Director Johnny Griffin credits the state's tax incentives with the strong film activity in recent years.

"We are thrilled with the results," said Griffin. "In previous years there were projects that wanted to film here, but they couldn't justify it. We just weren't competitive. Now, thanks to the hard work done by our state legislators and Governor, productions see our performance-based incentives as strong and stable. We've always had an outstanding crew base and excellent support services, and of course the studio, and now, it is much easier to build a case for productions to come here."

Unfortunately, the N.C. Governor and Legislature eliminated the successful film tax incentives as such in 2014 and switched to a grant system in January 2015 that set aside a maximum of $10 million that would be available to qualifying films. The result of this switch was devastating, at least in the short term. Film projects that had been investigating this area went elsewhere and few productions even bothered to inquire about the Wilmington film industry.

Still hoping for a promising future

Because the film and television industry is so important to Wilmington, the state of North Carolina (and the tourists who visit too) a very active group of concerned citizens as well as those who directly benefit from the film industry are working hard to encourage state officials to correct this decision. Although nothing is assured yet, many hope that the governor and legislators realize what a terrible mistake they made. Their action can salvage this critical industry and the jobs and economic benefits it produces, both directly and indirectly, but only if they act quickly.

There are spectacular views of the water from all vantage points on Figure Eight Island.

exclusive figure eight island

Figure Eight Island is a delightful oceanfront community located just 12 miles north of Wilmington, accessible only by crossing a guarded causeway bridge from North Carolina State Road 1402, (Edgewater Club Road) off Highway 17 and Porters Neck Road. The island is serene, peaceful, quiet and stunningly beautiful.

The island is unrecognizable from how it appeared just a bit over 100 years ago, when the only residents of the island were wild ponies who freely galloped the dunes.

That changed at the dawn of the 20th century and today admission to the private island is by invitation only. When you arrive, you'll be taken by the feeling of being in another world. You are.

Figure Eight Island is one of the most expensive places to live in the area.

Fabulous private estates

The five-mile, 1,300-acre island retreat features only private homes, most better defined as estates, each different from the next.

You won't find cookie-cutter developments among the approximately 475 homes here.

The highest price paid for a home sold in 2014 was $3.5 million dollars. The most expensive home for sale currently is on the market for $4.8 million dollars; the least expensive is $1.5 million dollars. Only five of the 23 properties for sale as this article is written are less than $2 million; most are $3.5 million or more. As one might expect, the homes are gorgeous, most with spectacular ocean, sound or marsh views. From luxurious, exquisite seven and eight bedroom homes to more modest three and four bedroom bungalows, all have their own personalities.

Vacation in style

Although the island has permanent residents, it is popular as a second home and vacation location, too, often as a haven for celebrities and politicians. Experienced agencies handle Figure Eight Island real estate sales, rentals and property management. Rentals range from $3,000 a week in the off-season to more than $13,000 a week in the height of the summer. Those prices include taxes and travel insurance.

First-class amenities

Figure Eight Island features tennis courts, boat ramps and miles of white sand beaches.

This is a perfect place to enjoy surfing, kayaking, windsurfing, paddleboarding and canoeing.

Other options include kite flying, biking, shelling, bird watching, crabbing, fishing, walking, and just plain doing nothing at all. Leave your stress at the guardhouse!

No traffic here!

Although cars are permitted, traffic is not a factor here primarily due to the absence of commercial centers, hotels, condos, and shopping. However, you're only minutes from the mainland where you'll find all the services, stores, restaurants, golf courses and other amenities you need.

Several excellent restaurants, golf courses and attractions are no more than 30 minutes away. That proximity enables those who stay on Figure Eight Island to enjoy the best of what the Cape Fear area offers.

When you choose a doctor, choose a health team backed by the hospital you trust

NHRMC Physician Group is welcoming new patients. Our patients have seamless access to **board-certified physicians** and **NHRMC's MyChart** which offers:

- 24/7 access to medical information
- prescription renewals
- appointment requests
- private and secure electronic communication with your provider

Visit **nhrmcphysiciangroup.org** for a comprehensive listing of providers, locations and contact information.

Even Stronger Together.

NHRMC Physician Group

Board-Certified Physicians, Specialty Practices, Convenient Locations – All In One Group.

FAMILY & INTERNAL MEDICINE

Coastal Family Medicine
- Janalynn F. Beste, MD, FAAFP
- Douglas J. Boss, MD, FAAFP
- Heather L. Davis, DO
- Karen M. Isaacs, MD, MPH
- Albert A. Meyer, MD, FAAFP
- Cecile T. Robes, DO
- Catherine L. Sotir, MD
- Lisa P. Edgerton, PharmD, BCPS, CPP
- Elizabeth L. Kyle, PharmD, BCACP
- Joseph W. Kertesz, MA, LPC, NBCC

2523 Delaney Avenue, Wilmington
910.763.5522

Internal Medicine Specialists
- Renuka M. Bhan, MD
- Martin J. Butler, MD
- Lucas Faulkenberry, MD
- Charin L. Hanlon, MD, FACP
- Maya Y. Peltsverger, MD, FACP
- Joseph Pino, MD, FAAP, FACP
- Edward Taylor, MD
- Mark E. Williams, MD, FACP
- Kim Thrasher, PharmD, BCPS, CPP
- Patricia Neilsen, RN, MSN, FNP
- Shannon C. Thompson, MSN, FNP-C
- Linda M. Wooley, RN, BSN, CDE

1725 New Hanover Medical Park Drive, Wilmington
910.662.9300

New Hanover Medical Group Central Office
- Charles M. Almond, MD
- Dewey H. Bridger III, MD
- Deborah S. Carter, MD
- J. Richard Corbett, MD, FACR
- Daniel P. Dawson, MD
- J. William Eakins, MD
- Charles B. Herring, MD, FACP
- J. Todd Kornegay, MD
- Clifford T. Lewis, MD
- Darcy J. Rezac, PA-C
- Elizabeth C. Ward, PA-C

1960 S. 16th Street, Wilmington
910.343.9991

New Hanover Medical Group Leland Office
- J. Wellington Adams, MD
- L. Kyle Horton, MD
- Eric Carter, MHS, PA-C
- Amanda Gettier, FNP-BC

1333 S. Dickinson Drive, Ste. 240, Leland
910.332.0241

New Hanover Medical Group Myrtle Grove Office
- Christian P. Daniel, MD
- D. Elijah Gregory, MD
- Dean H. Karras, MD
- Shona F. Martin, MD
- Neill H. Musselwhite, MD
- J. Greg Player, MD
- Christopher M. Sepich, MD
- Jeffrey L. Warhaftig, MD

5145 S. College Road, Wilmington
910.792.1144

New Hanover Medical Group Ogden Office
- John D. Boldizar, MD
- Bryan J.H. Broadbent, MD
- Janice F. Dickerson, MD
- Thomas G. Lee, MD
- Peter G. Manolukas, DO
- Amy E. Messier, MD
- Matthew R. Messier, MD
- Margaret W. Pierson, MD
- Noah R. Pierson, MD

7420 Market Street, Wilmington
910.686.2525

Pender Primary Care - Burgaw
- Pamela Smith, MD

Internal Medicine
Adult Medicine
209 B, US Hwy 117 N Bypass, Burgaw
910.259.0600

Pender Primary Care - Rocky Point
- Christi Ray, DO

Family Medicine - Infants, Children & Adults
7910 US Hwy. 117 S, Ste.120, Rocky Point
910.259.0400

Wrightsville Beach Family Medicine
- Peter Kramer, DO
- Amanda Ricker, FNP, CNM
- Kim Farmer, PA-C

1721 Allens Lane, Wilmington
910.344.8900

URGENT CARE

NHRMC Urgent Care
- Robert Penn, MD
- Ashley Pratt, PA-C

1135 Military Cutoff Rd.#103, Wilmington
910.256.6222

NHRMC Urgent Care
- Kern Barrow, PA-C
- Shanna Bradshaw, PA-C

112 G Medical Village Dr., Wallace
910.285.0333

CARDIOLOGY

Cape Fear Heart Associates
- Christopher C. Barber, MD, FACC
- William P. Buchanan, MD, FACC
- Linda P. Calhoun, MD, FACC
- P. Christopher Ellis, MD, FACC
- James S. Forrester Jr., MD, FACC
- James R. Harper Jr., MD, FACC
- Frank A. Hobart, MD, FACC
- W. Lance Lewis, MD, FACC, FSCAI